POLITICAL RACISM

POLITICAL RACISM
Brexit and its Aftermath

MARTIN SHAW

agenda
publishing

First published in 2022 by Agenda Publishing

Agenda Publishing Limited
The Core
Bath Lane
Newcastle Helix
Newcastle upon Tyne
NE4 5TF
www.agendapub.com

ISBN 978-1-78821-507-7 (hardcover)
ISBN 978-1-78821-508-4 (paperback)

British Library Cataloguing-in-Publication Data
A catalogue record for this book is available from the British Library

Typeset by JS Typesetting Ltd, Porthcawl, Mid Glamorgan
Printed and bound in the UK by CPI Group (UK) Ltd, Croydon, CR0 4YY

CONTENTS

ACKNOWLEDGEMENTS

The project which led to this book originated during the campaign period of the referendum on the United Kingdom's membership of the European Union, which took place on 23 June 2016. I am grateful to the editors of openDemocracy for publishing the articles in which I first articulated some of the ideas which are developed in this book, notably two opinion pieces, "BREXIT: the R is for Racism" and "What will happen after the referendum?" – the latter envisaging "a folksy new authoritarian populism" under Boris Johnson if Leave won – which both appeared on 10 June 2016; and a first version of my analysis of the propaganda, "Truly Project Hate: the third scandal of the official Vote Leave campaign headed by Boris Johnson", which appeared on 30 August 2018. My arguments were also presented in a seminar series at Roehampton University, London, in Autumn 2016, and revised for an edited volume which in the end did not appear; I am grateful to the colleagues who commented and encouraged me to develop the work. A conceptual approach, anticipating part of the argument in Chapter 2, was outlined in "Racial self-interest, Max Weber and the production of racism", published in *Patterns of Prejudice* in 2020; I am grateful to the editors and their reviewers for their advice, and to Gurminder Bhambra (who I inadvertently failed to thank in that publication) for her comments on a draft. Versions of two chapters were presented to the "identity" cluster of the Institut Barcelona d'Estudis Internacionals and I particularly thank Irina Ciornei, Lesley-Ann Daniels and Matthias vom Hau for their suggestions. I also presented these chapters to the Academic Advisory Group of Another Europe is Possible; I thank Luke Cooper for organizing the session and for his and his colleagues' comments. I am also grateful for the advice of my editors at Agenda, Alison Howson and Steven Gerrard, and two particularly helpful anonymous reviewers. My wife, Annabel, shared with me the first five difficult years of Brexit including the pandemic years, 2020 and 2021, in which this book was written; I am grateful to her for far more than I can say here. All of these people have helped me improve this book, but I alone am responsible for its contents and any errors or weaknesses.

Martin Shaw

INTRODUCTION

At the end of the twentieth century, the United Kingdom's withdrawal from the European Union was a fringe idea, even on the political right, and the name "Brexit" had not been invented. Yet by the 2020s, it was the new reality of British economics, society and politics, both domestic and internationally. This dramatic change is the result of the referendum of 23 June 2016, in which 51.9 per cent, out of the 72.2 per cent of the electorate who voted, supported leaving the EU. Although legally the vote was only advisory – and arguably a supermajority should have been required for such a fundamental constitutional change – this narrow result quickly had a decisive, structural character. Half a decade afterwards, therefore, important connections between Britain and continental Europe which had expanded over more than half a century were contracting. In particular, flows of people between the two which had grown throughout this period were being reversed to a significant degree. Brexit also led to a wide-ranging upheaval in the UK. The country's politics were transformed in the three and a half years after the referendum, with deep new conflicts and electoral realignments, leading in the general election of 12 December 2019 to a substantial majority in parliament for the Conservatives, who had changed from a largely Eurosceptic party which nevertheless favoured EU membership into a party which was fundamentally hostile to European integration, which we can describe as Europhobic (following the approach of Kopecký & Mudde 2002). This election led in turn to the implementation of a "hard" Brexit, which excluded the UK from the European Economic Area (EEA, or the "single market") as well as the EU itself, ending freedom of movement between Britain and the EU. Moreover, these changes did not stop with the UK's formal exits from the EU on 31 January 2020 and the single market on 31 December 2020. Brexit also radicalized the national conflicts in Scotland and Northern Ireland, threatening the very coherence of the UK state. The new administration (which itself emphasized its differences from its Conservative-led predecessors) operated in an authoritarian nationalist mode, and was widely seen as a hard-edged and ambitious (if somewhat inchoate) power formation, unusually prepared to dispense,

1

so far as the balance of forces allowed it to, with certain democratic and international conventions. It aimed to embed its power in order to rule throughout the 2020s, by simultaneously reinforcing the popularity of its ideas and subordinating the country's administrative regime, public services, cultural institutions and devolved governments to its rule. Despite many potential sources of instability for this formation, commentators widely credited the possibility that it would indeed retain power for the rest of the decade. It was particularly appropriate, therefore, to describe this as a new regime.

These British developments were of international significance. The new Toryism developed, after the Brexit vote, in the years of Donald Trump's presidency in the United States, as part of a global trend for the mainstream political right to move in an authoritarian direction (Cooper 2021). Even after his defeat in the 2020 presidential election, this tendency remained internationally powerful, not only in the USA – where the Trumpian hold on the Republican party continued growing after the failed insurrection in 2021 – but also in India, Brazil, the Philippines, Hungary, Poland, France, Italy and elsewhere, where authoritarian, far-right formations remained either in power or serious contenders. However, within the liberal-democratic heartland of North America and western Europe, the nationalist Conservative regime was the sole representative of this tendency in power in the early 2020s and needed to accommodate the Democratic administration of Joe Biden which had ousted Trump. In this situation, the ambiguities of the Tory regime's relationship to the wider trend came to the fore. Although Trump had called Johnson "Britain Trump [*sic*]", and Johnson leaned openly towards Trump until the latter's defeat neared, he was widely seen as rather different from his American counterpart; many believed that more than stylistic differences separated the urbane Etonian columnist and the thuggish New York property developer. Johnson was not a political outsider like Trump (although it sometimes suited him to present himself as one) but an established Conservative politician, and he was an obvious shapeshifter who had even toyed with the idea of supporting the other side in the referendum and appeared less committed to an ideological position than to the achievement and preservation of power. Although playing shamelessly to right-wing culture war themes, he cultivated ambiguity about his beliefs and even presented himself as a "liberal". Johnson and his ministers were unabashed Anglo-British nationalists, but where Trump tried to dispense with international allies, they emphasized the UK's alignment with the wider liberal-democratic West and proclaimed their government the standard-bearer of "Global Britain". As this vague concept was increasingly interpreted to mean hostility to China, the regime's geopolitical position began to converge with Biden's. The differences between Johnson and Trump partly reflected the obvious power disparity between the USA, still a superpower, and the UK, decidedly a state of the second rank, but also the different political and ideological cultures of the two countries and their right-wing elites, and they fed uncertainty in the evaluation of the government.

The elision of Brexit's racism

The new Tory regime quickly provided much material to its critics, including its shambolic handling of the Covid-19 pandemic, cronyism, corruption and crass culture war campaigns, while appearing (like Trump) almost immune to criticism. As it consolidated its power, British politics refocused. Brexit remained a potent source of Conservative electoral support, since the electorate continued to polarize around the fractures it had revealed, but the crisis of 2016–19 began to recede into history. Johnson's victory had been the result of the exhaustion of the voters with conflict as much as the popularity of his agenda, and afterwards his urging to "move on" from Brexit was echoed by many observers and opponents as well as voters. In this climate of the early 2020s, there was a widespread tendency to neglect some of the forces which had produced the new regime and the "hard" Brexit which it was implementing. This was particularly true, this book argues, of Brexit's *racial* element, which in any case had not been fully recognized by commentators and even academic analysts after 2016. As the economic difficulties caused by Brexit, together with the political difficulties they provoked in Northern Ireland, became a major focus of attention in the 2020s, Brexit's racial-nationalist roots often disappeared further from view. Even the major fallout in the UK from the worldwide Black Lives Matter protests in 2020 did not change this, as Johnson's government presented a multiracial face and made elaborate efforts to dissipate accusations of racism through a determined "anti-antiracism". As a British "culture war" emerged, many emphasized its broad character, encompassing issues of patriotism, gender, attitudes to authority, etc., rather than the central part which racial questions were playing. In this context, the regime had some success in simultaneously exploiting *and* obfuscating these dimensions of its politics. Even liberal commentators and academic analysts would euphemistically describe right-wing voters as "cultural conservatives" rather than racial nationalists, although anti-immigrant racism and Europhobic nationalism were key characteristics of the beliefs which bound them to Brexit and the Conservatives.

Moreover, although racial nationalism was a worldwide feature of the new right-wing movements, the new British right was unique in being forged simultaneously through the secessionist project of extracting the UK from the EU and opposition to major secessionist movements within its own borders. This led some to look for the roots of the new right more in Anglo-British nationalism, the instabilities in the territorial integrity and geopolitical positioning of the state, and indeed in socio-economic change, than in racism. Although it was widely recognized that, as with other new national far-right movements, the campaign to achieve Brexit had involved the issue of immigration, the claim that this could be separated from racism was given considerable credence even in scholarly accounts. In this light, Brexit's connections with racism were not widely seen as fundamental, the racial element of Brexit nationalism was obscured and there was what Gurminder Bhambra (2017) calls a "methodological whiteness" about much of the academic as well as public commentary. Even opponents of the 2016 Leave movement often minimized its racism as they focused instead on its deceptions, illegal electoral practices and economic irrationalities; typical Remainer critiques relied heavily on claims such as that Brexiters believed in things that "had no basis in fact and were impossible to deliver" (Grey 2021: 87). The fantastical character of some Brexiter beliefs is not in doubt, but their fusion of nationalism with racism, itself viewed as irrational by opponents, provided them with a grim logic which proved highly potent. A particular interpretative error seriously compounded this general failing: even when analysts recognized that the Leave campaign had involved racism, they often mistakenly ascribed it more to the secondary, radical right Leave.EU organization led by Nigel Farage, then leader of the United Kingdom Independence Party (UKIP), than to Vote Leave, the main campaign officially recognized by the Electoral Commission, which was led by Johnson, Michael Gove and the Labour MP Gisela Stuart and involved other Conservative cabinet ministers. In reality, anti-immigrant racism was a key element of both campaigns, but Vote Leave's operation was larger, more sophisticated and almost certainly more influential.

Aims of the book

This book aims to challenge these perceptions and elisions and to produce a more satisfactory analysis in two principal ways. First, it examines the particular forms of racism that were among the most important drivers of Brexit and the rise of nationalist Conservatism. It aims to show that rather than constituting a secondary factor, what this book calls "political racism", centred on the strategic orchestration of hostility by organized actors, has been a guiding thread of Brexit, from the rise of anti-European politics in the 2000s and early 2010s, through the 2016 referendum and the "hard" exit aimed for by both the May and Johnson governments and Johnson's accession to power, to the consolidation of the regime and its conflicts with the EU in the 2020s. The primary aim of this book is, therefore, to analyse, bringing together many kinds of academic research as well as other publicly available information, the extensive and often dominant roles of this type of racism in the structures of Brexit itself and of the new political and social realities which it helped to create, while also showing how this aspect has been repeatedly diminished in widely accepted academic and other interpretations. Moreover, because investigators have analysed aspects of this problem in a wide range of literatures, the book aims to bring them together for the first time in a systematic, integrated interrogation of the role of racism in Brexit and its aftermath.

Second, since racism is evidently a contested concept, and in any coherent understanding takes complex and multiple forms, the book enters into the debates about its meaning and scope and its role in today's international political right. In this context, it aims to show that specific forms of political-racist agency – rather than the individual, cultural and systemic forms of racism which are more widely studied – have been most at stake in the processes I analyse and should be accorded greater theoretical significance in understanding contemporary racism in general. This approach has distinct methodological implications. Unlike most political science and sociological accounts of these developments, which start from changes in society and the electorate, the book aims to show that – while such studies are valuable – we need to pay particular attention to how change has been promoted in racist political interventions by parties, campaigns, press and social media activists before we can understand how voters' ideas have changed in response to them. While political change is obviously a two-way process between organized political actors and electorates, the actions of these actors not only influence how voters behave, which helps determine key political events, but also contribute to creating racialized structures in political life and what Paul Gilroy (2019) calls the ongoing "sedimentation or embeddedness" of underlying racial attitudes, which too many scholars take as givens.

Origins of this study

I had been studying and writing about political phenomena, as a globally oriented historical sociologist, for several decades before 2016, working mainly on war and genocide, which are often considered primarily as topics of international relations but which I showed tend to consistently involve questions at the intersections of international and domestic politics – which is also, by definition, the case with Brexit. In conceptualizing genocide, race and ethnicity were obviously important elements, and as I moved beyond war and genocide, I began to write about the racialization of contemporary political situations (Shaw 2015). However, although research on British society and politics had played a role in my work on war and militarism (Shaw 1991: 109–62; 1996) and genocide (Shaw 2011), I had not worked on racial politics in the UK. This began to change as I observed developments in the Brexit referendum campaign. My first trigger was watching Vote Leave's (2016a) official election broadcast, which was first transmitted on 23 May 2016. This piece of propaganda was obviously racist (as I show in Chapter 4), and although I had followed the speeches of Leave leaders and the controversies around their claims, I was shocked that it was shown, repeatedly and almost without criticism, on the BBC and other public, terrestrial television channels. As it became evident that this approach also typified a torrent of material which Vote Leave, along with Leave.EU, was putting out on social media, my interest deepened. Then, on referendum day, I was present (in my capacity as a citizen rather than a social scientist) as people voted in a normally quiet, strongly pro-Brexit town in south-west England. There was verbal abuse from a minority of Leave supporters towards Remain activists, who were standing silently at a distance from the polling station, of a kind and frequency I had not seen in previous elections. A van driver shouted, "You people are disgraceful", as he drove past; an older man strode up to a young woman with short hair and told her, "You need to sort out your sexuality". Then a woman of around my own age came up to me and jabbed her fingers at my chest, shouting aggressively, "You're not English, you're not English". My first reaction was one of shock, my second, after she had gone into the polling station, of amusement, since I tend to take my Englishness for granted, having been born in England of English parents and lived in the country for most of my life. However, my considered response was: What if I had not felt so English? What if I had been born in Poland, or had Pakistani parents? Thinking it through, I realized that this verbal attack had been ethnic in character. If my accuser had said, "you're not British", she might have impugned only my patriotism, but "not English" was clearly an ethnic or racial slur: you're not one of us. The reader may think the incident barely worthy of mention. More serious threats and also violence were directed that same day and afterwards at people of Polish, Pakistani and other non-British backgrounds, as they are every day at people of colour in the UK and elsewhere. For me, however, it was a novel experience, the first time in a long life that I had personally received ethnic hostility in Britain, and ironically at the hands of another white English person on the day that a majority of the English were voting for Brexit.

This small attack, in the threatening climate of polling day, brought home to me the link between race and the aggression which accompanied the Leave movement, making me think even more about the Europeans and members of minorities who were suffering serious abuse at the hands of the racists whom Leavers had emboldened. A week earlier, the Labour MP Jo Cox had been assassinated by a far-right sympathizer who, echoing Leave ideas, shouted "Britain first" as he killed her. This high-profile event was not an isolated incident but part of a pattern of street-level and online racism which peaked just after the referendum. Alongside this, however, there was the organized threat, implicit in

Brexit and understood by those who promoted it, which the referendum posed to the patterns of life and legal rights of UK residents who had come from other EU countries, particularly by potentially exposing them to the officially proclaimed "hostile environment" from which migrants from outside the EU, and even some UK citizens of colour, already suffered. Most of this book is political analysis, social theory and history at a more general level, so I have introduced these experiences of the victims (and my own encounter) at the beginning in order to emphasize to readers that the argument refers to very real hostility which many men, women and children suffered – and are still suffering – not only from crude racists but also from state institutions. It is too easy, more than half a decade on, to treat the referendum as an abstract political decision and to ignore the discrimination, abuse and violence which it entailed. It is rather like treating the assault on the US Capitol on 6 January 2021 as a legitimate protest about the counting of votes, rather than a violent attempt to intimidate elected representatives into overthrowing the result of a presidential election.

Writing about racism in Brexit

I make no apology for taking sides against such harms, since I don't believe that social scientists can be neutral on issues which are closely connected to fundamental human values. I don't apologize, either, for presenting these harms in this book as manifestations of racism. Obviously "racism" is not a neutral concept, and in pursuing the argument that it is fundamental to Brexit this book enters a political minefield which many analysts have avoided. During the referendum campaign, some Remainers circulated the trope on social media that "not all Leavers are racists but all racists support Brexit", which while accepting that some Leavers were not racist implied general guilt by association. Clearly, suggesting that those who supported Leave (in the event, 17.4 million people compared to 16.1 million who backed Remain) were implicated in racism, even if only in an indirect way, was a politically explosive accusation. Even the serious spike in abuse involved only a small minority of these millions, most of whom would doubtless have dissociated themselves from it. The charge of "racism" was therefore resented by supporters of the successful Leave movement, some of whom – not least among the third of ethnic minority voters who supported Brexit – sincerely regarded themselves as antiracist. Moreover, this Remainer trope was sometimes combined with a kind of class condescension towards them, based on the idea that they were mostly the "left-behind", less educated northern working-class voters of whom much commentary spoke in the immediate aftermath of the vote (in fact, the largest group of Leavers were middle-class voters in southern England).

However, the fact that charges of "racism" have not always been made in appropriate ways does not mean that the idea should be avoided in attempts to understand Brexit, or cannot be addressed through academic analysis. Such Remainer attitudes, which tarred Leavers generally with ignorance, were certainly offensive; but they differed in two important ways from the hostility faced by Europeans and others which I discuss in this book and so cannot be understood as "racist" in the same way. First, they were not intended to, nor did they, result in systematic discrimination; and second, although they were undoubtedly widespread on social media, they were not orchestrated by organized actors like campaigns, parties or mainstream media outlets. Leaver hostility towards Europeans, on the other hand, was knowingly aroused or supported by the Leave leaders and Leave press in the knowledge that it was likely to result in formal and informal discrimination. Indeed, I show that the opposition to immigration which was central to Brexit was suffused with hostility to foreigners and ethnic minorities, and that the ideology of the movement was broadly informed by racial assumptions. Likewise, I demonstrate that the "hard" Brexit which the Theresa May government proposed, an extreme version of which was finally implemented by Johnson in 2020, was fundamentally shaped by the anti-immigrant politics of the movement which triumphed in 2016, which was also deeply embedded in the Conservative Party and ultimately Johnson's regime.

Thus, although "How many Leavers were racists?" is not a helpful question or one to which it is possible to give a meaningful answer, Brexit is a phenomenon of organized racism, which has remained a guiding thread of its institutionalization and the political regime to which it led. There is a popular belief that racism is about whether people are or are not "racists", and there are certainly some people whose racism is so blatant, consistent and central to their self-presentation that it is appropriate to describe them in this way. However, racism is about much more than these people. It involves complex and varied sets of ideas and practices, which operate under the surface of social life as well as in plain view, and it is highly possible to be involved in some of these without being an "overt" racist. People relate differently to the various types and expressions of racism, often accepting certain ideas or assumptions but not others, in many cases while regarding themselves as non-racist or even antiracist. This is particularly true in a society like the twenty-first century UK in which racism has been delegitimized. In this context, racism becomes something which tries to hide itself, even while seeking people's support – for example, the promoters of anti-immigration politics often present it neutrally as a matter of the total number of people in the country, rather than of hostility to immigrants or particular racial or ethnic groups, although it obviously involves this. By the time of the EU referendum, British society was certainly significantly more liberal, for example in the acceptance of diversity, than it had been in earlier historical periods – although it was far from being a "post-racial" society – and both Leave leaders and voters had accepted aspects of this liberalization. It would be as mistaken to ignore these changes as it would be to neglect the continuing salience of racism; and it would be as wrong to neglect how Brexit politicians' approaches have changed compared to that of Enoch Powell, the emblematic racist politician of the late twentieth century, as it would be to ignore the important continuities of their ideas with his.

Perhaps what both sides of the Brexit divide might agree on is that there is a conflict *over* racism, and that it is paradoxical that this has arisen in a country whose dominant self-image, accepted by many international observers – if not by all people of colour in the UK – was as one of the world's most diverse, open societies. The Leave leaders, like all mainstream British politicians and parties, proclaimed themselves to be opponents of racism; even on the extreme right, few were still openly proud of racial views. Four years before the referendum, the London Olympics had celebrated a diverse, progressive Britishness and Johnson, then mayor of London, had presented himself as in tune with its spirit; even as prime minister after 2019 he continued to evoke this part of his record while making unprecedented appointments of ethnic minority MPs to senior ministerial positions. These changes were not purely presentational but reflected real changes in society, in which the status of minorities had advanced and diversity was more widely, if by no means fully or universally, accepted than it was earlier. Part of the explanation for the paradox is certainly that some sections of society had not accommodated as fully as others to the changes which had taken place. While no one survey metric can capture the persistence of racism in society, it is striking that British Social Attitudes analysts argue that "when it comes to racial prejudice, we are not seeing the clear trend towards social 'liberalization' that is so marked in other areas", such as views on sexual orientation. When the survey asked people whether they considered themselves "prejudiced against people of other races", over three decades "the proportion of the public who described themselves as either 'very' or 'a little' racially prejudiced varied between a quarter and over a third of the population. It has never fallen below 25 per cent" (Kelley, Khan & Sharrock 2017: 3). This book will show that Brexiters[1] and the more nationalist Conservative Party aimed to mobilize the racially oriented section of the population.

---

1. I use the term "Brexiter" throughout. Although it might sometimes be appropriate to replace it with the more evocative "Brexiteer", it seems sensible to consistently deploy the more neutral version rather than switching between them when there is no clear basis for the distinction.

The approach and argument of the book

This book does not seek simply to substantiate a *charge* of racism against the Leave movement or the Brexit regime. Rather, it addresses a specific paradox which arises from the general one which we have just noted. This is that racist political strategies appear to have played a more important role in Brexit and the rise of the nationalist Tory administration – and contributed to more important constitutional, political, economic and social changes – than in earlier periods when racism was more obvious and widely accepted and there were more overt interventions, such as the speeches of Powell in 1968. To understand this problem, I explore how both racism itself and thinking about it have changed over the last half-century. In particular, I argue that we need the concept of political racism to distinguish racism's organized political use from its individual, everyday, institutional and structural forms; or to put it another way, we need to understand that racialized politics is a crucial element of agency, which sustains racialized structures in the political field and has major consequences for societal racism. While political racism certainly existed in earlier periods, I argue that we need to pay particular attention to the changed ways and contexts in which it operates in twenty-first-century democracies. In exploring these, I contend that rather than starting from the sentiments of the voters, important though they are, we need to begin by examining how parties, campaigns, leaders, ideologues, media outlets and other organized actors, together with their followers on social media as well as in the streets, deploy and mobilize hostility in the current period. There is, of course, no intention of arguing that political racism, by itself, fully explains Brexit or the wider rise of the far right. However, I suggest that it is almost perverse for scholars to be so concerned with "underlying" causes of Brexit and its support that they fail to adequately address the forms of political mobilization which produced them.

To put my argument at its simplest, racism and the understanding of it have changed; its widespread delegitimization has altered how it is used politically; and so political racism today often looks different from racism as it has been perceived historically. But – and this "but" is why the book is needed – it remains an extremely potent resource for, and method of, modern politics. As not only Brexit but also the international mainstreaming of far-right ideas suggests, it could even be more potent than in earlier periods. *Political Racism* therefore offers a new way of thinking about racism and politics which has wide applicability, but here it is applied to British politics with only passing illustrations of its role in other countries, although I offer some thoughts on its wider uses in the Conclusion. I draw on evidence which has been accumulated and analysed by many specialists in different social science and humanities disciplines, as well as reports and commentary of many kinds. Surprisingly, no one has brought together the material and arguments which specialists have produced into a general analysis of the role of racism in this major structural change. This absence results not only from the usual fragmentation of knowledge which accompanies academic specialization but also from the particularly low salience of racism in the political science field (compared to sociology, anthropology, etc.) and the technical rather than conceptual character of much analysis. However, I propose that it is also because of a widespread ideological reluctance to acknowledge that racism is constitutive of Brexit. The avoidance of racism, which amounts to *denial*, is implicit as well as explicit. It is not confined to the few overt apologists but also includes scholars who are critical of Brexit, the political right and anti-immigration politics. It would be worth investigating the reasons for this further than I am able to in this study. However, I suggest that many scholars internalize, rather as many journalists and broadcasters do, a taboo on defining powerful actors and their projects in this way. Formal and informal relationships with the political right and a right-wing government can be as useful to academics in studying them as to reporters in reporting them, and probably contribute to euphemism and terminological self-censorship. This book therefore aims to not only present a coherent and satisfying narrative of Brexit racism, based on the knowledge which has been produced, but also a critique of this widespread denial of its existence and scope.

This volume adopts a historical approach, but it it is not a straightforward history. Rather, I write as a sociologist, developing a historically structured analytical account. I examine the development of British political racism and Europhobia over time, leading up to the crucial moment of change in the 2016 referendum, and how their combination contributed to the transformation which Brexit produced. The book is therefore organized part-thematically and part-chronologically, but the major dimensions of political racism (which are outlined in Chapter 1) inform each stage of the analysis, and there is a recurring focus on the hostility which it produces towards migrants, minorities and people of colour. The book therefore develops in the following way. Chapter 1 explores key issues in the understanding of racism and outlines the concept of political racism. Chapter 2 analyses the development of post-Second World War British political racism, leading to an argument that its adaptation to liberalizing norms helped produce what I call "numerical racism", linked to new forms of targeted hostility against Muslims and eastern Europeans in the present century. In Chapter 3, I discuss the racialized dimensions of the Europhobic movement's post-imperialist, nationalist and free market ideologies. In Chapter 4, I present a detailed analysis of the role of political racism in the 2016 referendum, both in the Leave campaigns and the media, and its hostile implications for Europeans and other minorities in the UK. In Chapter 5, I look at how hostility towards European immigration was embedded in and decisively influenced the May and Johnson governments' approaches to negotiations with the EU, and how the consequences helped structure the Brexit crisis of the years 2016–19 and deepen the divisions in British politics and society. In Chapter 6, I examine how political racism continued to play a significant role in Johnson's rise to power, his 2019 election victory and the new nationalist Tory regime. In the Conclusion, I reflect on the lessons of this analysis for the wider understanding of political racism as well as for British politics.

While these are manifestly difficult subjects, I believe they deserve the careful examination which I try to give them in this book. It is impossible as well as wrong for a writer to ignore their own value and political commitments, but it is necessary to address the issues in a measured and evidence-driven way. This is what I have tried to achieve, and the reader will judge how far I have succeeded.

1
CONCEPTUALIZING RACISM AND POLITICAL RACISM

Racism cannot be weaponized because it is already a weapon. ... Racism can, however, be deployed. It may galvanize, distract, deflect, distort, scapegoat and marginalize. It is an incredibly effective tool for dividing people and giving a sense of superiority to those to whom you have nothing material to offer.   Gary Younge (2019)

In arguing that racism was a major driver of Brexit and the transformation of British politics in the 2010s, this book proposes an interpretation of racism in general which may be new to some readers, as well as a distinctive concept of political racism. Racism is an obviously contested idea, in the double sense that there is no clear consensus on its meaning and application and that the differences about it matter in social and political conflict. It is also a relatively recent idea: Mark Mazower (1998: 103) dates *racisme* in French to the early 1930s, but its English equivalent only took over from the now quaint-sounding "racialism" around 1970. The use of the harder-sounding "racism" to describe racial hostility emerged in the Western world, therefore, long after "race" became a prominent feature of social relations and power in the world empires of European states, and only at the tail end of what Dirk Moses (2002) calls the "racial century" between 1850 and 1950 during which racial hierarchies achieved their most rigid forms. Indeed, it was only after racist political ideologies achieved extreme impacts in Europe itself during the Second World War, rather than in the colonized world where these had been obvious for centuries, that the modern critical idea of racism truly came into its own. Only then were the ideas of race which developed in the previous period – distinctions between human groups through biological and cultural differences and the discrimination and cruelty which accompanied them – deeply and widely contested within Western societies. Priyamvada Gopal (2019: 209ff.) shows that in Britain, it was between the world wars that anti-imperial insurgency in the colonized world combined with widespread dissidence in the metropolis to challenge the foundations of the racialized empire.

However, it was only in the 1960s and 1970s, as Black people in the United States and elsewhere began to organize, that opposition to racial discrimination became genuinely widespread and increasingly mainstream among large sections of white society too (Virdee 2014: 123–44). The late emergence of a general term to describe racial hostility should be understood in this context.

Changing ideas of race and racism

In the last half-century this critical idea of racism has increasingly informed policy and analysis, including work across academia, and has been linked to both the formal and substantial delegitimization of racist ideas and practices. In this process, the social and intellectual climates around the ideas of "race" and "racism" have repeatedly changed. Originally, racism was widely assumed to concern the "colour question" and to be based on the idea of "racial groups" which were biologically determined. In the middle of the twentieth century, biological race was still widely accepted as real, but its stereotypical features such as skull shape and skin colour were discredited as markers of significant differences between human beings. Indeed, even earlier in the century, the sociologist Max Weber (1964: 138) had dismissed the idea that "common social relationships" were connected to "a common biological inheritance". Early recognition of racism therefore centred on the idea that discriminating along the lines of biological race was irrational, and UNESCO (1968: 365) defined the phenomenon as "antisocial beliefs and acts which are justified by the fallacy that discriminatory intergroup relations are justified on biological grounds". Yet race had often been conceived of in more than biological terms. In the nineteenth-century English-speaking world, Duncan Bell (2020: 28) argues, it "was typically configured as a *biocultural assemblage*, a hybrid compound of 'cultural' and 'biological' claims" (emphasis in original). Whiteness fixed the outer boundary of the race, but it was through culture that it was positively defined: "The racial identity of Anglo-America was most commonly described as 'Anglo-Saxon'. The term was usually employed to designate a human collectivity defined by a vague admixture of mythology, historical experience, shared values, institutions, language, religious commitment, and cultural symbolism, all circumscribed (but not fully specified) by whiteness." Race was "an insidious feature" of the Western political imaginary, so that "identifying the precise meanings of the term during the Victorian and Edwardian years is a thankless task. Racial thinking formed a shape-shifting amalgam of theories, vocabularies, practices, assumptions, and desires, and it both interdicted with and competed with other ways of conceptualizing human groups, most notably civilization and nationality" (Bell 2020: 26). Until the late twentieth century the dominant US racial group continued to be widely described as "White Anglo-Saxon Protestants", a term which has only faded from use as Catholic groups such as the Irish and Italians were accepted into a broader category of "white". Even after this, people of Latin American descent, "Hispanics", continued to be distinguished from them, and distinctions of Black and white remained fundamental because of how histories of slavery and racial oppression had informed the deepest hostility rather than the visibility of skin colour.

If race has remained a powerful definer of discrimination, by the end of the twentieth century biological "race" had long lost even any residual credibility as as an objective category, but it was still cultivated by right-wing ideologues (Saini 2019). As Stuart Hall (1997: 6) put it, "all attempts to ground this concept scientifically, to locate differences between the races, on what one might call scientific, biological, or genetic grounds, have been largely shown to be untenable". Yet new ways of fixing the concept continued to be sought, which Hall (1997: 7) saw as attempts to *replace* biology by culture: "We must therefore, it is said, substitute a socio-historical or cultural definition of race, for the biological one." This meant that "the biological, physiological, or genetic definition, having been shown out the front door, tends to sidle around the veranda and climb back in through the window". Against attempts to fix race either biologically or culturally, Hall insisted that it was "a floating signifier" or "a discursive category", "more like a language, than it is like the way in which we are biologically constituted … The meaning of a signifier can never be finally or trans-historically fixed" (Hall 1997: 8). Since race was not an objective category, "racism" increasingly became the key concept, describing discriminatory beliefs, cultural orientations and political values, together with the sets of practices and institutions which instantiated them in society. The hollowing out of the idea of race gradually transformed the understanding of racism, diminishing and even eliminating a necessary role for the "biological fallacy". Working in the same period, Floya Anthias and Nira Yuval-Davis (1983: 67) suggested that while racist discourse indicated an essential biological determination of cultural difference, its referent might be any group that had been "socially" constructed as having a different "origin", whether cultural, biological or historical. The focus of racism could be "Jewish", "Black", "foreign", "migrant", "minority"; any group that was located in ethnic terms could be subject to racism as a form of exclusion. Since that time, racism has been increasingly used as a general term for hostility on the grounds of group identity, whether or not biological determination is posited. However, as Alana Lentin contends, race as a project or a system of rule and legitimation nevertheless has widespread bodily effects: "Race is not biology … but it may become biology" (Lentin 2020: 110, summarizing Clarence Gravlee).

In a common contemporary understanding, therefore, anti-Muslim sentiment is as much an instance of racism as hostility to people of colour, as well as another way of reproducing the latter. There has also been a growing recognition of how fundamentally racism is connected with class and exploitation. While still directed mainly at people of colour, it particularly affects poorer and lower-status groups. This also means that some people who are "white" in terms of skin colour may experience a xenophobia which is, to all intents and purposes, a form of racism. At the turn of the twenty-first century, Ambalavaner Sivanandan (2001) argued that there was a new "xenoracism",

> not just directed at those with darker skins, from the former colonial territories, but at the newer categories of the displaced, the dispossessed and the uprooted, who are beating at western Europe's doors, the Europe that helped to displace them in the first place. It is a racism, that is, that cannot be colour-coded, directed as it is at poor whites as well, and is therefore passed off as xenophobia, a "natural" fear of strangers. But in the way it denigrates and reifies people before segregating and/ or expelling them, it is a xenophobia that bears all the marks of the old racism. It is racism in substance, but "xeno" in form. It is a racism that is meted out to impoverished strangers even if they are white.

However, what this understanding refers to was not really new. Robbie Shilliam (2018: 19–32) demonstrates how, in the early nineteenth century, even the English "undeserving poor" were racialized by analogy with slaves, while Satnam Virdee (2014: 12–17) shows how Irish Catholics were the main "racialized outsiders" in Britain later in the century, followed by Jews at the beginning of the twentieth. The way that "race" was linked to national culture in ideas like "the Anglo-Saxon race" already implied a hierarchy among white people as well as between white and Black people. However light their skins might be, during the racial century Jewish people were rarely seen as fully white; Nazism, which many see as the archetypal racist ideology, developed a comprehensive racial hierarchy in which not only Jews and Black people but also Slavs were slated for extreme violence because they were regarded as racially inferior to "Aryans". While each type of racism has specific roots and consequences, they overlap in contemporary societies; as Glynis Cousins and Robert Fine (2012: 166) put it, "prejudice and persecution in relation to Muslims, Jews and Black people are connected phenomena in the formation of European modernity". Racist ideologies and practices combine different types of hostility in varying, selective ways, and these combinations may cause contradictions. For example, Gilroy (2004: 110) suggests that "white" migrant minorities may simultaneously be subject to new forms of racialization themselves *and* try to "seek salvation by trying to embrace and inflate the ebbing privileges of whiteness". In the context of these intellectual developments, it is hardly a novel move to understand the hostilities towards eastern Europeans and Muslims – which we shall see played a central part in Brexit – as distinctive forms of racism, even if from a narrow "colour" standpoint Europeans could be seen as white and Muslims as belonging to a religious rather than a racial category.

Summarizing these changes in thinking, the fundamental problem with some older ideas of racism is that they make specific (biological, colour) grounds of irrational and harmful discrimination the definer, when it is the irrationality and harm of discriminating which is the problem. Certainly, all forms of racism have the capacity to make "race" real, so that Lentin (2020) is right to argue that "race still matters", the specific ways in which people are targeted always have serious consequences (as the slogan "Black Lives Matter" suggests), and in modern global society the history of racism both begins with and returns to the oppression of Black people by those who regard themselves as white. However, the core of racism is not discrimination because of colour, religion, nationality or ethnicity; rather it is the very *principle* of discrimination on the grounds of people's supposed membership of a group or category which the perpetrators treat as inferior to their own. This is usually thought of as being directed against particular groups, but "xenophobia", that is, hostility to "foreigners" or non-members of the perpetrators' own group, is also an important type. Gavan Titley (2020: 45) argues that the "shifting set of racializing practices cannot be adequately understood if analysis has to be accommodated in a 'definition of racism'". He is correct that narrow and rigid definitions are extensively deployed in denial, as I discuss below, but like any concept, the idea *is* capable of being defined, in a way which enables us to capture variation and change, if expressed at an adequate level of generality. It is therefore proposed here that racism can be defined, narrowly, as *ideas and practices which entail hostility to people on the grounds of their otherness*, and more expansively in terms of the patterning or structuring of such ideas and practices as they are developed and embedded in social life, together with the cultural and ideological panoplies which sustain the ideas of racial difference which underlie hostility.

Changing modalities, discourse and intentionality

Just as there are many different types of othering, there are many ways in which hostility may be manifested, and these have been changing. Racism is often associated with hatred, which implies a direct relationship between agent and target, but not all hostility is obviously "hateful" in this sense. It's also sometimes assumed that racism is necessarily overt; this idea is particularly developed by those who promote hostility, who often deny being involved in "overt racism". However, hostility or enmity may be covert, indirect, latent or concealed, as well as overt, direct, manifest or proclaimed. The less obvious forms of racism have always been important, even in societies openly organized on principles of racial dominance. As racism has been delegitimized over the last century, its most potent forms have often been those which are less obvious or openly designed. Sociologists and anthropologists still examine open forms of what Stokely Carmichael and Charles V. Hamilton (1967: 4), writing in 1967, called "individual racism", in which individuals directly express hostility to those from different backgrounds, and what Philomena Essed (1991: 11–53) later named "everyday" or "micro" as opposed to "macro" racism. These two concepts overlap, but they are not the same: for example, individual abuse and violence around the time of the 2016 referendum was not "everyday", because it was stimulated by a high-profile political event. Everyday racism refers to individual hostility which occurs regularly in routine social interaction, such as the hostility experienced by Muslims and eastern Europeans in the UK over the previous decade.

However, alongside individual and everyday racism, studies have increasingly emphasized types which are *typically* indirect or implicit, even occurring through mechanisms which are formally regulated by norms against discrimination. Carmichael and Hamilton (1967: 4) coined the term "institutional racism" for hostility which was "less overt, more subtle, and less identifiable in terms of specific individuals" committing acts. This type, they argued, "originates in the operation of established and respected forces in the society, and thus receives far less public condemnation" than overt racism. A classic example was identified by the official Macpherson report into how London's Metropolitan Police dealt with the killing of Stephen Lawrence. The inquiry defined institutional racism as the "collective failure of an organization to provide an appropriate and professional service to people because of their colour, culture, or ethnic origin. It can be seen or detected in processes, attitudes and behaviour that amount to discrimination through prejudice, ignorance, thoughtlessness, and racist stereotyping which disadvantage minority ethnic people" (Home Office 1999). Many see such failures, however, as representing more than the ways in which organizational cultures permit bigoted individuals to practice violence or produce negative outcomes for minority groups. Police racism can also be seen as part of larger patterns, both of "state" racism (Goldberg 2002) and more broadly of what has been variously termed "societal", "structural" or "systemic" racism. From this perspective, racism is built into the ways in which global and national social systems operate in their deep structures, and how many forms of power, entrenched in institutions, practices and ideas, combine to reproduce patterns of discrimination against specific groups. Economic and social inequalities, deeply rooted in long historical processes, work against minorities, while cultures of hostility persist in organizations and everyday social milieux. As Stephen Ashe's (2021) survey shows, structural racism continues to be reproduced *despite* laws, norms, policies and institutions designed to prevent racial discrimination. Shilliam (2018: 119) argues that when discrimination in systematic forms (informal as well as formal) is outlawed, it continues in "individualized and fractured" forms.

Alongside these transformations in the practices and effects of racism and how they are understood, there have been significant changes in the discourse around it. As biological racism was recognized as "irrational" and "overt" discrimination became illegitimate, new discursive moves implied that we already lived in "post-racial" societies in which racial inequalities no longer needed special attention but could be addressed merely by treating everyone equally. This led, as writers like Reni Eddo-Lodge (2017) and Meghan Burke (2019) argue, to "colour-blind" racism, which by treating minorities as though they were already equal allowed structural discrimination against them to continue. A typical idea of this kind is that "All Lives Matter", which claims to equalize all groups' experiences but actually diminishes the significance of continuing discrimination and violence against Black people. In that context, all lives are *not* equal; indeed, as Priyamvada Gopal puts it, "White lives don't matter. As white lives", because white people are not oppressed as Black people are (Guéron-Gabrielle 2020).

What is going on in such ideological ploys, Lentin (2016: 35) proposes, is that "the understanding of what racism is becomes narrower", so that "proper" racism is "often thought of in the past tense" and even "frozen" in those "examples from the past about whose horror there is universal consensus", such as the Nazi genocide. Yet while the idea is solidified in this way, racism actually becomes "more and more motile", allowing "discrimination and abuse to continue polyvalently under the guise of purportedly post-racial arguments about cultural incompatibility, secularism versus religion, or sovereignty and security". Official rejections of frozen racism allow motile racism to continue, and we are left with "an inability to see, let alone understand, what fuels racism's apparently continual drive". Racism also appears to become debatable, "not because the racisms of the past are called into question, but precisely because by fixing 'real' racism solely in historical events, the continuities between racisms past and present are *made* undecidable" (emphasis in original). As Titley (2020: 61) argues, "postracial denial says you can talk about racism as much as you like, as long as it does not exceed the terms of a definition that we control". It can even be seen, Sara Ahmed (2010) points out, as wilful to name racism, "as if the talk about divisions is what is divisive". Increasingly, the gambit of the right is "to empty the idea of racism of any political purchase, to ensure that it is always subsumed to the meta-debate, primed as the trigger of patterned controversies where the 'accusation' becomes as controversial as the substantive issue" (Titley 2020: 61).

The systemic approach leads Titley to critique "dehistoricized understandings of racism" which "have made it possible to extract racism from political economy and social structures, locating it principally in the realm of ideas", where it is "expressed through intentional speech acts and actions" (Titley 2020: 18, 40). He is right that racism is neither a purely ideological form nor wholly a matter of intentional acts, that these ideas are frequently used – together with a "frozen" historical approach – to limit racism to acts marked by overtly hostile intentions and that we need to examine the "shifting set of racializing practices", recognizing that race "is a technique of power ... always in formation" (Titley 2020: 44–5). However, the fact that racism is not by definition ideological or intentional does not mean that ideology or intentions are unimportant to it; indeed, we must also beware of frozen concepts of ideology and intention. Ideas which imply or protect racism – such as the abuse of "free speech" which Titley analyses – are as much racist ideology as doctrines which proclaim racial hatred. Campaigns which strategically mobilize racial hostility in indirect or covert ways, even while trumpeting their antiracist credentials, are as much forms of intentional racism as are open appeals to prejudice. A one-sided emphasis on structural racism, especially if it is conceived in socio-economic terms, can imply that racism is more or less immutable and that actors mainly reproduce patterns which have long existed. Yet this minimizes the ways in which racist agency transforms these patterns and creates new structures of racism. Contemporary racism is not only systemic and a routine technique of power but also has a powerful, hard and repeatedly renewed edge in the *organized, intentional use of race* by major political actors. It is the argument of this book that these strategic forms of racism, which we can see at work in Brexit, Trump and other recent developments, have been increasingly influential and help create new structures of political racism, which in turn both sustain and modify the overall pattern of racism in society.

Nationalism, nativism and selective racism

The changes to which the critique of frozen racism draws our attention have also been identified in studies of political ideologies, especially in the relationship between racism and nationalism. In principle, we can distinguish between nationalism, which typically defines nations as being in conflictual relationships with other nations, states and international organizations, and racism, which defines social communities through hostility to other racial, ethnic or other social groups. However, nationalism has often worked through racial ideas and at the same time has been the prime, overt ideological frame within which organized political racism has operated, because the nation is the principal modern "imagined community" and excluding others from that community has often been the manifest goal of racist politics. While the distinction between inclusive "civic" and exclusive "ethnic" nationalisms is widely invoked, this has always been a simplification; as Michael Mann (2005: 3–4) shows, democracies have generally defined their "demos" (people) in terms of an "ethnos", and discriminated against ethnic others both inside and outside the national society. Even "civic" nations always involved such boundaries, which intersected with class divisions and were constantly negotiated and contested. Writing about Britain, Gilroy (1987: 57) notes that "statements about nation are invariably statements about 'race'"; Shilliam (2018: 46) argues that "as the deserving English working class became enfranchized they also became racialized as Anglo-Saxon"; and Virdee (2014: 9–71) shows that successive immigrant groups had to fight to extend these boundaries in order to be included in the nation. Historically, both right and left often linked nationalism and racism; however, as working- and middle-class constituencies for antiracism grew, social-democratic and liberal parties increasingly internalized its norms, ideologically rejecting the equation of nation and race and redefining the civic nation in more explicitly inclusive ways, often differentiating themselves from the right through this definition – even while still, as Maya Goodfellow (2019) shows in the British case, responding to right-wing mobilization by defensively or pre-emptively continuing policy racism. In this context, it became more important for civic nationalists to distinguish their causes from racism, as secessionist movements in countries such as Scotland and Catalonia have done. Taking this trend to its logical conclusion, Anthony Barnett (2021) sees "small country" nationalism as a route to emancipation from the authoritarianism and racism of multinational states like the UK; however, even small-nation imagined communities exist in constant tensions with their underlying ethnic identities and produce othering of the dominant nationalities (Macintosh, Sim & Robertson 2004) which tends to be expressed during secessionist conflicts.

The tendencies to delegitimize overt racism and distinguish nationalism from racism have had important implications for the global far right. Racism has always involved supranational identities – for example, whiteness, Christendom, Europe and the Anglo-Saxon race – and ideological racism now circulates ever more across borders, generating transnational networks. At a mobilization level, however, the nation-state context has remained central; indeed, the nation is even more important as a legitimate ideological frame. Yet because of the growing stigma attached to race, far-right movements have developed new terms in which they specify nations' racial communities. Early in this century, scholars began to use the term "nativism" to describe a distinctive type of ideology which was emerging in the West. According to Cas Mudde (2007: 19) this was "an ideology which holds that states should be inhabited exclusively by members of the native group ('the nation') and that nonnative elements (persons and ideas) are fundamentally threatening to the homogeneous nation-state". As a form of racism, nativism's key characteristic was that it represented a *generalized* exclusion

21

of others, typically linked to a view that immigration was the overriding problem, which was framed in religious, security, economic and above all cultural terms, as nativists claimed to speak for "indigenous" white nations (Mudde 2012: 9–17). Many nativists used frozen concepts to differentiate themselves from overt racism, but their main ideas had long been advocated in conjunction with overt racist themes; as George Newth (2021: 1) puts it, nativism is "a racist and xenophobic discourse structured around an exclusionary vision of the nation".

The principal novelty was in fact the way in which nativism was deployed by new "radical right" populist parties, which differentiated themselves from older extreme right parties that carried overt racist, fascist and antisemitic ideological baggage, as well as from mainstream conservative parties which were anchored in more traditional forms of nationalism. Radical right parties were the type of party, Mudde (2012: 9) argues, for whom nativism was "a core ideological feature". However, in the last decade, this approach has also been widely mobilized by mainstream parties which have entered populist phases or acquired extreme populist leaders (although of course not all have done so: for a survey of European cases, see Bale & Kaltwasser 2021). In later work, Mudde (2019: 165) argues that "mainstream and populist radical right parties not only address the same issues, they also increasingly offer similar positions. Research shows that this is the consequence more of the radicalization of mainstream parties than of the moderation of populist radical right parties." Conservative leaders have often been willing to convert immigration into a political problem, but today many are exploiting its potential more systematically and in innovative ways, explicitly or implicitly espousing nativist ideas. Hence, Mudde (2019: 1–2) argues, the "mainstreaming and normalization" of radical right nativist populism was a key development in the 2010s, as the translation of immigration into a political issue moved to the centre of mainstream right politics. It is also important to underline that although nativism represents a particular ideological fusion of racism and nationalism, the two may still need to be distinguished in the analysis of political mobilization in order to establish their dynamic relationships, as the Brexit case shows. Although (as Chapter 2 shows) the Europhobic movement emerged from milieux in which nativism was a powerful tradition, it developed specifically (as Chapter 3 discusses) out of Euroscepticism, with a nationalist ideology which increasingly specified the EU as the enemy. It was therefore necessary for Europhobic nationalism and racist nativism to be fused for the nationalist cause to become popular. We shall also see that in turn, the deepening of Europhobic nationalism helped to generalize new forms of anti-European racism.

Moreover, "nativism" does not fully describe the ideological racism of the anti-immigrant right, either radical or mainstream. This is partly because ideology alone does not drive political racism; it is above all a *strategic resource* for mobile political actors. From the point of view of political mobilization, the important thing is to define enemies and to create an effective coalition against them. Hence, while some nativists are strictly mono-ethnic, in practice many interpret the nation – which notionally at least they often define civically – in particular pan-ethnic terms, according to the demands of the political situation. The nation is therefore defined as much by those it excludes as those it includes; the enemy can be all those who are not "us", that is, "immigrants" in general, poorer migrants, particular ethnic and religious groups or some combination of these. "We", the nation, can therefore be strategically adapted to the particular constellation of ethnicity and class within the state, often incorporating some minorities in order to be more effective against another minority (or even majority) which is excluded. This is not a new phenomenon, since it was the essence of colonial divide and rule over several centuries and has been a normal process in Western democracies, as shown by the incorporation of successive migrant nationalities into the white majority in the USA while Black people remained excluded. However, today in Western countries, while racial nationalism is still predominantly steered by whiteness, there is a tendency towards a "pick 'n' mix" approach, which may involve some minorities of colour being partially included and some white groups excluded.

Peter Pomerantsev (2019: 381) even suggests: "In an age in which all the old ideologies have vanished and there is no competition over coherent political ideas, the idea becomes to lasso together disparate groups around a new notion of the people, an amorphous but powerful emotion that each can interpret in their own way, and then seal it by conjuring up phantom enemies who threaten to undermine it." Certainly the prevalence of antiracist norms places a higher premium on this kind of selectivity; Pomerantsev might have added that if some "good" minorities are added to the mix, it makes it all the easier to conjure the others as enemies, and by highlighting the minorities which they include, political entrepreneurs can insulate themselves against charges of racism and even present themselves as antiracist. Keith Kahn-Harris (2019: 10–11) goes so far as to argue that in the twenty-first century, what he calls "selective anti/racism" is normal, as racists and "antiracists" choose ethnic groups, and indeed sections of groups, to favour and show hostility towards. In this way, some immigrants and minorities become "worthy" while others remain "unworthy". Jews, historically the ultimate outsiders in Christian countries, have now been adopted by the right – especially the Christian right – while Muslims are demonized, although some continuity antisemites have it both ways by blaming Jews for Muslim immigration. Anti-Muslim racism, which like antisemitism has a long history in both Europe and Asia, has become increasingly important to nationalist politics in many countries where Muslims are minorities; in India, the right defines the Hindu nation by its exclusion of Muslims as well as through the hierarchy of caste.

Social media, demography and denial

The other transformations which have been widely noted concern the typical practices and social bases of political racism. If its ideological content can be identified in a combination of nativism and selective anti/racism, its primary mode of expression often appears to be posts on social media. Political racism in democracies has always been validated through feedback which allows racist ideas to be represented as the spontaneous choices of voters, but traditionally this occurred through formal mechanisms like elections and polling. In the last digital decade, however, much feedback has become direct. Increasingly, fluid informal collectivities actively contribute to shaping political trends, through platforms such as Twitter and Facebook, leading to what Helen Margetts *et al.* (2016) call unprecedented "political turbulence". The digital scholar Eugenia Siapera (2019: 2, 27) suggests that in terms of content, "there are very few differences" between ambient and organized racism, which "are often combined and circulated in tandem", resulting in a situation where supremacist discourses "have blended with racial and ethno-nationalistic common sense". In contrast to Mudde's emphasis on the role of radical right parties in furthering nativism, Stephen Albrecht, Maik Fielitz and Nick Thurston (2019: 8) argue that "the quantity, sophistication and inter-connectedness of both unofficial activists and official party channels on-line has made it more and more difficult to carry forwards established academic categories to explain the far-right's renewal", while Philip N. Howard (2015: 224) even claims that "the state, the political party, the civic group, the citizen ... are all old categories from a pre-digital world", and Siapera (2019: 3) concludes that "conceptual and operational distinctions between organized, extreme racism and ambient, banal everyday race talk, do not in fact hold, and may even contribute to the circulation of racism in digital environments". Yet, while the extensive visibility and apparently everyday character of racism on social media sometimes obscure the continuing importance of the organized elements which are at work, these are still playing different roles from those of ambient actors. We still need the conceptual distinction between collective political actors and their leaders, for whom racism is primarily a *strategic tool*, and individual users of social media, for whom it is chiefly a *mode of expression* even if this includes support for strategic initiatives. Without this distinction, we cannot capture the interactions and continuing power imbalance between the two, which are reproduced even as they appear to be involved in a seamlessly harmonized circulation of themes through instantaneous feedback loops.

The tendency to reduce racism to its everyday and popular manifestations is also very strong in electoral analysis, centred around the idea that underlying "ethnocentric" attitudes have crystallized into "demographic" realities which in turn are the main drivers of political change. According to Maria Sobolewska and Rob Ford's (2020: 4–7) synthesis of recent research, the British electorate has followed the American in dividing between "identity conservatives", who are mainly white "school leavers" without higher education, and an "identity liberal" alliance of graduate "conviction liberals" and ethnic minority "necessity liberals". These identities have been forming, they argue, since the earlier period of mass immigration in the mid-twentieth century, so that developments like Brexit are a matter of "the activation of ethnocentric hostilities to out-groups *which had been there all along*" (Sobolewska & Ford 2020: 151, emphasis added). Yet these authors, like many other students of electoral trends, find no serious conceptual place for "racism", which (following a frozen approach) they reserve for historical figures like Powell. Even "nativism" is passed over as the euphemistic terms "identity conservatism", which stresses in-group identity rather than the rejection of out-groups, and at best "ethnocentrism" are used to describe anti-immigrant attitudes. In addition, direct contact with immigrants is ascribed the central role in shaping the attitudes of pre-existing populations. For Sobolewska and Ford (2020: 41–2), Margaret Stacey's classic (1960) sociological study of responses to domestic incomers in one English town in the 1930s provides a model for understanding current nationwide hostility to international migrants. However, the arrival and physical visibility of immigrants cannot, in itself, create anti-immigrant sentiment even at a local level; they need to be discursively represented to facilitate this response. *A fortiori*, the arrival of immigrants in *some areas* cannot be the direct driver of hostile national sentiment which is spread fairly evenly across areas without, as well as those with, significant numbers. As Mudde (2012: 1–2) points out, "rising numbers of immigrants do not automatically translate into increasing extremism in a country; immigration has to be *translated* into a political issue" (emphasis in original).

Sobolewska and Ford offer the caveat that "demography is not destiny", emphasizing that identity conservatism needs to be "activated", but it is clear that "demography" is the main driver in their account. While they trace the formation of today's British "identity conservative" group to Powell, they almost wholly ignore the underlying production and reproduction of racial attitudes, over the previous decades, to which he himself responded. As Kathleen Paul's (1997) persuasive analysis of policy-making (discussed in Chapter 2) had shown, it was not popular racism which first created Britain's "race relations problem". Rather it was policy-makers' "racialized understandings of population" and their long search for a way of limiting colonial "immigration" of people of colour without being overtly racist which helped, with the assistance of the press, precipitate the racialized immigration politics of the 1960s. The first opinion polls on immigration, which Sobolewska and Ford cite as evidence of the original racism of the "identity conservative" majority, were taken "only after ten years of government discouragement of colonial migration" (Paul 1997: 139). Sobolewska and Ford's demographic account of polarization also takes little account of how substantial sections of the "school-leaver" white population remained part of working-class movements alongside members of ethnic minorities, and sometimes shared in these movements' growing resistance to nativism.

Sobolewska and Ford's analytical biases are taken radically further by a small group of political scientists who – if they have not "gone native" with the far right they study – have become "academic populists" in their zeal to popularize the idea that its parties and electorates are expressing "legitimate" racial concerns (Shaw 2019). Although we shall see in Chapter 2 that in the early 2010s Matthew Goodwin had been involved in much of the research which documented British far-right parties' mobilization of racism, in his co-authored potboiler such parties only sometimes "veer into racism and xenophobia", which are not fundamental components of their appeal; they have merely "tapped into" concerns about immigration which already existed (Eatwell & Goodwin 2018: xii, 156). The labelling of far-right parties as "national" populists is particularly insidious, accepting as it does their leaders' claims to speak for whole nations rather than indicating their ideological drivers, as would alternative qualifiers like "nativist" or even plain "national*ist*". It is accompanied by a hyperbolic legitimation of nativism in claims such as that "immigration and hyper ethnic change are cultivating strong fears about the possible *destruction* of the national group's historic identity and established ways of life" (Eatwell & Goodwin 2018: xxiii, emphasis in original). The idea that the mere arrival of people from different backgrounds causes fears of the "destruction" of group identity and ways of life – terminology which evokes the definition of genocide – is backed by little more than mundane facts like, "by 2011 white Britons in London had become a minority" (Eatwell & Goodwin 2018: 141). Similarly, Eric Kaufmann (2018: 7) claims that anti-immigration politics is caused by the "cultural instability" resulting from the declining white "share" of the population: "Demography and culture, not economic and political developments, hold the key to understanding the populist moment. Immigration is central. Ethnic change – the size and nature of the immigrant inflow and its capacity to challenge ethnic boundaries – is the story." Kaufmann's (2018: 10) concern with racial mixing even leads him to emphasize that "only those with at least some European ancestry can identify as members of the white majority"; he therefore sees Brexit as a "racial" response by the "white British" (Kaufmann 2017; Shaw 2020), although only one political orientation in the white population is involved, and research shows that white people who regard their ethnicity as important or a matter of pride are a minority (Juan-Torres, Dixon & Kimaram 2020: 91–2).

Both Eatwell and Goodwin (2018: 74–5) and Kaufmann (2018: 145) also advance incoherent definitions of racism. The former say it refers to "the erroneous and dangerous belief that the world is divided into hierarchically ordered races, to antisemitism which plays more on conspiracy theory, and to violence and aggressive attitudes towards others based on their ethnicity", the latter that it is "an irrational fear or hate of or prejudice against a member of another ethnic group, a violation of citizens' right to equal treatment without regard to race, or a desire for race purity". Here we have two different lists, each of three elements, and neither explains what links them together as instances of racism. The effect, however, in both cases is to narrow racism to frozen historical manifestations, so that Eatwell and Goodwin (2018: 76, 122) assert apologetically that Trump "does not fit the systematically racist mould" and that "blatant racism is actually in decline", while Kaufmann (2017: 21–2) argues for "cordoning off" racism from mainstream anti-immigrant ideas. His argument, which is developed in more openly racial terms than his colleagues', contends that when a white majority is "ethnicized" by immigration and racial mixing they merely seek to maintain their "share" of the population through a legitimate defensive attitude which he calls "racial self-interest", which he argues is "normal" in contrast to racism which is "taboo". Kaufmann (2017: 10) tries to ground the distinction in social theory, claiming that racial self-interest is "a form of group partiality Max Weber might classify as 'substantively rational'".

The reference is curiously unexplained, but as I have argued elsewhere (Shaw 2020), it points to Weber's (1964: 15) well-known distinction between purpose-rational action, which is instrumentally rational as a means to an end, and value-rational action, which is absolutely oriented to a value. Applied to racially oriented action, this would imply that hostility which is conditional on a particular "threat" could be regarded as instrumentally "rational", while hostility to out-group people *tout court* would be an expression of an absolute negative value. Clearly actors could hold these different types of racial attitude, but to the extent that they did, the idea does not remove "instrumental" anti-immigrant action from the field of racism, nor establish that they are distinct rather than overlapping in voters' minds. Rather, "racial interests" can only be second-order projections, emphasizing contingent realities and objectives, of values which prioritize a white collectivity against racial others. To further block the interpretation of racial "self-interest" as racist, Kaufmann (2017: 3) quotes David Goodhart's (2017: 251) view that we need to distinguish "between the greater comfort people often feel among familiar people and places and active hostility towards outsider ethnic groups". Yet opposition to international immigration can never be merely a reflection of inward-looking group feeling since its rationale is outward-looking and relational, defining group interests *against* actual or potential immigrants, whether because of their particular identities or simply because they are non-members of the group. Contesting immigration therefore necessarily transforms any benign group feeling into hostility towards others whose arrival or presence is opposed.

Even when not accompanied by apologetics, the widely expressed analytical priority for electoral demography largely takes anti-immigrant attitudes as given and minimizes the significance of racist anti-immigrant mobilization. It exemplifies what Mattijs Roudijnn (2019: 364) calls a general "shift from the supply side of the political spectrum to the demand side" in populism studies, which does not address the realities of power. The longstanding existence of racial attitudes in all Western populations is hardly in dispute; as Mudde (2010: 1178) pointed out, "populist radical right attitudes are not just shared by a tiny minority of the European population. In fact, the populist radical right is better perceived as a pathological normalcy ... well connected to mainstream ideas and much in tune with broadly shared mass attitudes and policy positions." Yet precisely because these attitudes are longstanding, they cannot explain the rise of the *new* right-wing nativism. Mudde argued instead that it was the supply from the radical right which was novel and needed to be examined. His proposal is even more relevant now that some radicalized mainstream parties have also moved racist anti-immigration politics centre stage. The increased importance of immigration as an issue, in societies which are slowly becoming more accepting of migrants in practice, does not reflect increasingly racist attitudes so much as the success of right-wing nationalists in persuading those who oppose immigration to focus on the issue and to vote in accordance with their concerns. Even Eatwell and Goodwin (2018: 271) acknowledge, when their hyperbole subsides, that "much of our focus has been on the key 'bottom-up' trends, or ... the 'demand side' ... Critics might argue that we have not looked enough at the 'supply side', at how national populists themselves tap into these currents."

Defining political racism and its main elements

Looking at the supply side of racial politics means looking beyond ideological, media and electorate-level developments to the *strategic role* of racism for political actors. Even if radical right parties have a degree of ideological coherence around nativism, power remains their *raison d'être* and leaders like Farage, France's Marine le Pen and Italy's Mario Salvini are ambitious politicians as much as ideologues; mainstream conservative leaders like Trump and Johnson who have picked up their mantle even more so; indeed, even extreme right leaders are hardly pure ideologues. Like "pick 'n' mix" approaches to racial nationalism, the tendency of all these leaders to turn the strength of racist appeals up and down, according to the demands of the political situation, reflects their essential opportunism when it comes to race. It is mistaken to see political racism as driven primarily by either politicians' nativist ideologies or the mass electoral support for nativist ideas. Rather, these are primarily resources in the struggle for power, even if the different types of right-wing party (and single-issue coalitions like the Leave campaigns) engage in this struggle from different vantage points.

As Gary Younge implies in the epigraph to this chapter, all racism involves relationships of power; indeed, race can generally be seen, as Alana Lentin (2020: 110, 14) argues, as a "technology" of power and in this sense a "political project". However, something distinctive is involved when it is deployed instrumentally to achieve specifically political goals. We can therefore identify a specific form, political racism, which we can define as *the deployment of hostility to achieve, maintain or transform political power*. This is a particular type of organized hostility, involving powerful collective actors, for a specific set of purposes, typically in mass democracies. It has a new and distinctive importance in societies where racism has been delegitimized and other types of intentional, consciously organized racism are in relative decline. Recognizing political racism alters the overall picture: today racism is produced not only by structural inequalities which persist *despite* official norms and policies designed to prevent them but also through organized hostility promoted *in conjunction with* nominal or partial adherence to antiracist norms. In this sense, specifying political racism adds a new dimension to the analyses of the embedded forms of societal racism – individual, everyday, institutional and structural – which sociologists, anthropologists, historians and post/decolonial scholars have emphasized. Since consciously organized systems of racial domination like slavery, apartheid and Nazism have been largely superseded, political racism represents *the principal continuing element of intentional, organized racism*, especially in democracies. It is important to be clear about the meaning of this distinction. Structural racism operates through the conscious actions of individuals, but no organized actor consciously directs it, and it persists despite racism being officially rejected and mitigated. Political racism, in contrast, is directed by organized actors and seeks to *manage* the normative rejection of racism so that racist attitudes can still be exploited for political purposes.

A political racism focus therefore leads us to examine the *active* forces which *mobilize* hostility and thereby help to produce new inequalities and reinforce old ones. Its core mode is the strategic use of hostility to conquer political power and control state apparatuses by winning elections, referendums, intra-party contests, key political decisions, etc. Collective actors such as parties, campaigns and partisan media, as well as their individual leaders, are the prime movers, who most directly express its relationships to power. This strategic use is a traditional form, developed in many countries through two centuries of electoral democracy, but it is deployed in distinctive ways in today's conditions. Contemporary political racism is used flexibly in combination with other resources and, as always, is closely entwined with nationalism which provides it with an essential legitimate cloak, so that in many contexts it makes sense to talk about "racial nationalism" rather than, or as well as, racism as such. While political racism is an organized, intentional element it is also partially covert, albeit hiding in plain sight. Strategic actors seek to stimulate and exploit racist attitudes among sections of the population, as well as the resentment the holders of these attitudes feel about their delegitimization. They therefore shape racist sentiments for their political ends, but in today's society they also need to appear to respect antiracist norms. To build winning electoral coalitions, they often cultivate ambiguity in their appeals: while appealing to those who are consciously racist, they also need to reassure supporters who think of themselves as non-racist and tell both that it is not racist to want to exclude migrants, to reject reforms which tackle structural racism, to cherish racist symbols, etc. A superficial antiracism, often in colour-blind forms, may be projected even in tandem with the most blatant racist appeals, as Trump repeatedly showed during his presidency.

Political leaders today rarely systematize racism as some did in the "racial century". When racism was widely accepted as legitimate, major political movements developed fully blown racist doctrines, like those of Nazism and apartheid, which capitalized on the widespread acceptance of racial versions of Christianity, racial "sciences" like eugenics and other racialized ideological forms. In contrast, in today's "post-ideological" as well as "post-racial" societies – where overt racism contradicts antiracist norms and diminishes the strategic value of racism – major actors rarely elaborate systematic ideologies. For today's racist entrepreneurs, agility and flexibility are necessary for political success. Ambiguity is the normal ideological mode not only of what John Keane (2020: 41) calls "the new despotism" pursued by authoritarian, semi-democratic rulers but also of authoritarian-inclined conservatism in Western democracies. Yet *ideological development* – the production of more or less coherent sets of ideas – remains important to motivate and justify strategic racism. Because racism and antiracism have been made debatable, there is a constant ideological battle in both mainstream and social media over their legitimacy. Social media have enormously expanded the scope for the diffuse elaboration of racist thought, which is no longer confined mainly to people conventionally regarded as "intellectuals" or "ideologues". They have provided big new opportunities for party figures, journalists and others to expand their audiences and the frequency and speed of their communication with them, but racial ideas – including what we can call *anti-antiracism* – are also elaborated, contested and circulated daily by people we can truly call the "organic intellectuals" of contemporary racial-nationalist movements, in the sense originally proposed by Antonio Gramsci (2011: 199–211). Countless threads, many originated by recognized figures but others by "ordinary" users who have no prior political standing (but who may become figures in their own right as they accumulate followings), constantly shape and reshape the ideologies of contemporary racism, updating ideas with the turns of events and testing them against antiracist responses. This development of racism in social media is an example of what Sven Engesser *et al.* (2017) call "fragmented ideology", in contrast to the more systematic forms of the past.

Moreover, because social media has become a prime arena in which racism is expressed, hostility towards groups tends increasingly to be *identified* through the ideological assumptions of the political positions which are expressed in opinion pieces and posts, rather than through offline discrimination, although of course the latter often accompanies online hostility. Politicians respond to these ideological debates and learn from them the kinds of tropes which work. Indeed, the dividing line between mainstream politicians and celebrity ideologues is perhaps even finer than ever; politicians like Trump and Farage have been media personalities and adept Twitter users, while former journalistic operators like Johnson and Gove become political leaders. While political parties are formally defined by their constitutions, they also have broader existences through social milieux which are not formally incorporated. Tim Bale (2016: 2) argues that one cannot understand the British Conservatives without acknowledging the existence of "the party in the media", the editors, commentators and journalists who have had "a huge impact" on strategy. However, we need to pay equally close attention to the role of social media activists in parties' milieux. Indeed, Farage established his Brexit Party in 2019 as a purely "digital party", a wholly owned company with no members in the traditional sense but only online supporters and donors, taking to its logical conclusion the model pioneered by Italy's Five Star Movement which is analysed by Paolo Gerbaudo (2019) in his pioneering discussion of this new type.

The continuing role of ideological development now overlaps more than ever with the function of the *popularization of racism*, which remains a third key dimension. Popularization brings racist images, tropes and arguments to a mass audience who are mostly *not* proactively engaged, typically combining hostile representations of immigrants and particular ethnicities with generalized claims about the racial threat of immigration and attacks on antiracists. Historically, this role has been carried out primarily by partisan mass media outlets, such as the tabloid press in the UK and right-wing radio stations in the USA, which still offer daily negative coverage of individual migrant and minority stories merged with editorial content. Despite the literature which shows the roles that the press and broadcasting played in cultivating racial and anti-migrant sentiment at the beginning of this century (Threadgold 2009), political science accounts of the emergence of racial-nationalist "identity conservative" electorates largely ignore them; in over 300 pages, Sobolewska and Ford (2020: 154) make only one passing reference to how "anxieties about the arrival of a large new out-group were stoked and reinforced by persistent negative media attention". Despite the relative decline of the printed newspaper, mainstream media remain very important in popularizing racist nationalism, with relatively new television operations like Fox News (established in 1996) playing major roles. Overall, these media are now ever more integrated with social media, and the online "organic intellectuals" who play key roles in developing racist ideas are also hugely important to the dissemination of "mainstream" content. The distinction between the development and the popularization of racist ideas remains a useful way of thinking about different functions, but today they are more combined than ever.

A fourth dimension of political racism is its *expression in active popular hostility*. For the mainstream and radical right, the most important expressions are the votes of the mass electorate, even if the extreme right relies more on street mobilization and violence. However, every form of political mobilization needs active involvement by committed supporters. Crude direct hostility is now mostly expressed online, but this hardly makes it more benign; as a study of hate crime shows, internet hostility can and does "migrate to the real world" (Williams *et al.* 2020: 117). Extreme right organizations often mobilize activists to orchestrate racist hostility in communities and to attack, even physically, the "enemy" groups and antiracists. The most important contemporary example is the Rashtriya Swayamsevak Sangh paramilitary movement linked to India's ruling Bharatiya Janata Party (BJP), which has been implicated in violence against Muslims and others from the mid-twentieth century to the present day (Jaffrelot 2009). Right-wing paramilitarism also plays a significant role in the USA, and Trump helped bring this closer to the mainstream of the Republican Party through his support for violence in Charlottesville in 2017, the attacks on Black Lives Matters protesters in 2020 and the assault on the Capitol in 2021. In European countries, violent extreme right organizations are generally more marginal, but they play an important ongoing role in sustaining street-level, face-to-face hostility, even if some of this is unorganized. Of course, face-to-face aggression in general has very significant effects on individual victims and minority communities, but it is ambiguously related to the goals of strategic racists. On the one hand, it reinforces at a local level the climate of hostility which their propaganda fosters for electoral reasons, but on the other hand, it potentially threatens their respectability and ability to maintain broad electoral coalitions.

Last but not least, political racism entails the development of *policy hostility*, sometimes described as bureaucratic racism, through which state legal and administrative practices produce hostile effects. Historically, overtly racist parties and politicians embedded racial ideas in comprehensive legal frameworks, the most notorious of which included the Nuremberg Laws, apartheid legislation and segregation laws in the USA, although these had counterparts in most countries. Today, in contrast, antiracist norms are embedded in human rights, equality and anti-discrimination legislation, but strategic racist actors still need to show their supporters that power delivers results in ways which align with their ideology. Political racism implies discriminatory policies, which most often nominally target non-citizens, immigrants and refugees but may also entail harm to citizen minorities, for example the Modi government's use of an anti-immigrant campaign to target Indian Muslims and the widespread tendency of "counterterrorism" policies to bleed into discrimination against Muslims. Brexit, as we shall see, is a case in which political racism has helped steer, via migration policy, the whole geopolitical and geoeconomic orientation of the state. Indeed, since political racism is more a power resource than a policy framework, its policy effects often follow strategic political as well as ideological and policy logics. These effects can also be seen where right-wing parties are not in power, as left-wing and centrist administrations respond to the pressure of political racism and elaborate their own defensive and pre-emptive versions, as in the cases of the Blair government in the UK and Macron's in France.

These different modalities of political racism reinforce each other, and while there are typical actors corresponding to each, actors operate across them. Political racism also crystallizes variably in different political contexts. In organized contests like elections and referendums, as we shall see in the case of Brexit, it tends to generate a more or less coherent system in which the strategic racism of leaders, parties and campaigns acts as an organizing centre around which other actors coalesce. However, outside electoral periods, ideological, mass media and popular action can often set the pace for parties and politicians. Major ideological interventions, like those of Enoch Powell which I consider in Chapter 2, can change the terms of political debate. Mass and social media provide continuous space for ideological elaboration as well as developing tropes which are later mobilized by strategic actors. In some moments popular racism, like the antisemitism of some Labour supporters which I discuss in Chapter 6, can become the story and create issues for strategic actors and ideologues. Moreover, it should not be thought that because political racism is primarily a means of producing political effects such as votes, it does not have societal effects, or that they are less dangerous. On the contrary, through its electorally and media-driven campaigns, political racism contributes to specific harms such as ostracization, abuse and denial of rights; individual racism by providing occasions for anger; everyday racism by relegitimating existing prejudices, identifying new enemies and circulating new tropes; and specific forms of institutional racism in parties and movements.

2
POLITICAL RACISM AND IMMIGRATION

I knew that touching the immigration issue was going to be very difficult. ... [T]he only thing that upsets me about it is that, had it been
wilfully and overtly a racist message, I might have deserved some of
[the criticism]. But it wasn't. It never was. It never, ever was. It was a
logical argument about numbers, society.

Nigel Farage (quoted by Cowley 2017).

[H]ostility to one out-group tends to correlate with hostility to others;
those who dislike immigrants tend to dislike racial minorities and to
dislike the "foreigners" from the EU encroaching on British politics.
Robert Ford, Matthew J. Goodwin and David Cutts (2012: 211)

The intensity of racial politics around the 2016 referendum shocked those observers who had accepted the narrative of positive change in British society. Yet,
while some forms of liberalization were real, overall the country was far from
being "post-racial", and many sources of continuing racism were embedded in
social relations, institutions, beliefs and attitudes. However, the constant renewal
of a tradition of political racism had also played a crucial role in perpetuating
the general level of racism and blocking fuller liberalization. This tradition, orig-
inating in the nineteenth century, was revived in the context of non-white immigration in the second half of the twentieth, most notoriously through Powell's
speeches in 1968. As we have seen, race is a "floating signifier", and it tends to
be constantly filled with new meanings, especially by political actors who need
to adapt to changing circumstances and the challenges which these pose for the
achievement of their goals. It was possible for Brexit to catalyse racist tendencies
in society because political racism had been regularly reproduced by sections
of the political right and the press, and fed by the immigration policies of both
Labour and Conservative governments. Although this tradition was "Powellite"
in the sense that his example was seminal for most of the actors, contemporary racemongers are not simply Powell tribute acts, even if that is how some

present themselves at times. While they attempt to emulate his considerable success in popularizing racism, they have also learned from the problems which he encountered and the political dead ends in which the extreme right – who followed him in overt racism – also found themselves.

This chapter therefore analyses the "tradition" of political racism through the idea that traditions are invented and constantly reinvented (Hobsbawm & Ranger 1983), examining the *mutation* of political racism in the half-century before Brexit, as new promoters adapted it to the increasing normative prevalence of antiracism. The discussion emphasizes how racist entrepreneurs in the Conservative Party, as well as smaller right-wing parties and campaign groups, attempted to distinguish opposition to immigration from "overt racism" by re-configuring it in the largely numerical terms to which Farage refers and simultaneously focusing on new targets, especially Muslims and eastern Europeans. This longer trajectory of political racism in the UK is essential to understanding Brexit, because it helps explain why and how the Europhobic movement (discussed in Chapter 3) was able to prevail in the EU referendum, producing the greatest ever mobilization of racism as a political resource, despite – and even to some extent because of – the social changes of the preceding years. The discussion shows that while the Conservatives tried but largely failed to harness anti-immigration politics in the early and mid-Blair years, UKIP under Farage developed a winning formula linking political racism and opposition to the EU in the decade after 2006, which in turn influenced Conservative policies on immigration and Europe, leading in 2016 (we shall see in Chapter 4) to the Conservative-led Vote Leave campaign adopting a Faragist approach in order to win Brexit.

Enoch Powell and his legacies

The discussion mainly considers British political racism from the mid-twentieth century onwards, but it is important to understand its longer history. Britain entered the twentieth century as an emerging democracy – many male workers gained the vote in the late nineteenth century, while universal suffrage was achieved for men in 1918 and for women in 1929 – at the heart of a global empire. Following the abolition of slavery in 1833, racial hierarchies had actually been strengthened and naturalized across the colonial world in the later nineteenth century, despite an important history of opposition in Britain informed by colonial resisters themselves (Gopal 2019: 41–208). Within Britain, the oligarchic parties inherited from the eighteenth century transformed themselves into mass parties to win the support of the expanding working-class electorate. From the mid-nineteenth century, Satnam Virdee (2014: 31, 5, 66) argues, there was "a growing penetration of racist and nationalist sentiment in British public life", as a British national identity was repeatedly "constructed in opposition to the racialized other". Each time "the boundary of the nation was extended to encompass ever more members of the working class, it was accompanied and legitimized through the further racialization of nationalism which prevented another more recently-arrived social group from being included". As the labour movement itself increasingly embraced this commitment, democratization "bound the working class ever more to the politics of nationalism, and a shared commitment to race and empire". However, in the more radical form of what Bill Schwarz (2019: 54–5) calls the "new ethnic populism" of the years before the First World War, which linked a specifically English nationalism to Ulster Unionist hyper-patriotism, race was especially a resource which Conservatives mobilized in the face of Liberal and Labour challenges. Robert McKenzie and Allan Silver (1968: 60), writing during the heyday of class-based electoral partisanship about the apparent anomaly of working-class Toryism, reproduce a leaflet from 1904 which warned that

> the Radicals, by their obstruction to the Aliens Bill, are evidently glad to see all foreigners who are criminals; who suffer from loathsome diseases; who are turned out in disgrace by their fellow countrymen; who are paupers; who fill our streets with profligacy and disorder. The Unionist Government wants to keep these creatures out of Great Britain. They don't want to see the honest Britisher turned out by these scourings of European slums. They brought in a bill to check this evil flow of aliens.[1]

The targets of this Tory tirade were Jews, who had been forced out of the Russian empire by pogroms and were the prominent new "racialized outsiders" of the time. Like the Catholic Irish in the nineteenth century, Jews were racialized although they were not dark-skinned.

Anti-Black racism had spread in British society through the history of the empire, but the Black and "mixed-race" minority in the UK itself still numbered only around 30,000 in the mid-1940s, and only after the war did the "colour question" become politically central. Kathleen Paul's (1997) study of cabinet papers shows how this developed between 1945 and 1965. The initiative for the control of "coloured immigration" came from officials and politicians, with their "racialization of the imperial population", rather than the public or even the press.

---

1. Conservatives called themselves Unionists in this period because of their opposition to Irish Home Rule. The party's official name remains The Conservative and Unionist Party. "Radicals" referred to a section of the Liberal Party.

"The significance attached to skin colour" in this period "cannot be overstated", she argues; for the elite, "by simple logic, if the British population was white and the colonials were black, colonials could not be British" (Paul 1997: 124–5). Struggling to hold together the empire/Commonwealth which secured the UK's status as a great power, the Labour government of Clement Attlee simultaneously promoted transplanting British "stock" to the white dominions and assimilating white European and Irish workers into the domestic or what Paul calls the "familial" community of Britishness while restricting Black colonial people to its "political community" (Paul 1997: 64–110). In view of anti-European hostility in the twenty-first century, it is striking to note that in the aftermath of the war, even "enemy" civilians such as Germans and Italians were considered desirable and assimilable immigrants, who were candidates for a full membership of society denied to Black or Asian British colonial citizens. Although the British Nationality Act 1948 introduced a single United Kingdom and Colonial citizenship, Labour ministers and their officials, in an approach which was maintained under the Conservative government after 1951, pursued in parallel an *informal* nationality policy which excluded colonial citizens from full membership of British society. The very arrival of the *Empire Windrush* in the same year as the act – with its complement of British citizens from Jamaica who had taken autonomous decisions to travel to England – produced a "panic" among policy-makers which "matured into a clear-cut and fixed" determination to limit colonial migration as it grew in scale in the 1950s and early 1960s (Paul 1997: 112ff.).

It was not a matter of "isolated cases of bureaucratic racism" but of "a general climate of hostility towards the prospect of colonial migration" (Paul 1997: 127). Initially, "boxed in by their ideological commitment to [white] Old Commonwealth citizens' rights to come to Britain, Conservatives opted for no controls" (Hansen 2000: 18), but by 1955 Prime Minister Winston Churchill was urging them to use the slogan "Keep England White" for that year's general election. While his cabinet declined to adopt this blatant racist appeal, ministers increasingly opted to publicize the "dangers" to a general public "perceived to be as yet too liberal to initiate change on their own behalf" (Paul 1997: 32). In terms of the categories introduced in Chapter 1, the ideological and policy racism of the elite was increasingly directed towards generating popular racism, even if Tory reticence inhibited a clear policy of strategic racism. Central to this process was that "what was perceived as a 'race' problem had to be disguised as an 'immigration' problem", "transforming migrants of colour from British subjects into Commonwealth immigrants while racializing the term 'Commonwealth immigrant' to refer only to migrants of colour" (Paul 1997: 134). However, this racialization of the idea of "immigrant" was a fundamental move which *would* shortly enable a strategic racist approach. It has since permeated politics, the press and public opinion for three-quarters of a century, even surviving (as we shall see) the expansion of hostility to include white European as well as Black "immigrants" in the twenty-first century.

Although Whitehall's version of events, accepted by some scholars, was that "a liberal UK government was forced by a frightened and hostile public to impose immigration controls", Paul (1997: 31) demonstrates that the politics of migration "shifted from the private to the public sphere" only through a decade of increasingly open official manoeuvring to limit the arrivals of colonial citizens. By 1956, policy-makers' attempts to hold a racialized Commonwealth together were wearing thin, as their humiliation in the Suez crisis "symbolically marked the beginning of the end of the British empire" (Virdee 2014: 102). Press and popular opinion also began to express the official consensus against immigration, as discrimination and racial hostility reinforced a "white" identity in a large section of the population, although social-scientific studies showed that a "potential base for education in tolerance persisted as late as the 1960s" (Paul 1997: 140). In 1958, race riots centred on Notting Hill in west London gave the prewar fascist leader, Oswald Mosley, a brief new prominence. The "language of the Cabinet room and parliamentary chamber had finally moved to the public highway", Paul argues, but the cabinet did not want to be seen to giving in to the mob and prevaricated further about immigration controls. Only in 1962 did the Conservatives introduce a Commonwealth Immigrants Act, with a voucher scheme designed "to most effectively limit the entry of blacks without being seen to discriminate"; they relied on the press to stimulate public demand for this (Paul 1997: 147, 149). With this legislation, the politics of immigration became more prominent, and the Tory candidate for Smethwick in the 1964 election, Peter Griffiths, won against the trend after his supporters used the slogan, "If you want a n****r for your neighbour, vote Labour", which he refused to repudiate (Foot 1965: 44). He was ostracized by his party; Virdee (2014: 113) argues that "the ideology of racializing nationalism was losing some of its force among key elements of the political class" in the context of their "realist accommodation to the forced relinquishment of empire". However, it was clear that parts of the working class "were not disinterested bystanders in these debates, but helped inform them with their everyday practices and attitudes" (Virdee 2014: 102). An informal colour bar "ran the length of British society", enforced by "ordinary" people as well as institutions, with a "racialized division of labour" across most employment, widely sustained by the trade unions (Shilliam 2018: 92, 103). The new Labour government of Harold Wilson responded to this climate by sharpening the Tory controls in 1965 and introducing a second Commonwealth Immigrants Act in 1968.[2]

---

2. At the age of 17, I had canvassed for a left-wing Labour MP in the 1964 election; his support for the 1965 Immigration White Paper, after being appointed to a junior ministerial

However, Labour was pursuing a twin-track approach, combining policy racism on immigration with legal antiracism, as the Race Relations Act, the first to outlaw racial discrimination, was passed in the same year. This became the de facto bipartisan framework of the Labour and Conservative leaderships for the next half-century. Yet the new elite accommodation was disrupted as it was launched by Enoch Powell, a Conservative shadow cabinet minister and former minister of health, who sought to restore the earlier unqualified hostility to immigration in his speech of 20 April 1968 (reproduced in Hansen 2000: 181–5, from which the following quotations are taken). Raising the spectre of "rivers of blood" if it was not curtailed, his rhetoric was highly emotive but – in a standard ploy of racist politicians, used more recently by Farage and Johnson – claimed to ventriloquize popular thinking. He started from the views of "a constituent, a middle-aged, quite ordinary working man", who had told him, "[i]n this country in fifteen or twenty years time the black man will have the whip-hand over the white man". As he moved towards his bloody crescendo, Powell evoked the situation of the "one white (a woman old-age pensioner)" remaining in a Wolverhampton street: "she is becoming afraid to go out. Windows are broken. She finds excreta pushed through her letter-box. When she goes out to the shops, she is followed by children, charming, wide-grinning piccaninnies. They cannot speak English, but one word they know, 'Racialist.'" Defending the citizen's "right to discriminate", Powell argued that, far from immigrants being victims, it was the white majority who were victims of Labour's Race Relations Bill. Yet he also claimed to address "the natural and rational first question for a nation confronted by such a prospect is to ask, 'how can its dimensions be reduced?'" Therefore, he argued, "numbers are of the essence: the significance and consequences of an alien element introduced into a country or population are profoundly different according to whether that element is 1 per cent or 10 per cent". So he proposed an "equally simple and rational answer: ... stopping, or virtually stopping, further inflow, and ... promoting the maximum outflow". He warned against "the immigrant and his descendants" being "elevated into a privileged or special class".

Thus Powell's rhetoric combined two main appeals. There were explicit attacks on "Negroes", a term which he applied to the people from the Indian subcontinent who were the majority of immigrants in his constituency, with white people presented as their victims. This speech provided a template for racist propaganda which would be used, as we shall see, by Vote Leave half a century later, even down to an election broadcast which featured a vulnerable old white women being edged out by a foreigner; similarly, Johnson's comments about "piccaninnies" in 2008 and "letterboxes" in 2018 look like paying homage to the

---

position, was a significant factor in the disillusionment which led me to leave the party the following year.

master's rhetoric. But Powell also presented what he called a "rational" policy concern, focused on the numerical level of immigration. He always claimed to be "ignorant of the term 'race'", and even suggested that clusters of Italians or Germans in British cities would constitute the same sort of "alien" presence as large numbers of Black people (Hansen 2000: 181n.2), a stance which departed from the 1940s idea that European migrants could become British and anticipated later Europhobia. However, the fundamental driver of his speech was its overt anti-Black racism, which served to turn what Randolph Hansen calls the "abstract stuff" about numbers into the emotive stuff of effective propaganda. As is well known, Powell elicited a huge popular response; workers struck and marched and polls showed large majority support. His impact is ascribed by Schwarz (2019: 55) to an "unexhausted reservoir of ethnic populism" from earlier in the century, while Sobolewska and Ford (2020: 93, 95) explain it through "the demographics of the 1960s British electorate, which was dominated ... by identity conservatives. White school-leavers ... formed a large majority of the population", so that there was a "clash of outlooks between more cosmopolitan political elites and a more ethnocentric electorate".

"More" is doing a lot of work here: as we have seen, the elites were hardly cosmopolitan, and while racism had been sedimented since the nineteenth century, Powell's support did not reflect a timeless or homogenous ethnocentrism among the less educated British masses. The response had also been prepared by the increasingly open expression of elite hostility to immigration by people of colour, and even as the Conservative leadership disowned Griffiths and Powell for their proactive stances, the latter were by no means ideological outliers; more or less unreconstructed racism remained a significant force among MPs, local politicians and party members. Likewise, immigration had been accompanied for over a decade by hostile, sensational and often openly racist reporting in the tabloid press, then in its heyday. Therefore the pre-Powell, anti-immigration polling majorities which Sobolewska and Ford (2020: 91) describe were steered by powerful organized forces, as well as reflecting the benefits which many white people perceived in discrimination. Yet Gopal (2019: 245–309) shows that sections of liberal and left-wing opinion had already learned antiracism from anticolonial resistance before the Second World War, and while racism remained significant in the Labour movement, antiracism continued to slowly strengthen. Indeed, Sobolewska and Ford (2020: 101–7) rightly identify Powell's speech as a turning point: the Conservatives were now seen as the more anti-immigration party and benefited accordingly in the popular vote, while Labour became gradually more liberal. Yet Labour's antiracism, like Powell's racism, drew on pre-existing political traditions; and while his effect on public opinion was strong, class voting still mattered. Labour won elections in the 1970s and later, despite its increasing handicap with the racial-nationalist section of the working class.

Powell repurposed the old imperialist, Anglo-Saxon racial nationalism of the Conservative right for the post-imperial, mass immigration and emerging European age. As Virdee (2014: 114) summarizes, the "confident racism that had accompanied the high-imperial moment mutated into a defensive racism, a racism of the vanquished who no longer wanted to dominate but to physically expel the racialized other"; Powell invoked a primordial, pre-imperial Englishness to construct a post-imperial "nation for whites only", attempting to "revive the unquestioning consensus over the association between British national belonging and whiteness in the face of contemporary non-white settlement". Or, as Tom Nairn (2021: 259) commented, "[i]n the obscene form of racism, English nationalism had been reborn". Yet despite attempting to foment, as Shilliam (2018: 102) describes it, "a specifically populist form of nationalism" against the partly liberalizing party leaderships, Powell lacked a coherent political-racist *strategy* and did not *directly* achieve significant political change; he certainly failed in his manifest aims of halting and reversing the increase of the non-white population. The overt racist language which magnified his public impact also limited his leverage in the Conservative Party, whose top layer was sufficiently committed to the two-track policy that Powell, like Griffiths four years earlier, was forced into the wilderness. Lacking an alternative political vehicle in Great Britain, he become a Unionist MP representing a Northern Irish constituency in 1974.

While Powell showed the Conservatives the electoral potential of anti-immigrant politics, his interventions, Bale (2013: 27) argues, "ruled out a thoroughgoing populist approach by the Party, not least because [party leader Edward] Heath made a point of distinguishing himself from a man he regarded as a dangerous maverick"; over the following decades, the party would consistently demonstrate a "historic reluctance to go all-out" on immigration, stemming "partly from the social and economic liberalism of some of its leaders (and from their concern to act 'responsibly' on the issue) and partly from their concern not to alienate the well-heeled and well-educated middle-class voters whose support was (and is) crucial to electoral success". Yet, although Heath disowned Powell, he moved policy in a Powellite direction, bringing in the 1971 Immigration Act which introduced the racial notion of "patriality" as the basis of citizenship, giving legal expression to the previously informal familial concept which largely excluded non-white people (Paul 1997: 180–81). Two years later, the European Economic Community (EEC), in the face of the UK's accession, needed to be satisfied that Commonwealth citizens who possessed the right of abode in the UK were not UK citizens for the purposes of free movement; the Court of Justice of the European Union accepted "patriality" as defined in the 1971 Immigration Act as the legitimate basis for belonging in the EEC (El-Enany 2020: 193–6). This episode shows, as Nadine El-Enany (2020: 190) notes, that European citizenship rights, while internally non-discriminatory, were effectively linked to the whiteness of the formerly imperial founding member states. The British acceptance of increasingly open European migration, while non-white Commonwealth citizens faced severe obstacles, was also in line with the racialized conceptions of population which had driven British policy since the Second World War (Paul 1997: 187) and indeed were involved in European integration itself (Benson 2020).

The tabloids whose coverage of immigration had helped create Powellism continued to feed it in the following years; a 1974 survey showed that many journalists depicted immigrants as a "threat and a problem ... conducive to the development of hostility toward them" (Goodfellow 2019: 28), while Stuart Hall *et al.* (1978) analysed the press's role in a moral panic about "mugging" by young Black men, which reinforced hostility towards the minority population. While media and popular racism kept the Powellite spirit alive, his political capital was directly exploited by the neo-fascist National Front (NF) with its openly racist policies. The NF had some limited electoral success, but attracted strong antiracist opposition and failed to break through under the first-past-the-post voting system – a pattern later repeated by the British National Party (BNP), which peaked in 2008–10. Some working-class racists supported the extreme right, but left-wing opposition to it combined with the growing assertiveness of workers from Asian and Caribbean backgrounds also produced "the first, modest indications that socialist pressure was finally beginning to shift the mainstream organized labour movement" towards active antiracism (Virdee 2014: 127).

Powell's major medium-term influence on British politics was his contribution to Thatcherism, as the ideology of Margaret Thatcher's historically transformative Tory leadership (1975–90; she was prime minister from 1979) came to be called. Although this may indeed have been "an iconoclastic instinct more than a clearly thought-out or consistently executed ideological project" (Bale 2016: 24), the leader herself and the coterie of politicians and writers around her developed a fairly coherent set of ideas in reaction against the liberalism of the 1960s. As Hall (1983: 29) summarized them, these combined "the resonant themes of organic Toryism – nation, family, duty, authority, standards, traditionalism – with the aggressive themes of a revived neo-liberalism – self-interest, competitive individualism anti-statism", amounting to what he called a distinctive "authoritarian populism". In this ideology, he argued, "Powellism won" through "the magical connections and short-circuits which [it] was able to establish between the themes of race and immigration control and the images of the nation, the British people and the destruction of 'our culture, our way of life'" (Hall 1983: 138). Thatcher clearly indicated her sympathies when she said in 1978 that "people are really rather afraid that this country might be rather swamped by people with a different culture", but there was a disjuncture between her demonstrated ideological affinity with Powellism – which Sobolewska and

Ford (2020: 108–13) show helped the Tories electorally – and her overt strategies for winning elections. She did not directly focus on immigration or race in the 1979 election, when she won power, or in the campaigns which consolidated her rule in 1983 – even if the tabloid racialization of Argentinians as "Argies" during the 1982 Falklands/Malvinas War contributed to her nationalist thrust – or 1987. Therefore Powellism impacted Thatcherite *ideology*, which dominated the Conservative, tabloid and popular right wing long after Thatcher's own departure, but this was not matched by strongly developed *strategic* racist electoral interventions. Hansen (2000: 212) could even claim that "at no point since the 1970s has Commonwealth immigration been more than a fleeting issue" in elections. Even in this populist phase, therefore, the Tories continued to pull their punches. In policy terms, too, Thatcher's 1981 British Nationality Act had a mixed significance: while it finally severed the link between British and Commonwealth citizenship, it also dispensed with "patriality", albeit providing a way for former patrial subjects from the white dominions to continue to register as UK citizens even as that right was denied to colonial British citizens like Hong Kongers (Paul 1997: 182, 185–7).

The numerical turn in British political racism

In response to Powell's marginalization, the overt racism of the extreme right and the rise of antiracism, mainstream anti-immigration politics increasingly evolved in a new direction in the last decades of the twentieth century. Conservative and UKIP politicians and governments aimed to insulate themselves against charges of racism by separating (at least on the surface) Powell's "rational" case about the numbers of immigrants from his "emotive" case about the effects of Black people on white communities. The reviving right were mostly careful to highlight the claim that "the problem is the current scale of immigration, which is simply unsustainable", as a prominent campaigning organization founded in 2002 would put it (Migration Watch 2018). Reflecting this shift, as the immigration lawyer Colin Yeo (2020: 269) would later point out, an "obsession with numbers" was official government policy from "at least 1981". The need for adaptation was reinforced by New Labour's landslide victory in 1997, which seemed to usher in a new multicultural age, even if the immigration policies of Blair and his successor Gordon Brown remained restrictive and its antiracism "hypocritical" (Goodfellow 2019: 92–128). The case for a new deracialized Britishness advocated in a Runnymede report chaired by Bhikhu Parekh (2010) set the tone, even if it was not fully endorsed by the government. It appeared that Labour had successfully annexed much of the economic programme of Thatcherism while dispensing with some of its reactionary social ideas, and the Conservatives struggled to respond.

Bill Schwarz (2019: 56) expresses a widespread view when he writes that the subsequent renewal of racialized ethnic populism came largely from "the political right outside (or largely outside) the Conservative Party". Yet this perception distorts the true relationship between the two forces; the Tories themselves played the crucial role in relaunching anti-immigration politics after their defeat. Bale (2013: 25), the historian of the party in this period, goes so far as to comment that "anyone who thinks that it takes a fringe (or formerly-fringe) party to prompt its bigger, older rivals ... into talking and sometimes even acting tough in this regard has either a very short memory or is ideologically-blinkered". Rather, Bale *et al.* (2017: 265) argue, it was the Tories who first highlighted immigration in their search for issues to counter New Labour's apparently unchallengeable hegemony; they "did not ignore voters' cultural anxieties but ... sought, deliberately if somewhat desperately, to appeal to them". This was certainly the period in which UKIP also began to promote anti-immigration politics, but "it was the Conservative Party and not its radical right rival that, between 1997 and 2005, achieved the fusion of populism and Euroscepticism". In these early stages of the "25-year, essentially symbiotic relationship" between these two parties, the mainstream party, which had "a long history of emptying populist (and more centrally Eurosceptic) frames in its discourse – particularly its discourse on immigration", was also "deeply implicated in [UKIP's] rise" (Bale *et al.* 2017: 264–5).

In opposition between 1997 and 2005, the Tories were led by a succession of right-wing anti-Europeans who intermittently indulged in populist campaigns around issues such as restricting asylum, law and order, and "saving the pound". William Hague turned on the "liberal elite" after the Macpherson report criticized the Metropolitan Police for institutional racism in its handling of the Stephen Lawrence murder; he also dog-whistled about immigration, appealing to endemic racism among Tory members and voters (Bale 2016: 110, 112). Michael Howard backed a pioneering tabloid campaign linking Europe with migration against alleged "benefit tourists" from the eastern European states which joined the EU in 2004; he "attempted to insulate himself from the inevitable accusations that he was 'playing the race card' by stressing his family background" as the son of Jewish immigrants (Bale 2016: 193). In the face of a growing UKIP threat in European elections in the same year, Howard cranked up his Eurosceptic rhetoric, and after the latter won 16.1 per cent of the votes, the Tories shifted "to an almost wholly populist appeal" to win back voters who "were channelling their essentially xenophobic views into the more socially acceptable form of Euroscepticism" (Bale 2016: 212). Therefore, he also majored on immigration, and "took out extra insurance, first, by ensuring he was flanked during the speech by a couple of the Party's ethnic minority candidates and, second, by attending, a few days later, a big meeting of Britain's Sikh community" (Bale 2016: 213). With this cover, by the 2005 general election, Howard – who employed the firm run by Australian electoral strategist Lynton Crosby, who was later to serve Cameron, May and Johnson – was talking about immigration "in classically populist terms", while Tory adverts asked, "Are you thinking what we're thinking?" and proclaimed, "It's not racist to impose limits on immigration" (Bale 2016: 223, 226). However, despite this clear pitch for the anti-immigrant vote, immigration was by no means "the sole feature of the Conservatives' campaign" (Bale 2016: 233) and was not deployed in anything like the ruthless and concentrated way that both Leave campaigns would use it in 2016. Concern about immigration had not yet been whipped up as strongly as it would be after 2005, immigration remained a second-order issue for most voters and the Labour government had insulated itself against Howard's attack with its own immigration controls. Bale (2016: 235) even concluded that with his 2005 defeat, Howard had "tested to destruction" the idea that the Conservatives "could win power on a platform of populist promises and simply taking up where Thatcher left off".

This judgement would prove premature. In the first years of the twenty-first century, anti-immigration politics was becoming increasingly central for all sections of the right, but a significant shift had taken place (compared to Powell) in the manner in which they approached it, which would pave the way for its more successful use in the following decade. In the New Labour era, right-wing Tories, UKIP and even the extreme right (who viewed immigration as "their ticket into the mainstream", according to Mulhall 2019: 1) were taking much greater care to cover themselves against the charge of racism. They adopted a primarily *numerical* approach, which appeared to turn immigration control into an abstract question free from hostility to particular groups, and even a question about the overall size of the population, which they presented as a reason for objecting to the level of international migration. Farage summarized this pitch in his post-2016 reflection with which I preface this chapter, and in the 2015 election his party's slogan was "Immigration is not about race; it is about space" (Goodfellow 2019: 125). His claim that immigration control was "a logical argument about numbers" is a classic case of what Hall (1995: 20, emphasis in original) called "inferential racism", that is, "those apparently naturalized representations of events and situations relating to race ... which have racist premises and propositions inscribed in them as a set of *unquestioned assumptions*". The concern about the numbers of immigrants was not, as it appeared to be, a concern with the total numbers of people in the country or even the total number of immigrants. As Maya Goodfellow (2019: 63) points out, one of its earliest uses, by Tory prime minister, Harold Macmillan, in 1962, had come as immigration control was directed at Commonwealth citizens of colour but not Irish citizens, who were entering the UK in larger numbers.

At the national level, the UK population had grown consistently since the Second World War but there had been no politically articulated concern about the natural increase (which still accounted for over a third of the total in 2015–16), only about international immigration. Numerical concern therefore drew on the well-established racialization of the idea of "immigrant" itself while extending it to "asylum seekers" (Favell 2020). In some areas with high levels of immigration, there were certainly local concerns relating to socio-economic issues (effects on jobs, wages, services, etc.) believed to be caused by immigrants, but even in these areas, anti-immigration politics were largely premised on "identity" concerns, and it was also strong in areas with low international immigration. Evidence on the relationships of internal and international migration at regional and district levels underlines the identity basis of opposition. The Office of National Statistics (2016a, 2016b) shows that in 2015–16 the region with the highest rate of net domestic migration, the south-west, saw an annual population rise of 0.55 per cent because of this, the same level as the UK-wide increase because of net international migration. Yet even south-western districts with the highest domestic migration saw little or no opposition to it in principle, incomers were not labelled "immigrants" and there were none of the tensions seen in some areas of high international migration. In my district, east Devon, for example, the population rose by 1.79 per cent because of internal but only 0.01 per cent because of international migration (ONS 2016a), yet the area still saw expressions of hostility to international immigration, while the issues around domestic migration were expressed only as questions of development planning. Therefore, concern about the level of immigration did not reference, as Migration Watch implied, the overall size of the national or local population but its ethnic composition. As we have seen, even academics sympathetic to anti-immigration politics, such as Kaufmann, Eatwell and Goodwin, clearly acknowledge the ethnic and racial basis of concerns about population "shares".

Numerical anti-immigration politics extended political racists' usual abstract representation of target groups, which mobilize populations against groups with whom they have little direct contact and against groups rather than individuals, by appearing to dispense with group targets altogether and so denaturing the "problem". This was a form of racial politics particularly suited to a society like the UK where overt racism had been widely delegitimized; it was a catch-all, readily understood through the racialization of "immigrant" by those who had a particular animus, and providing a lowest common denominator for all types of racial attitude and hostility. The demand to lower the level of immigration could be supported by those who were hostile to Black people, Asians, Muslims or eastern Europeans, or to any mixture of these, as well as by those who didn't strongly feel a specific hostility but agreed that there were too many non-British people. It could be supported by those who wanted to get rid of established minority populations as well as those who distinguished them from immigrants. It could be supported by out-and-out racists, people who didn't believe they were racist and people who saw themselves as antiracist but understood racism narrowly. Indeed, it could be supported by ethnic minorities as well as the white British, provided they understood it as directed against new immigrants rather than existing residents or against members of minorities other than their own. Yet, while numerical reduction provided a common platform for all who wished to diminish the numbers of non-British incomers or register a protest against established minorities, historically support for control had always been connected, as in Powell's speeches, with targeting particular groups. If the targets changed over time, there was usually an understanding that particular groups were creating the alleged numerical "problem". By talking about numbers, anti-immigrant politicians maximized the breadth and legitimacy of their support, but by targeting particular groups they struck stronger chords in the minds of the resentful.

Therefore few twenty-first-century racemongers confined themselves entirely to numbers; like Powell, they felt the need from time to time to touch on the "emotive stuff". Farage frequently expressed concerns about Muslims and eastern Europeans, saying in 2014 that "any normal and fair-minded person would have a perfect right to be concerned if a group of Romanian people suddenly moved in next door". The language was more moderate, but the underlying sentiment was the one that Smethwick Conservatives expressed about their Black neighbours 50 years earlier. His other rhetorical ploy, linking the numerical and targeted approaches, was to label Muslims "immigrants" even when they were British born (Favell 2020). Similarly, Johnson, knowing that anti-Muslim feeling was strong among Tory and Brexit supporters, notoriously used a *Daily Telegraph* column in 2018 to attack women who wear the burqa (this case is analysed in Chapter 6). These leaders will have understood that, taken up by the people they were appealing to, their remarks could have abusive or even violent consequences for individuals, families and communities, just as when translated into restrictive state policies they might lead to individuals being incarcerated, deported, separated from their families or stressed by the bureaucratic harassment which these would encourage officials to deploy. Like all those who justified tighter immigration control without considering these consequences, they denied racism, but this was implicit in numerical goals as well as explicit in targeted remarks. The widespread pattern of overt racist comments, by right-wing activists, councillors and supporters even more frequently than their leaders, and their general diffusion through the press and social media, meant that abstract proposals for numerical control could be readily interpreted by their consumers as expressions of hostility to both potential migrants and established minority communities who were identified with past migration.

Hostility to Muslims and Eastern Europeans and the rise of UKIP

Farage's and Johnson's comments reflected the fact that by the twenty-first century, targeted political racism had reoriented in two specific directions, both of which would play crucial roles in how the right-wing tabloids and UKIP honed their amalgam of immigration and Europhobia. First, as colour racism was delegitimized, the targeted racism of the right-wing politicians and press had become more obviously selective. Hostility to non-white minorities was increasingly refocused against Muslims, especially after the 9/11 terrorist attacks in 2001. The timeline of Roger Scruton, a right-wing philosopher much celebrated by Conservatives on his death in 2020, indicates the shift: as late as 1982, as editor of the *Salisbury Review*, he published an article which suggested that the presence of West Indians "offends the sense of what English life should be like"; by 2006, while still defending Powell, he was warning against "pious Muslims from the hinterland of Asia" who could never "produce children loyal to a European secular state" (quoted by Malik 2020). Second, for the first time since the Second World War a "white" group – eastern Europeans and within it particular nationalities such as Poles and Romanians – became a major target of hostility after EU expansion in 2004 and 2007 allowed many to move freely to the UK. Although both kinds of racism were common across the right-wing spectrum from the Tories to the extreme right, it was the press which played the main role in fanning them and UKIP which made the most effective strategic use of them in the drive towards Brexit. We shall see in Chapter 4 that both played an important role in the Leave campaigns of 2016.

Anti-Muslim sentiment, which was of course an ancient current, had already been substantially mobilized before 2001. In part, it was a response to the increasing political organization of Muslims both in Britain and globally in the final quarter of the twentieth century. Until the 1980s, "British Muslims were viewed primarily in terms of their ethnicity and countries of origin, rather than as members of a collective faith group" (Hussein 2017: 17), since their communities were initially organized along national lines, as Indians, Pakistanis, Bangladeshis and others. However, as communities became more established, faith-based organizations such as the Muslim Council of Britain became increasingly important, and Muslim opinion was increasingly recognized as a political factor after the protests against Salman Rushdie's 1988 book *The Satanic Verses* emphasized the divergence of Islam from the UK's increasingly dominant secular liberalism and after protests against the 1991 Gulf War (Shaw 1996: 65–9). The growing representation of minority communities on a religious basis corresponded, moreover, to the rise of Islamism at the expense of secular nationalism in the Middle East, a complex set of processes which included the rise of a Shi'ite theocracy after the Iranian revolution of 1979 and of radical Sunni

Islamism in the opposition to the Soviet occupation of Afghanistan in the 1980s. In Western reactions to these developments, Islamist political movements were often not coherently distinguished from each other or from Islam as a religion, and of course Islamists' own ideologies conflated the two.

All of these factors contributed to a growing identification of "Muslims" and "Islam" as enemies in the UK, so that the Runnymede Trust (1997) had already identified anti-Muslim racism, or "Islamophobia", as a significant form, arguing that Muslims suffered "unfounded" hostility towards their religion, discrimination both as individuals and communities and exclusion from mainstream political and social life. Nevertheless, 9/11 dramatically broadened these hostile perceptions; during the "war on terror", Muslims were widely portrayed as potential terrorists and a civilizational threat to the West. Within a decade, Gilroy (2019) comments, "Muslim" would "become fixed as a racial trope rather like Jew in the interwar years of the 20th century". A "Muslim otherly mix" developed in which "securitarian and cultural suspicions bleed into and sustain each other" (Hage 2017: 6). Crucially for the movement towards Brexit, "many right-wing political parties, protest movements and advocacy groups across Europe and North America [came] to view themselves as part of a transnational 'counter-jihad' movement dedicated to resisting what they perceive as the 'Islamization of the west'" (Pertwee 2017: 56). Anti-Muslim racism harnessed the ideas of Western societies as liberal, secular, gender-equal and spaces for sexual freedom, values which were allegedly "violated" by Islam. Indeed, "freedom of speech" became a "dominant political imaginary" for the right, which, argues Titley (2020: 66), "cannot be fully understood without examining the racializing work it has, since the early 2000s, been pressed to perform".

Sexual liberalization and even women's rights sometimes played a similar role for political Islamophobia, and internationally many radical right supporters became "sexually modern nativists" (Lancaster 2019), although the right's anti-feminism and misogyny had far from disappeared. Although the US and British governments were officially clear that they were fighting extreme Islamists, not Muslims in general, anti-radicalization programmes also blurred this distinction. In the UK, Cameron partly resiled from New Labour's multiculturalism as far as Muslims were concerned, proclaiming in 2011 a turn towards "muscular liberalism" (Shilliam 2018: 128). Meanwhile, extreme right organizations like the BNP, Britain First (BF) and the English Defence League promoted explicitly Islamophobic views. As they adapted and modernized (eschewing Nazism, fascism and classical racist politics), they focused on "a narrower anti-Muslim, pro-free speech platform, coupled with the populist notion that they, 'the people', are being oppressed by a tyrannical elite", so that Muslims were seen as "uniquely different from the majority of the British public" (Mulhall 2019). A study of Muslims in the press during the 1997, 2001 and 2005 general elections demonstrated that increases in the numbers and hostility of the reports could be attributed to 9/11 and the invasion of Iraq (Richardson 2009); Goodfellow (2019: 26) reports a journalist on the *Daily Star* during this decade recounting a constant pressure to find stories that fitted in with an anti-immigrant or anti-Muslim narrative.

UKIP played heavily and strategically into these themes. Robert Ford and Matthew Goodwin (2014: 283), in a major study of the party, noted its "strident and often emotive language about the effects of immigration", and that "members of ethnic minority groups who do support [UKIP] have ... been wheeled out to counter claims that UKIP are racist, or to front their election broadcasts. Yet such efforts are continually hampered by the less than welcoming views held by many UKIP members and voters." In fact, these comments underestimate UKIP racism, which was increasingly strategic. Not only did UKIP's elected representatives (MEPs and councillors) also express racist views (Deacon & Wring 2016: 173–5) but Farage, who became leader in 2006, also developed a clear anti-Muslim orientation, supporting a ban on the wearing of the burqa, blaming Muslims for antisemitism and highlighting the role of Muslim men in grooming girls for sexual exploitation. However, he calibrated his comments to avoid explicit hostility to Muslims as such, instead citing public opinion evidence to suggest that there was "a problem with some of the Muslim community", that British Muslims experienced a "tremendous conflict and a split of loyalties", and even, "people do see a fifth column living within our country, who hate us and want to kill us" (Dathan 2015).

Goodwin and Jocelyn Evans (2012: 23) showed that BNP and UKIP supporters were driven by a similar set of concerns; both groups identified Muslims in British society as the third "most important issue facing the country" after immigration and the economy; although fewer UKIP than BNP supporters selected Muslims as the most important issue, "on the whole, they would also feel bothered by the presence of a mosque and view Islam as threatening". Similarly, Thomas Davidson and Mabel Berezin (2018: 485) demonstrated that the absence of a leadership-level relationship between UKIP and BF "belied a substantial connection between BF and UKIP's rank-and-file supporters, including many people who were active in support of the agendas of both groups. From UKIP's initial electoral breakthrough in 2014 until the Brexit referendum in 2016, we observed frequent interactions between their supporters. Many promoted the cause of leaving the EU and attempted to connect this to grievances towards Islam." On the mainstream right, Cameron – despite his "detoxification" of the Conservative Party after 2005 – talked of a "swarm" of immigrants (Goodfellow 2019: 9) and allowed Crosby to target anti-Muslim propaganda at Hindu and Sikh voters in an attempt to defeat Labour's Muslim candidate, Sadiq Khan, in the London mayoral election six weeks before the 2016 referendum (Chakelian 2016; Mason 2016).

The increase in Islamophobia after 2001 was followed within a few years by increasing hostility to eastern European immigrants, again across the right including the press. As we have seen, unlike colonial citizens of colour, European workers had been viewed in the late 1940s as being capable of assimilation as Britons, and similarly their increasing numbers in the 1980s and 1990s were not met with organized hostility. Unlike even the long-settled Black population, they were not widely represented as "immigrants"; instead, mostly younger incomers from mainly western European countries were largely "invisible" (Favell 2008). However, after EU enlargement in 2004 and Blair's decision (unlike other western European governments) not to place an interim restriction on numbers, migrants from Poland and other countries, who often entered skilled and unskilled working-class occupations, became the focus of right-wing press and political attention. Negative tabloid coverage towards eastern Europeans became a major phenomenon and for the first time they were widely racialized. In the six months before Romania and Bulgaria joined the EU on 1 January 2007, Irina Mădroane (2018: 144) writes,

> the right-wing, Eurosceptic tabloid media (*Sun, Daily Mail, Express*) raged against unrestricted labour migration from Romania and Bulgaria … They employed statistics and expert knowledge to make predictions about an "invasion" of Romanian and Bulgarian nationals, depicted through metaphors of deluge and siege …. The rhetoric of numbers was coupled with representations of Romanians and Bulgarians as criminals, carriers of disease (AIDS and tuberculosis), or impoverished, lazy people, who were looking forward to British welfare.

A "panoply of negative characters (the Romanian homeless migrant, the Romanian beggar, the Romanian gangster, the Romanian benefit scrounger) essentialize[d] Romania as a source of crime for the UK, via EU mobility rights" (Mădroane 2018: 165). Rising opinion poll opposition to eastern European migration was directly attributable to this kind of media coverage: using the *Daily Mail* as a measure, the statistical "links between immigration, media coverage, and public concern are impressively strong" (Evans & Mellon 2019: 80). The message cut through politically, notably when the pensioner Gillian Duffy asked Labour prime minister Gordon Brown during the 2010 election, "these eastern Europeans, where are they all flocking from?" This became an iconic moment of the campaign after Brown was recorded calling Duffy "that bigoted woman"; the right-wing press defended her for expressing "genuine concerns about immigration". However, in 2007, Brown himself had crassly proposed "British jobs for British workers".

This press and polling momentum created a major political opening for those ready to highlight the eastern European "threat". Although a Conservative minister, Peter Lilley, had attacked Europeans coming to the UK as "scroungers" as early as 1994, becoming "the first major politician … to apply classic xenophobic tropes to European citizens" (Yeo 2020: 188), in the decade before Brexit it was UKIP which chiefly mobilized this narrative. The party's overt support in the press was limited until the *Express* titles backed it in 2014–15, but it capitalized on their negative coverage of the eastern European migrants, making Romanians its main scapegoats (Deacon & Wring 2016) and using them to forge a decisive link between immigration and its core Europhobic goals. In 2009, it broke through to get the second-highest share of the vote in the European Parliament elections in the UK. Analysing this advance, Ford, Goodwin and David Cutts (2012: 209) saw UKIP's "emphasis on opposition to immigration, multiculturalism and Islam" as playing a crucial part. Their research showed that while its voters were primarily motivated by Euroscepticism, xenophobia was also an "important driver"; the party was "particularly successful at attracting votes from citizens who are alarmed about immigration and hostile to immigrants". While not all UKIP's anti-immigrant supporters were openly hostile to British ethnic minorities, "relatively strong" statistical correlations between xenophobia and Euroscepticism and between racial prejudice and xenophobia suggested that "hostility to one out-group tends to correlate with hostility to others; those who dislike immigrants tend to dislike racial minorities and to dislike the 'foreigners' from the EU encroaching on British politics" (Ford, Goodwin & Cutts 2012: 211).

The BNP also advanced strongly in these elections, drawing support which was still largely motivated by overt racism but beginning to build a larger coalition (Cutts, Ford & Goodwin 2011), becoming at this point "the most successful extreme right party in Britain's electoral history" (Ford & Goodwin 2010). Although UKIP's core support was akin to the BNP's – economically struggling working-class voters from traditional Labour backgrounds – in the European elections it also attracted better-off "strategic" voters who normally supported the Conservatives in general elections (Ford, Goodwin & Cutts 2012). UKIP was more than a polite version of the extreme right, or the "BNP in blazers"; rooted in the politically legitimate tradition of British Euroscepticism – with a substantial overlap with the Conservatives to whom Farage and other party leaders had earlier belonged – the party's self-presentation as non-racist, non-sectarian civic nationalists meant they were able to mobilize widespread anti-immigration sentiment among voters who previously or concurrently supported both main parties. Using hostility to EU immigration to mobilize this coalition, UKIP moved from being a marginal electoral player to a serious challenger party.

In the 2010 general election, the Tories were partially successful in containing this threat. At a leadership level they "made relatively little noise about immigration", but it featured in the 17 million pieces of direct mail they sent out, which "helped to ensure the Conservatives emerged as the single biggest party" (Bale 2016: 356). This low-key operation anticipated the much more extensive and largely online activities of Vote Leave in 2016. Under the first-past-the-post system which penalized minor parties (it was a proportional party list system which had enabled its success in the European elections), UKIP won only 3.5 per cent of the votes, but this was the largest national percentage vote of any smaller right-wing party in general election history, while the BNP's 2.1 per cent was the largest for an extreme right party. Together this was enough to deprive the Conservatives of an overall majority, forcing them into coalition with the Liberal Democrats. For the Tories, the far right now represented a serious threat, which escalated after the election. Earlier in 2010, Cameron had made his seminal commitment to reduce net immigration (discussed further below). By 2013, as Farage was threatening the Tory position by fanning fears about the ending of transitional controls on immigration from Romania and Bulgaria, Cameron gave his pledge to hold an in–out EU referendum. Despite his "hostile environ-ment" policy (also discussed later), the Conservatives "had essentially lost own-ership" of the immigration issue to UKIP (Bale 2016: 395). Farage's party topped the polls in the 2014 European elections; two Tory MPs defected to it, going on to win by-elections for their new party; and in the 2015 general election, it gained an unprecedented 13 per cent of the votes although only one seat. UKIP's burgeoning support in these years not only helped the Tory right extract key policy concessions from Cameron; it would also hugely inform the 2016 major-ity for Brexit. After the referendum, support for Leave closely mapped support for UKIP in this period (Goodwin & Heath 2016: 323), while fully "67.1% of the leave vote consist[ed] of voters who have at least dabbled with UKIP" by voting for them once or more in 2014–16 or expressing a strong likelihood of voting for them (Mellon & Evans 2016).

Indeed, UKIP's arguments in the years before the referendum closely antici-pated those of the Conservative-led Vote Leave campaign in 2016, which are ex-amined in Chapter 4. A 2014 European election poster asked, "26 million people in Europe are looking for work, and whose jobs are they after?" The same year, Farage proposed "an immigration policy that is non-discriminatory, because at the moment we discriminate in favour of people from Poland, or Romania, or Bulgaria, regardless [of] who they are, we discriminate against people from New Zealand … or from India, or Canada, or whatever else it may be. We've got our, I think, our priorities completely wrong here. And we should not be discriminating on grounds of nationality." Yet by 2015 he was openly supporting a discriminatory policy: "I do have a slight preference. I do think, naturally, that people from India and Australia are in some ways more likely to speak English, understand common law and have a connection with this country than some people that come perhaps from countries that haven't fully recovered from being behind the iron curtain." UKIP's proposal of an "Australian-style points system" for immigration, with which the Tories' Howard had earlier flirted, would be picked up by Vote Leave and finally used to frame the new system which the Johnson government announced in 2020. Although the UK had had a nominal points-based system in place since 2008 – it was "literally called 'the points-based system' in the Immigration Rules" (Yeo 2020: 34) – it was convenient for the right to propose modelling UK policy on Australia, the archetypal white Commonwealth country, which was later to be similarly invoked to label the kind of trade arrangement with the EU (or lack of it) which Brexiters desired. As Peter Mitchell (2021: 93) comments, "the details of the actual Australian immigration policy [were] unimportant: Australia becomes shorthand for a certain kind of violence deployed in defence of a certain kind of whiteness. That whiteness is situated within probably the purest form of the queerly nostalgic place Australia holds in the British popular imaginary: a place that's still white *in the right way*, which is to say Anglo, eerily masculinist, and not inclined to share" (emphasis in original).

Policy racism: the numerical target and the hostile environment

If UKIP was making the running in the early 2010s, adding attacks on asylum seekers to its portfolio (Favell 2020), the demand for immigration control had been fed during half a century – and especially since the late 1990s – by Conservative politicians, the right-wing press and the citizenship policies of successive Labour as well as Tory governments (Yeo 2020: xvii). The system had long been based on the idea that migrants were threats to be securitized, and its operation had had great personal costs for many. However, as anti-immigration campaigning was increasingly linked to Europhobia, numerical racism became more prominent in Conservative policy, with policy effects which further worsened the already hostile environment for migrants and minorities. In 2005, Howard committed to an annual limit on all forms of migration. Although when Cameron took over after the Tories' election defeat that year, he initially talked only about "annual limits on non-EU economic migration" – that is, not on refugees or EU migrants (formally, this remained the policy even in 2015) – media pressure, sharpened by UKIP's advance in 2009, led him in January 2010 (months before a general election in which he hoped to gain power) to talk about a general numerical limit, reducing immigration from the "hundreds" to the "tens of thousands" (Yeo 2020: 23–34). He did not commit to a figure, but "the perception gradually spread that a target had been set, restricting net migration to 100,000, to be applied to all forms of migration, EU and non-EU alike. Cameron never said or intended this, yet the perception was so widespread that he and his Home Secretary, Theresa May, felt bound to embrace it" (Yeo 2020: xxiii). Woolly words, assisted by the *Daily Telegraph*'s reporting of its interview with Cameron, morphed into a solid pledge and this "accidental target", as Yeo (2020: 15) calls it, enshrined numerical racism in immigration policy, providing a fixed reference point for future anti-immigration campaigning and proving an albatross round Cameron's neck in 2016. Yet originally, "the advantage of focusing on net migration, rather than solely on inward immigration, [was] that the policy can be represented as one of overall population management, rather than one of keeping foreigners out – with the connotations of racism and xenophobia that might be implied"; it was "a tactician's gambit for winning an election rather than a strategist's plan for governing effectively and retaining power", and Cameron "had been a little *too* successful in moving the discussion from immigration to net migration" (Yeo 2020: 23, emphasis in original). Like Heath following Powell's speech, in countering UKIP Cameron "dialled down the rhetoric" but "pumped up the policy, moving away from the populist words but simultaneously (and very unusually) risking a commitment to a specific and highly restrictive target" in "an attempt to have his cake and eat it too" (Bale 2013: 32).

The target would never be reached; Johnson would quietly abandon it in 2020. Yet for almost a decade, rather than "resile from the impossible policy", Cameron and May "felt it was better to at least look like they were trying. The result was an all-out assault on immigration in which not just migrants but lawfully resident and even British citizen ethnic minorities became collateral damage" (Yeo 2020: 26). As a new system was launched in 2012, the "hostile environment" of bureaucratic reality became the official name for the government's immigration policy: "the idea was to make life in the UK intolerable for those who were unlawfully resident by cutting them off from the necessities of life and preventing access to public services" (Yeo 2020: 29). Policing this environment was outsourced to public bodies, companies and individuals who came into contact with migrants, through a new Immigration Act in 2014 (which Labour failed to oppose) and additional rules expanding the system from employment into landlord–tenant relations, banking, vehicle licensing and even children's records in schools. An Immigration Enforcement Hotline encouraged Soviet-style informing by citizens. The system encouraged racial discrimination and produced huge "collateral damage" to people who were not illegal immigrants or even migrants at all.

The most notorious example of this was the treatment of longstanding "Windrush" citizens of Caribbean and other Commonwealth origin, many of whom were forced out their jobs, denied medical treatment and even deported, some of them dying as a result, for lack of documentary evidence of citizenship (Gentleman 2019). The exclusion of colonial citizens from "familial" Britishness for which politicians and officials had worked so hard in the middle of the twentieth century was gruesomely reflected in these extreme bureaucratic cruelties, involving the denial even of people's formal political citizenship, to which many were subjected in middle and old age. The government argued that these were not the intentions of the policy, but most of its effects were predictable and widely predicted (Holloway 2018). Furthermore, since the real goal of this policy (rebranded "the compliant environment" in 2018) was to reduce the politically hypersensitive net migration figure, its success in removing illegal immigrants was not even effectively measured (Yeo 2020: 58). Likewise, the asylum policy did not deter asylum seekers but could better be explained by aims of reassuring public opinion, manufacturing public concern for political gain and throwing "red meat" to the right wing of the Conservative Party (Yeo 2020: 133–6). Institutionalized cruelty even against Britons, for example in family separations, supported the policy's numerical goals: "If a British citizen was forced out of Britain, all the better, as this was an even greater contribution towards the net migration target, given that net migration counts both immigration and emigration" (Yeo 2020: 80). This example is a good illustration of how numerical racism operated at the policy level: the racism lay in the intention to limit the numbers of ethnic minorities and non-British, but because it was numerically defined it worked through abstract rules which also caught some white British. Equally significantly, as the Europhobes harnessed anti-immigration politics, they also reinforced the increasingly exclusive idea of citizenship which had developed over previous decades. The purpose behind British citizenship laws had increasingly become "to restrict and preserve the existing ethnic origins of the already established citizenry", so that successive governments had been "content to first create and later allow the growth of a sizeable population of long-term resident non-citizens" (Yeo 2020: 273). More than three million people who had moved from other EU countries through their common EU citizenship enjoyed almost all the rights of UK citizens. Yet Brexit intrinsically threatened the meaning of that citizenship in the UK, potentially turning their formal lack of British citizenship into a substantive lack and loss of rights.

Popular racism against eastern Europeans and Muslims

Media and campaigning-driven racism helped stimulate popular as well as policy hostility to these target populations. Bindi Shah and Jessica Ogden's (2021: 1) analysis of "non-elite" participants in Twitter discussions (around the time of the 2014 lifting of transitional controls on Romanian and Bulgarian migrants to the UK) revealed "a cohesive set of anti-immigrant or anti-immigration sentiments linked to UKIP and that express an exclusionary nationalism based on assumptions about race, 'whiteness' and entitlement"; while some pro-immigration sentiments contested racialized understandings of the nation, they did not "coalesce in ways to disrupt the dominance of right-wing anti-immigrant sentiments". This analysis matches accounts of eastern Europeans' experiences before Brexit, which reveal that they were widely racialized (Fox, Morosanu & Szilassy 2012). "Racism is something we learn", note Jon Fox and Magda Mogilnicka (2017: 1–2), "and some people in Britain have learned to be racist toward East Europeans, just as previous generations learned to be racist to other immigrants." For Poles, the largest national group, "racism and xenophobia were well established before the Brexit vote", according to Alina Rzepnikowska (2018: 74), whose research analysed the "overlapping racism and xenophobia discussed and experienced by migrant women coming from a predominantly white society". She argues that in the early years of the new migration, "some media focused on the positive work ethics of Polish migrants by emphasizing hard-workingness, value for money and diligence. They were constructed as a 'desirable' migrant group and seen as 'invisible' due to their whiteness." However, she dates a "rhetorical shift" to the outbreak of the economic crisis in 2008, as Polish migrants "started to be perceived as an economic threat responsible for society's malaise: job shortages, unemployment and the strain on social services". In 2012–13, Polish women in Manchester regularly experienced harassment and verbal abuse, and this got worse in the run-up to the referendum. Visible and audible markers of difference, "such as Polish registration plates, Polish satellite dish or Polish language [made] their Otherness visible and audible"; not "looking Polish" was considered as a way to be less stigmatized, and the women "were often surprised that they experienced racism and xenophobia despite being white", attributing this to poor and uneducated Britons (Rzepnikowska 2018: 66, 69, 72). Romanians and Bulgarians, Polina Manolova (2017: 4) argues, suffered even greater stigmatization and consequent insecurity than rather more settled eastern European communities like the Poles.

However, Fox and Mogilnicka echo Gilroy's (2004: 110–11) comment that the new immigrants, unconnected with the British history of empire, also become "caught up in a pattern of hostility and conflict that belongs emphatically to its lingering aftermath" and might follow "a well-trodden path pioneered by the most vulnerable and marginal members of the host community". They would "seek salvation by trying to embrace and inflate the ebbing privileges of whiteness. That racialized identification is presumably the best way to prove they are not really immigrants at all but somehow already belong to the home-space in ways that black and brown people against whom they have to compete in the labour market will never be recognized as doing" (Fox & Mogilnicka 2017: 1). In a "pathological" kind of integration, eastern Europeans in the UK were learning British racism: "Acquiring and using local variants of racism is one way East Europeans can manoeuvre and manipulate Britain's shifting and contingent status hierarchies in their favour. Racism in this view is not something separate from (or antithetical to) integration, but something that is also a part of integration." Poles, Hungarians and Romanians not only imported "home-grown" racist practices but were also "acquiring specifically British competencies of racism" vis-à-vis Black people, Asians and Muslims (Fox & Mogilnicka 2017: 1). The Romanian-born researcher Alexandra Bulat (2017) captured a similar tension in her paper's title, "We Are Not Tolerant as a Nation, but We Want Others to Tolerate Us".

These contradictions testify to how, as ever in the history of racism, new racializations are overlain on and interact with the old. For British Muslims, this experience was extremely overdetermined. Not only did most of them suffer from the deeply embedded colour racism in British society and the even older Christian hostility to Islam; these were now reinforced by the fear of Islamist terror. Muslims were now the most feared other (Modood 2005): young Muslim men were subjected to corrosive stereotyping as potential terrorists (Lynch 2015), Muslim women were frequently targeted for wearing Islamic dress (Copsey *et al.* 2013: 21) and polling showed twice as much opposition to white–Muslim as to white–Black marriage (Ford 2014). Extreme right organizations focused their hostility on Muslims, and BNP support was concentrated in towns with large Muslim populations (Ford & Goodwin 2010). In online anti-Muslim abuse, which accounted for three-quarters of all cases, almost 70 per cent was linked to the extreme right and principally the English Defence League (Tell MAMA 2018). Moreover, as Farah Elahi and Omar Khan (2017: 13) comment, reflecting on the two decades since the Runnymede Trust first recognized Islamophobia as a type of racism, "dangerous sophistications in Islamophobic discourse" had attempted to separate "Islamophobia as ideology from Muslims themselves and, in a parallel move, ... anti-Muslimism from the longer and broader historical and social context of racial discrimination and racism".

These general tendencies were exacerbated by the increasing polarization of identities within the group of communities defined as "British Asian". The development of British Muslim identity "left those who had at one time shared the British Asian category to consider where they now stand, and whether 'British Asian' [was] a socially meaningful identity"; many Indians "decided that 'British Hindu' was a good descriptor of their identity, but this remain[ed] contested and mutable" (Runnymede Trust 2006: 27, 29). If the growing salience of distinct religiously defined communal identities partly responded to "local civic pressures and the intensification of government rhetoric on harnessing the capacity of religious bodies in support of public policy", especially under Blair, it was also an expression of nationalism (Knott 2009). The emergence of separate Hindu and Muslim identities reflected continuing communal hostilities in the South Asian context from which the majority originated. In the decade before the Brexit referendum, while Hindus continued to support umbrella communal organizations, Hindutva (nationalist) influence was strengthening (Zavos 2010). Likewise, British Sikhs, Katy Sian (2013: 93) explains, increasingly projected the anxieties associated with the diaspora situation "onto the figure of a Muslim 'other' that has become the main antagonist within these narratives". She identifies "a specific Sikh Islamophobia" which played a "constitutive role" in "articulations of Sikhness against the backdrop of postcolonial Britain". As we have seen, the Conservatives perceived anti-Muslim sentiment among Hindus and Sikhs as sufficiently potent to pitch Islamophobic material to them in the 2016 London mayoral election.

Changing racism, new political viability

This chapter has argued that the forms of British political racism inherited from the nineteenth and early twentieth centuries mutated repeatedly in the three-quarters of a century after 1945, as actors across the right sought to exploit new waves of immigration in the context of imperial decline, the increasing importance of antiracist norms and changing political situations. We have seen that in the first decade after the Second World War, ministers of both main parties together with civil servants, operating with racialized conceptions of the imperial population, turned colonial citizens into "Commonwealth immigrants" whose entry into the UK needed to be blocked. This racialization of "immigrants", which originally reflected elite hesitancy about overt racial politics, became the central theme in the expanding popularization of racial politics, after Powell's interventions showed its huge political potential but also the pitfalls for mainstream politicians of crude and overt appeals. The chapter has argued that the combination of immigration control legislation with laws to outlaw discrimination represented a twin-track approach, in principle shared by Labour and Conservative governments into the twenty-first century. However, Tory leaders from Thatcher onwards sought to exploit immigration but more subtly than Powell and without ever making it overtly dominant in their election campaigns. As the mainstream right moved to mobilize it against New Labour in the 2000s, they sought to neutralize further the inferential racism of anti-immigration nativism by making it a matter of numbers, but I have shown that numerical racism was most successful when it was linked, particularly in the challenge which the radical right UKIP posed to the Tory mainstream, to new selective anti-Muslim and anti-eastern European racisms. The change in the approach to migrants from other European countries is particularly striking: they were transformed from racial equals who could be absorbed into white Britishness in the 1940s and were widely accepted as European integration deepened in the last quarter of the twentieth century into racialized others in the twenty-first, as immigration was annexed to the drive to withdraw the UK from the EU. This linkage, pioneered by the press and exploited most effectively by Farage, enabled the once-marginal Europhobic movement, which I discuss in Chapter 3, to move into the mainstream, laying the foundations for the 2016 referendum and the Leave victory.

3

THE EUROPHOBIC MOVEMENT AND ITS IDEOLOGY

> Brexit is a recent phenomenon, with causes in the here and now, and is opposed by roughly half the population. Brexit has nothing to do with deep history. David Edgerton (2018, xx)

As the Vote Leave slogan, "Take Back Control", suggested, the overt meaning of the project for British exit from the EU, developed by the British right-wing over a quarter of a century, was a nationalist attempt to recover autonomous sovereign power for the UK state from its enmeshment in the shared sovereignty of EU legal and state institutions.[1] "Regaining" sovereignty was also the most widely acknowledged motivation for voting Leave in 2016 (Centre for Social Investigation 2018), but since restricting immigration – long described as immigration "control" – was not only the second most popular reason for voting Leave but also (as we shall see in Chapter 4) the dominant way in which regaining sovereignty was justified by the Leave campaigns and the Brexit press, the majority for Brexit was both widely informed and in its narrow margin (51.9 versus 48.1 per cent) probably also decided by anti-immigration politics. While racism and hostility to immigration did not *define* Brexit as a project or process, they are central to *understanding* it, and no serious appraisal can avoid comprehensively examining their relationships to its overtly dominant nationalist theme. This I do over three chapters: this chapter discusses the ideas behind Brexit and the Eurosceptic/Europhobic campaign in the decades up to 2016; Chapter 4 analyses the referendum itself; and Chapter 5 examines the Brexit process and conflict following the referendum, between 2016 and the UK's formal exit in 2020.

---

1. There was of course also a left-wing version of the UK's exit, dubbed "Lexit", which emphasized socio-economic goals. However, this was very much a secondary movement in 2016, playing a minor supporting, if notionally critical, role alongside the dominant right-wing project. The longer-term weakening of left-wing opposition to the EU, which explains this situation, is discussed below.

British nationalism, Atlanticism and Europe

The movement for Brexit is part of a wider tendency towards economic and political nationalism in powerful states in the twenty-first century, which has increasingly threatened international cooperation. In this sense, Brexit can be compared to other policies, especially but by no means only of authoritarian regimes; but as the only secession from the unique international state entity which is the European Union, it is also very distinctive. Likewise, Euroscepticism is a major European political current and exists in most member states, but nowhere else has a Europhobic movement become dominant or come close to producing withdrawal from the EU; indeed, so far the British experience has acted as a deterrent rather than an incentive to others. Geopolitical repositioning linked to changes in ruling parties and regimes can also be found elsewhere, but Brexit is unique in its simultaneous transformation of international and domestic constitutional arrangements. Therefore, it has also involved a very different set of processes from the most consequential parliamentary or presidential election, not least because it has been and continues to be drawn out over a substantial period of time. The elections of leaders like Donald Trump, Narendra Modi, Jair Bolsonaro and Viktor Orbán are likely to have serious medium-term effects, some of them constitutional, but none of them *depended on* a comprehensive set of constitutional changes like Johnson's nationalist Tory regime, which would probably not have come to power without the more profound change which had already been set in motion by the vote for Brexit in 2016. As a nationalist leader, he was a creature as well as a creator of Brexit, which he embraced after considering opposing it. While racist strategies such as the electoral manipulation of anti-immigrant sentiment, discriminatory policies and laws, and stimulating abuse are common to the new right-wing regimes, in Brexit they are implicated in what will probably be a long-lasting transformation of the state and citizenship which has only limited parallels elsewhere. The installation of authoritarian racial-nationalist regimes may be reversible – as Trump's ejection showed – but Brexit is not, at least in a similar way; to overcome it would require a different kind of mobilization, far more difficult to achieve, from those required merely to remove a government from office even in the most challenging democratic conditions.

As David Edgerton suggests in the comments with which I preface this chapter, Brexit is a recent movement and draws on the past in the ways which suit its contemporary purposes, but it has emerged from the distinctive history of the British state and politics. It is striking that a regressive, Europhobic nationalism has arisen from a political elite which underwent, in the third quarter of the twentieth century, a slow but at the time apparently definitive conversion to European integration, and from the right wing of British politics which was then the more pro-European. As is well known, the original adjustment to "Europe" was difficult for both politicians and society in the UK, and the falling out is proving more so. It is useful to locate these processes in the longer-term trajectory of the state, which went from being the pre-eminent world empire at the beginning of the twentieth century to a member state of the EU in a world increasingly dominated by the US and emergent Chinese superpowers at the beginning of the twenty-first, and is now becoming an "independent" state again as a result of Brexit. This is manifestly the history of a state which remained powerful with considerable international status – one of the five recognized nuclear weapon states and permanent members of the United Nations Security Council – but was greatly reduced in relative power, having become militarily and financially dependent on the much more powerful USA during the Second World War and having lost its empire in the following decades.

An important paradox of Brexit is that like other major European states, the UK ceded much of its military autonomy to the US-led North Atlantic Treaty Organization (NATO) after 1949, and that even while fighting bitterly to end the sharing of economic authority in the EU, the British right has continued to support this fundamental pooling of military sovereignty which effectively subordinates the UK to the USA. Although Europhobes claim to uphold the principle that national sovereignty must be absolute, it is striking that all along they have conceded the pooling of the most fundamental dimension of sovereignty, which Max Weber (1978: 54) called the "monopoly of the legitimate use of physical force" (or violence) and defined as the core of the state's authority. Even if in practice states have rarely held such a monopoly, this is the central myth of modern statehood and, since the British right has consistently valued its military power as a reason why internationally it punches above its weight, it is a very significant concession. For all the Brexiters' talk about sovereignty, it is the pooling of sovereignty in a *European* union, rather than the principle of pooling, to which they object.

This paradox is an important indication of the ideological direction of the British nationalism which this movement espouses. In belatedly acceding to the EEC in 1973, the UK acknowledged a common process of change in western European states, which had become second-tier members not just of NATO but of a larger, US-led Western bloc, which operated through a growing web of international organizations as well as bilateral relations. Major adjustments of state and society which were taking place as a result: democracy was normalized, social expenditures were expanded, economies were becoming more national than imperial and ideas of the nation were increasingly centred on economic and social compacts of the state and the population. If Britain was exceptional, as Edgerton (2018: xxvii–xxx) argues, it was because only in this period was a "British nation" consolidated as "a distinctive economic, social and political unit within the borders of the United Kingdom", rather than as the centre of a more cosmopolitan empire. This was the high point of an economically based nationalism, centred on national productivism and full employment, and widely thought of in terms of its "welfare state", although as we have seen it also reproduced the empire's racialized population policies within the borders of the UK. In most countries of western Europe, this kind of nationalism proved compatible with cooperation in common European institutions, but in Britain it motivated the left-wing opposition to the EU which was strong until the 1980s, as well as opposition from the right. In general, the British adjustment to being merely an important nation-state was exceptionally demanding: the UK had had the largest empire, had remained a world-class military power until the war and had emerged from it victorious and uninvaded. In reality, Edgerton argues, it was more of a warfare than a welfare state, keen to maintain its global military rank, which makes the compromising of the "monopoly of violence" all the more noteworthy. Yet European integration had begun in the interstices of the Western bloc, with encouragement from the USA, so it was possible for British leaders to join European institutions without making them a primary commitment, or abandoning the "special relationship" with the USA or indeed the Commonwealth. For both Conservative and Labour leaders, membership was more a pragmatic than an ideological decision, to prevent the UK falling economically further behind a recovering Germany and other continental states. It was certainly true that large sections of both parties, including prominent figures of the left and right, remained opposed to UK membership, and the majority of voters remained sceptical even as they ratified accession in a 1975 referendum. Ideological Europeanism was initially confined to parts of the two parties' centrist wings and the smaller Liberal Party, later the Liberal Democrats, and probably only two prime ministers, Heath (who oversaw EEC accession) and later Blair, could be described as belonging to that tendency.

A curiosity of British nationalism was that, at least in the mainstream, it was less overt than many. However, the country had developed a deep national myth which only became more pervasive over time, celebrating its supposedly unique role in the defeat of Nazism; in reality, of course, its US and Soviet allies had played more important roles. British national self-images failed to correspond fully to its changed global position, and the UK's leaders often acted as though it were more powerful than it was. Its capacity for independent military action was found wanting not only in the failed Suez invasion of 1956, which the USA disowned, but also in the Falklands victory of 1982, which only succeeded with tacit US support. France, which shared the Suez humiliation, was the only country in a somewhat comparable position, but its defeat and invasion in 1940 led its leaders to define partnership with Germany through European integration as a fundamental strategic commitment. For British leaders, in contrast, a belief in their own distinctive contribution to world leadership remained undimmed despite the transformation of the UK's economic, political and military position; the soft power of its shared language with the USA enabled Britain to punch above its weight, for example, in science, media and education. The US commitment generally overrode European loyalties; even for Blair, it trumped them over Iraq in 2003. As European integration deepened in the 1990s and 2000s, British leaders continued to see it primarily as an economic project which should not involve geopolitical competition with the USA. From Thatcher onwards they were committed to a primarily economic view of integration: "driving forward the Single Market project and deepening internal liberalization notably by tackling behind the border barriers to trade in goods and services, was core for all British Governments from the 80s to 2016" (Rogers 2017). So too was the enlargement of the EU to the east and south-east: the British supported expansion, seeing the new eastern European members (who depended on US military guarantees) as allies who would dilute centralizing tendencies and Franco-German dominance. As the union deepened, the UK remained semi-detached, outside the eurozone and the Schengen area, retaining a unique budget rebate and opposing European military integration which it saw as undermining NATO. However, the financial crash and the eurozone crisis, with the institutional developments which it spawned, sharpened the structural problems of the UK's position in the EU economy, narrowing the Cameron government's choices just at the point when anti-European pressure was growing within the Conservative Party (Thompson 2017). As Rogers (2019a: 9) puts it, "the UK political establishment's main objectives in the EU, from money, to external migration and asylum and the securing of Schengen borders, to the avoidance of taxpayer liabilities which belonged to the Eurozone, became essentially defensive ones. Preserving carve outs and opt outs, avoiding liabilities, building firewalls against contagion."

Rise of the Europhobes

Even on the anti-Atlanticist left, many shared a belief in Britain's distinctive capacity for moral world leadership derived from its imperial past (Hinton 1989: viii–ix); scepticism towards the EU remained a significant minority current, often linked to anti-American, pro-Third World internationalism (this section of the left included Jeremy Corbyn, the Labour leader during the Brexit crisis). Yet, despite these broader roots, when "Euroscepticism" was named in the 1980s it was an increasingly right-wing tendency. In reaction to Thatcherism and famously attracted by Jacques Delors' promise of a "social market", the majority of the Labour Party shifted to support the UK's membership of the European Community, while left-wing pro-Europeanism also grew as a result of cooperation in the peace movements (Kaldor 1991). Overall, left-wing Euroscepticism was a weaker current than before, as the marginalization of the "Lexit" position in 2016 would confirm. Meanwhile, what Paul Taggart and Alex Szczerbiak (2004) called "soft" Eurosceptics – who accepted European integration but in a qualified way, as opposed to "hard" Eurosceptics (whom I have called Europhobes) who opposed it in principle – had become the majority in the Conservative Party. Thatcher herself accepted the economic rationale for European integration and played a major part in bringing the single market into existence, but as a British nationalist laid down a marker against further treaty integration and political "federalism" in her Bruges speech of 1988. After she was forced from office two years later, many of her followers, supported by much of the right-wing press and a few Labour MPs, fought a bitter parliamentary battle in 1992–93 against the ratification of the Maastricht Treaty which established the European Union, despite John Major's government securing an opt-out from the protocol on the treaty's Social Chapter. The "Black Wednesday" financial crisis of 16 September 1992, resulting from the UK's membership of the European Exchange Rate Mechanism, also energized Tory hostility to Europe (Bale 2016: 41).

In this context, the Europhobic tendency became a serious political force for the first time, and a referendum on the UK's EU membership became its key demand. While it gained more support among Conservatives than previously, its early political expression was chiefly through two new radical right parties: UKIP, founded in 1993, and a short-lived Referendum Party led by Sir James Goldsmith which gained 2.6 per cent of the votes in the 1997 general election, helping to compound the scale of the Tory defeat. Following this election, 85 per cent of Tory MPs were Eurosceptics (Bale 2016: 72), but EU withdrawal remained a minority position as opposition to the emerging European currency became the mainstream focus. Iain Duncan Smith, Tory leader from 2001 to 2003, largely avoided European issues but called in 2003 for referendums on any proposal for euro membership and on the EU's proposed Constitutional Treaty (Bale 2016: 166). As we have seen, in 2004 his successor Howard supported a tabloid campaign against "benefit tourists" and escalated his Eurosceptic rhetoric in the face of the UKIP threat. Howard's own successor Cameron, in contrast, was "continually calibrating" centrist and rightist positions (Bale 2016: 304), trying to steer the Tories away from their failed focus on Europe but also opposing the EU's Lisbon Treaty and, in a move which was popular with the Europhobes, withdrawing Tory MEPs from the main centre-right parliamentary group. In 2011, 81 Conservative MPs defied Cameron to vote for an in–out referendum on the UK's EU membership, and in 2013, as we have seen, he finally promised to hold a referendum before 2017. As Peter J. Anderson (2004) showed, the "party in the media" was playing a key role in cultivating a Europhobic common sense on the British right. The tabloids, with their "vernacular ventriloquism", using language, style and vocabulary similar to those of their readerships (Conboy 2006: 14), demonized the EU as an overregulating institution at best, and a totalitarian, suppressing and threatening power at worst. Cécile Leconte (2010: 204) documented their simplistic code words – "Brussels", "federalism", "dictatorship" and "unaccountable" versus "British values", "sovereignty" and "independence" – which fostered deep Euroscepticism and were easily turned in an openly Europhobic direction as anti-European politics radicalized.

Therefore, while the word Brexit was only coined in 2012, a substantial bloc of right-wing forces both inside and outside the Conservative Party, with a substantial following in the media and through them a wide popular audience, had never been fully reconciled to UK membership of the EU and increasingly envisaged a referendum which would lead to its departure; they were supported by a significant but less influential current which advocated Lexit. There was never a single Europhobic programme or organization with a shared vision of what leaving would mean but rather a network of groups, straddling Conservative and non-Conservative opinion, which supported a fully "independent", exclusively "sovereign" UK, outside the EU's political and legal institutions but within NATO. Even after a referendum became a real possibility when Cameron committed the Tories to it in 2013, and probable when he achieved an unexpected majority in 2015, Leavers failed to produce a single programme and notoriously entered the 2016 campaign without a clear prospectus. Most Europhobic politicians both in the Conservative Party and UKIP harked back to Britain as it had been before EU entry, but as to what an "independent" UK now meant, especially in economic terms, there was no clear agreement. What Ivan Rogers (2019a: 9) called the "most thoughtful sceptic attempt to map an exit route", which did "at least to grapple with what insider experts knew were inordinately complex issues", was the "Flexcit" plan. This made very clear the trade-offs between sovereignty, continuing economic strength and the political acceptability of exit, arguing that:

> No matter how attractive the eventual outcome, exit will never be tolerated if the immediate effect is to damage trade and plunge us into recession. In our view, that means we must – in the short to medium term – stay in the EU's Single Market. However, the EU has made it abundantly clear that if we want to stay in the Single Market, acceptance of the principle freedom of movement is non-negotiable. We can abolish freedom of movement or we can stay in the single market. We can't do both. On that basis, we have come to the conclusion that, in order to leave the EU and secure the medium and long-term gains that accrue from so doing, we must accept a short-term compromise over freedom of movement.   (North & Oulds 2016: 9–10)

It noted, indeed, that "the adoption of freedom of movement does not totally remove the ability of member states to control the flow of migrants from other EU member states" (North & Oulds 2016: 17). Major Leave politicians, from Johnson to Farage, associated themselves from time to time with this "Norway option" of single market membership, and none of them ruled it out before the referendum, although Lexiters opposed it primarily because it appeared to tie the UK to EU state aid rules. However, Flexcit was far from being a firm programmatic commitment by any major section of Europhobic opinion, and its economically rational, politically centrist approach was being pushed aside by the strategic racism through which, we saw in Chapter 2, UKIP had transformed Brexit from a fringe option into a real possibility. The 2016 referendum would demonstrate that, in its drive to succeed, the Brexit movement was radicalizing well beyond this approach, whose ideas would be spurned not only by the Leave leaders but also by Theresa May, the ex-Remainer who would become prime minister after the vote.

Free markets, empire and the Anglosphere

Flexcit also sat uncomfortably with the dominant ideological rationales for Brexit. It is important not to overideologize the Europhobic movement, which was a loose coalition of forces constantly adapting to changing political conditions. However, it needed justifications for the exit which it proposed, and these reflected the diffuse intellectual traditions of the British right. The rejection of European integration as a violation of sovereignty – while the pooling of sovereignty in NATO was embraced – reflected a deeper anti-Europeanism than simple anti-Brussels rhetoric suggested. Indeed, as Robert Harmsen and Menno Spiering (2004: 16) argue, British Euroscepticism was never merely a matter of critical views towards European institutions. Rather, it invoked the entrenched sense of otherness towards the continent and suspicion of the dominant roles of France and Germany, long cultivated through representations of the Second World War. In this context, Germanophobia was significant at many levels of anti-European discourse, from the speeches of Thatcher and her ministers in the 1980s to the tabloid comparisons of today's voluntary union of European nations to the Nazi European empire of the early 1940s (Leconte 2010: 141), a theme echoed by Johnson in 2016. Although Thatcher's Bruges speech had broadly acknowledged Britain's historic engagement with Europe, Johnson's frequent references to "our European friends" appeared ritualistic. It is partly in the light of this deep-rooted political-cultural suspicion that we must make sense of how easily the Europhobes dispensed with the single market, which was partly Thatcher's achievement and could be seen as the apotheosis of her focus on free trade and markets. This deeper anti-Europeanism also helped defeat the rational economic case against radical withdrawal, leading to the single market being seen through the prism of the economic regulation which underpinned it rather than the trade which it enabled, and to free trade agreements being celebrated as the meaning of Brexit in every case *except* the EEA, the world's most ambitious free trade project. This strangely anti-European free market stance was prominently expressed in *Britannia Unchained*, a collection linked to the Institute for Economic Affairs and published by five aspiring Tory MPs (Kwarteng *et al.* 2012), four of whom later became leading members of Johnson's government; Anand Menon (2021) argues that it has increasingly been clarified as the dominant rationale for Brexit in the trade policy decisions of the Johnson government. Free market Europhobia reflected how the anti-state, anti-tax and small-government ethos, which was dominant in the Conservative Party, UKIP and the right-wing press after Thatcher, had developed through close entanglements with the networks of right-wing think tanks – many of them lobbyists for corporate interests – closely linked with and modelled on similar outfits in the USA. As Peter Geoghegan (2020: 102) points out, "a small group on the libertarian and Eurosceptic right of British politics has long looked to the United States for inspiration. The transatlantic connections grew and strengthened rapidly, away from the public view, in the years before and after the EU referendum." These connections were about interests as much as ideas: as Robbie Shilliam (2021: 247) sharply puts it, "[n]ot all neoliberals are racist populists, but today's racist populists are all neoliberals – by intention or by effect. Most are also the spoilt sons of Thatcher who are less concerned by grand philosophical designs for remaking the human subject and far more interested in scams and short-term financial leveraging."

In line with these connections, as the Conservative Party made its populist, Eurosceptic turn in opposition between 1997 and 2005, it was also maximally pro-American; when most of Blair's own party were reluctant, Duncan Smith was a cheerleader for the UK's participation in the US invasion of Iraq in 2003. However, the problem with pro-Americanism as a rationale for Brexit was not only the toxicity of US demands like allowing healthcare companies access to the NHS and the sale of "chlorinated chicken" into the UK market, or even the unpopularity of Trump in the UK, both of which became apparent after Johnson became prime minister. More fundamentally, it was that the US alliance inevitably cast the UK in a subordinate position, much as Brexiters claimed it existed in relation to the EU. They therefore needed alternative geopolitical and cultural frames for their project. There were, of course, obvious echoes of empire in Brexiter thought – the very title of *Britannia Unchained*, Finton O'Toole (2018: 81) points out, "evoked images of enslavement" – and a still-influential Duncan Smith (2020) would proclaim, as the UK prepared to leave the single market, "I just wish I was 21 again, frankly, because my goodness what prospects lie ahead of us for young people now. To be out there buccaneering, trading, dominating the world again." Yet the empire was gone and although "the Commonwealth" was much invoked – as what Gopal (2019: 11) calls "a euphemism for regions once colonized by Britain, enshrining as it does the cherished mythology of an Empire that ruled in order to free" – in reality it was only a loose international association (Murphy 2018), which could not provide the Europhobes with the geopolitical and economic alternative that they needed as they hardened their opposition to the EU, even if it would prove to be a useful secondary campaigning trope, as we shall see in Chapter 4.

A notion which bridged Brexiters' pro-American and Commonwealth orientations was that of the "Anglosphere", an idealized English-speaking world in which Britain played a unique role by mediating between the USA and the former British dominions. The idea, which can be traced back to Winston Churchill's notion of the "English-speaking peoples" (Vucetic 2011: 2–3), represents a tradition of military cooperation and thought, invoked for example by Duncan Smith in frequent references to the "five eyes" intelligence cooperation system (the USA, UK, Australia, New Zealand and Canada), which constitute a power network inside the larger system of Western military alliances that excludes the other European NATO members. Srdjan Vucetic (2011) describes this as "a racialized identity in international relations", and Jack Holland (2020) shows it working through US, UK and Australian operations in the Syrian civil war. However, the idea has broader roots in racial thinking, reflecting "a deep-rooted sense of cultural commitment and civilizational vision, and it has always been anchored by strong beliefs … about who belongs authentically to it and who does not" (Kenny & Pearce 2018: 174). Its origins lie in widely shared notions of racial hierarchy in Victorian-era imperial ideology, which put not only Black people but also white non-English-speaking peoples within the empire, such as Boers and French Canadians, outside the core. In the late nineteenth century, as Duncan Bell (2020: 29, 30) shows, "a transnational ideology of white supremacism infused political culture" in both the USA and the empire; "the colour line delimited the space in which variability could be expressed. Not all white people were Anglo-Saxons, but all Anglo-Saxons were white. The fusion of biological and cultural arguments created an unstable compound that helped structure the political imagination." This Anglo-Saxon outlook had produced not only projects for a "Greater Britain", a union of the UK with its settler colonies (Bell 2011), but also transatlantic "dreamworlds" in which influential thinkers promoted Anglo-Saxon unification between the UK and the USA. However, fantasies of racialized reunion between the empire/Commonwealth and the USA – which even early in the twentieth century foundered on the realities of American power, British decline and colonial independence – now have to cope with even greater geopolitical challenges.

The global dominance of the English language makes a larger Anglosphere theoretically conceivable but, since most speakers use English as a second language, only if a broad multiculturalism were embraced. Yet within this ideology, people of colour remain problematic however much they acculturate (Kenny & Pearce 2018: 174), as can be seen in the case of India, the largest Commonwealth country with far more English speakers than the UK itself. Alexander E. Davis (2018: 2) underscores the persistence of the racial divide, which he claims leave this school of thought with a fundamental "India problem", indeed "the impossibility of drawing India into Anglosphere-type relationships". The "assertion of a shared cultural superiority" which "has long guided the foreign policies of the US, the UK, Canada and Australia", together with "the erasure of colonial violence", has in response produced a fundamental Indian "ambivalence towards the English-speaking world". The nationalism of the India's ruling BJP is centred on the idea of a Hindu, not an English-speaking, civilization (Davis 2018: 12). While the BJP have forged a tactical alliance with the Conservatives in recent UK elections, reinforcing Hindu voting for the party while Hindu-origin politicians have risen within the Tory leadership, there has been no real ideological accommodation between Anglosphere thought and Hindu nationalism. Ironically, the Anglosphere is a fundamentally *Eurocentric* idea; it harks back to the age when British were happy to think of themselves as white "Europeans" within the racially mixed colonial world, and offers a post-imperial, Anglophone version of racial Europeanism.

No more than pro-Americanism, the Commonwealth or the free market, moreover, could the Anglosphere provide a credible prospectus for Brexit. The loose proposals it generated for enhanced "networks" to reinforce the racial cultural commonalities at its heart were evidently insufficient from the point of view of defining the UK's post-EU international relations in an economic as well as a military sense. There was a more focused version known as CANZUK (Canada, Australia, New Zealand, UK), which reverted to the notion of a union of the white Commonwealth (Bell & Vucetic 2019); but since the three settler countries have a combined population which barely equals the UK's, and all have more important ties in their widely separated regions, it was little more than a historical curiosity. Probably recognizing the limitations of all these ideas, in 2016 Johnson and other Conservative Leavers adopted instead the term "Global Britain" to combine their extra-European trade ambitions with pretensions to a new geopolitical role. Its key notion was that the UK must escape the limits of a "declining" EU by forging independent trade deals with more "dynamic" powers, including China, India and Japan. Yet the idea remained insubstantial; it was described as little more than an "aspiration" and a "slogan" by the House of Commons Foreign Affairs Committee (2018: 3). Despite this, Johnson (2020) would double down on it after he became prime minister; his Global Britain based claims of a "glorious" future on a hoped-for patchwork of trade arrangements, designed to replace the EU's own system of global free trade agreements which Brexiters rejected in principle while recycling in practice. If the idea had economic substance, this appeared to be – until late 2020 when it became clear that Trump would not win a second term – a pivot to the USA and the hope of a quick deal with his administration. Its most viable meaning, especially after Trump's defeat, was clearly a renewal of the military links between the UK and the USA, and in 2021 a new nuclear submarine collaboration between Australia and the USA would provide Johnson with the opportunity to insert the UK into a military arrangement to be called AUKUS. While some saw this merely as a strategic pivot, it also reflected a racialized Anglo-Saxon view of the world (Holland 2021) and threatened to sharpen the dealignment of the UK from France and other NATO allies within the EU.

Englishness and the debt to Powell

As it came to fruition, the Brexit project therefore wrapped free market ideas in a racialized, post-imperial internationalism under the superficial branding of Global Britain. However, these ideas were insufficient either to define the economic direction of a post-EU UK or to win it wide political support. As far as economics and domestic politics were concerned, Brexit's Anglo-British nationalism owed as much to Powell as anyone. His belief that free markets were a peculiarly English value provided the link between their racial nationalism and their economic liberalism, even if, as Shilliam (2021: 247) acidly remarks, their "use of Powell's play-book draws on none of his philosophical depth: it is ... a political scam and an electoral leveraging. Zombie Powellism: the Anglo-Saxon race eats its own". Most importantly, of course, Powell's anti-immigration politics opened up the path most likely to make Europhobia popular, and his racism – which, "for all its roots in the past, was a self-consciously post-imperial nationalist one" (Edgerton 2020) – was a key reference point for right-wing Conservatives, UKIP and tabloid editors alike. At an ideological level, Powellite discomfort that many of Britain's former colonial subjects were now entrenched in its own society remained a potent source of resentment but one which mainstream Brexiters could only indirectly express. O'Toole (2018: 17) argues that the EU partly occupied "the space where open racism had once flourished", and "much of the animosity was never really about the EU itself – it was a sublimated or displaced rage at Them. The black and brown Other fused with the European Other."

The EU was itself a bordered entity in which the management of immigration was significantly racialized (Garner 2007), but even the idea of "Fortress Europe", aiming to restrict the entry of the global non-white masses, would not satisfy the Brexiters. Germany's admission, under Angela Merkel, of hundreds of thousands of Syrians and others during the refugee crisis of 2015–16 was for them a striking indication that the EU could not be trusted on immigration, even though the UK under Cameron was able to opt out of the collective European response and permitted only a token 5,000 refugees to enter the UK each year. It was no accident that Farage's infamous "Breaking Point" poster (discussed in Chapter 4) used a picture of a line of Syrian refugees to warn of the immigrant "threat" to the UK. In Brexit nationalism, "a crucial ingredient is the transference of victimhood: the claim that white men, rather than being (as they are) relatively privileged, are in fact victims" (O'Toole 2018: 85). This sense of white English victimization, which Powell had forcefully articulated in the context of Black immigration, was now applied to Britain's membership of the EU. Britain was repeatedly reimagined by right-wing politicians and commentators as a "colony", its historic victory in the Second World War transformed into "defeat" through EU membership (O'Toole 2018: 21). In their attempt at "bloodless revolution", the Brexiters mobilized "the political erotica of imaginary domination and imaginary submission" but also relied on "a deeper structure of feeling in England" (O'Toole 2018: 25, 29). In their eyes, a weird idea of invasion and submission was needed "to reassure Britain that it had a meaningful collective existence"; the EU's role was to be "a more insidious form of Nazism" permeating British institutions (O'Toole 2018: 39, 46). This idea had to be taken, many Europhobes believed, to the almost fantastical extent of expunging every last influence of the EU from British law, and separating the British from the European economy even at the cost of radical harm to many UK sectors and businesses: as proved, indeed, to be the result of Johnson's trade negotiations (Foster 2021).

The most disturbing development was that these Brexiter fantasies of EU power came to entail hostility towards *Europeans* from other countries living in the UK. O'Toole (2018: 90) offers this explanation: "If there is on the one hand a need to think of oneself as being invaded and colonized and on the other no tangible enemy to fill this need, the job has to be given to somebody more visibly present." In any case, this was a radical departure, even in racist terms; despite the old idea of Anglo-Saxon superiority and the anti-German and anti-French traditions of the Tory right-wing and press, people from these major western European countries had previously been accepted by white Britons as (more or less) racial equals. As we saw in Chapter 2, after 1945 the British elite had even taken the view that European workers could become naturalized Britons, and western European migrants in the last quarter of the twentieth century had been largely accepted. Yet during and after the referendum, Europhobia broadened to Europeans in general the hostility previously cultivated by the press and UKIP towards eastern Europeans. It was this hostility which the Cameron government, in what Rogers (2019b: 15) calls the "last attempt to amplify and entrench British exceptionalism within the EU legal order", repeatedly tried to pacify prior to the referendum. The government limited the rights of EU citizens in the UK with new requirements such as non-workers needing private health insurance or a European health insurance card to be lawfully resident, "street level bureaucrats" in the Home Office attempted to "make it as difficult as possible for EU citizens to rely on their EU law rights" and the number of EU citizens who were in immigration detention and deported shot up (Yeo 2020: 197–8, 218). In 2015–16, Cameron's renegotiation and referendum project for the UK's EU membership "degenerated into a desperate search of a means to limit the numbers of EU citizens moving to the United Kingdom", especially for alleged "benefit tourism" (Yeo 2020: 199).

Therefore, while Brexit had many sources in the ideological and political history of the British right, as the referendum approached its debt to Powell was undoubtedly coming to the fore. This was also the case with the *Anglo*-British form of Europhobic nationalism. Even if the Europhobes avoided Powell's dated language of "the English race" and lacked his emotional connection to Ulster Unionism, they operated with his sense of England as the core of Britain, and increasingly found Scottish and Irish identities suspect as they were linked to demands for autonomy and even withdrawal from the British union. If Brexit nationalism was primarily defined by opposition to Europe, it was also a reaction to the Labour government's devolution within the UK which had given Scotland and Wales significant autonomy (Wellings 2012), and its Englishness became much more pronounced as the Brexit movement grew simultaneously with the strengthening of the Scottish National Party's (SNP) pursuit of "independence within Europe". Although Unionists won the 2014 Scottish referendum by 55 to 45 per cent, there had been a huge popular pro-independence mobilization – especially among younger people – leading to an unprecedented 84.6 per cent turnout, a striking 12.4 per cent higher than in the Brexit referendum. Yet, in response to the Scottish referendum result, far from adopting an inclusive pose, Cameron responded by appealing to English nationalism, first by calling for "English votes for English laws",[2] and then, during the 2015 election, by campaigning on the fear that the SNP would "control" a minority Labour government. This message, distilled in a poster showing Labour leader Ed Miliband in the pocket of the SNP's Alex Salmond, "dominated the Conservatives' 'air war' and 'ground war' alike … reaching a fevered crescendo in the week before polling day" (Henderson & Wyn Jones 2021: 17). While there had been a

---

2. This is the idea that since the non-English nations have devolved parliaments or assemblies, which England lacks, legislation on English matters in the UK parliament should be voted on only by MPs from English constituencies.

secondary, grassroots anti-English element in the Scottish movement, now the Tories stirred a largely dormant English resentment against the Scots, picking up once again the idea of English national victimization. Significantly, critics argued that the Tories' anti-SNP line "was shading into – and fanning – a more general anti-Scottishness" (Henderson & Wyn Jones 2021: 17), that is, a racialization of the Scots. Backing up this strategy, the right-wing tabloids played on English ignorance and fears of Scottish nationalism, with the *Mail* dubbing Salmond's deputy Nicola Sturgeon "the most dangerous woman in Britain". Crosby, who directed the Tories' 2015 campaign, believed that playing on fears of Scottish nationalism had made a significant difference to the election result in England, helping the Tories to wipe out their Liberal Democrat coalition partners (Bale 2016: 407); but perhaps the most important contribution of the post-referendum polarization was that it assisted the SNP in destroying Labour's parliamentary representation in Scotland. Together these post-2014 developments played an enabling role for the EU referendum, since without the narrow overall majority that Cameron won in 2015, he would probably have been unable to stage the vote in 2016. In this sense, the increasing polarization between Anglo-British and Scottish nationalisms may have tipped the balance towards Brexit, just as the latter made it increasingly possible that the British union itself would be undone.

Michael Kenny (2014) sees economic and cultural trends strengthening "Englishness" as the root of Anglo-British nationalism. However, this nationalism primarily reflected how the British right responded to the challenges and opportunities which it perceived. Devolution and the demand for Scottish independence sharpened their sense of Englishness, but the hostility to Europe was more deeply felt, and it was around the Brexit project rather than English autonomy – which remains as ill-defined as Brexit itself was before 2016 – that Anglo-British nationalism cohered. Ben Wellings (2015: 373) pointed out that "nationalism is at times a relatively capacious ideological vessel that needs to be filled with other sources and bases of support, which can at times be contradictory". We saw in Chapter 2 how racist anti-immigration politics helped accomplish this for Brexit nationalism, and in this chapter how various racially informed ideological sources contributed. Wellings added, however, that contradictory elements in nationalism tend to "put aside political differences in a temporary alliance to force through change … . All this means that, despite the claims of nationalists, nationalism does not necessarily need to be representative, but it does need to be organized." We shall see in Chapter 4 how, in 2016, that was achieved.

4

RACISM IN THE REFERENDUM

Would we have won without immigration? No. It is true that we did not do much on immigration before the 10 week official campaign. That is because ... we did not need to. It was far more important to plant other seeds and recruit support that would have been put off if we had focused early on immigration. Immigration was a baseball bat that just needed picking up at the right time and in the right way.

Dominic Cummings (2016)

When, in the preparations for the referendum, Brexit moved from the ideological to the strategic level, the global elements of its ideas were too loose, thin and politically untested to win widespread popular consent for the project. Withdrawal from the EU had not been a priority for most voters; even during the 2015 general election, only a year beforehand, less than 10 per cent "identified the EU as among the two most important issues facing Britain, and the issue of the EU played a minimal role in the election campaign" (Hobolt, Leeper & Tilley 2020: 3). As we have seen, the referendum had only become possible because it had been linked with racist anti-immigration politics, and the 2016 campaign would underline the centrality of this connection. After the vote, the Brexit-supporting journalist Brendan O'Neill (2017) denied "the narrative [which] says the referendum was a swirl of racial fears". It was not, he argued:

Aside from one dodgy UKIP poster, swiftly taken down, the debate was principled, not prejudiced. Lord Ashcroft's post-referendum poll found only 33 percent of Leave voters gave immigration as their "main reason" for voting out. Subsequent polls show big majorities of Brits, including Leaver Brits, want EU migrants to stay here. A majority of Leave voters, just shy of 50 percent, said they voted on the principle that "decisions about the UK should be taken in the UK". They acted from democratic conviction, not racial panic.

In this chapter we shall see that there was a great deal more racist propaganda than "one poster", while the fact that a third of voters *volunteered* immigration as their main reason for exit – compared to fewer than half who gave Leave's manifest main theme of sovereignty – was actually strong evidence for the salience of the issue. Between 14 April and 4 May 2016, the British Election Study asked their panel of voters the open-ended question, "What matters to you most when deciding how to vote in the EU referendum?", and created word clouds which scaled the size of the text to how frequently words were used; the cloud for those clearly favouring Leave showed "immigration" hugely dominant (Prosser, Mellor & Green 2016). In this period before the official campaign, the right-wing tabloids, with Romanian and other eastern European migrants once more their "entry point into the debate on EU immigration", mobilized the same negative, essentialized identity categories and discursive strategies that they had used in the previous decade as the basis for claims about the EU and its principle of free movement (Mădroane 2018: 165). Reflecting this sustained coverage, as the referendum neared, opinion polls recorded the highest-ever level of support for immigration as the most important political issue. Matthew Goodwin and Caitlin Milazzo (2017: 453) argue that there were two ways in which immigration may have influenced the result: not only by creating "more identity-based hostility towards the EU and European immigration" but also by fuelling the drive for "control", that is, informing support for Brexit's sovereignty or "democratic" demand. They conclude that "the decision taken by the Leave campaigns to focus heavily on the immigration issue, particularly during the latter part of the referendum campaign, helped to drive public support for leaving the EU" (Goodwin & Milazzo 2017: 462). Martin Moore and Gordon Ramsay (2017), in the most comprehensive study of media during the referendum, draw different conclusions to O'Leary about the relationships between the issues: "sovereignty was not, as has been claimed, a more important issue during the campaign than immigration. Sovereignty was a secondary issue, discussed in the context of primary issues like the economy, immigration and healthcare."

In fact, we shall see, the Leave side largely presented sovereignty or "taking back control" as an issue of *immigration* control. Jennifer Saul (2019) describes a pattern of racial "dogwhistles", but it was more than that: there was a concerted, strategic attempt to mobilize anti-immigrant racism. In this context, it is important to note Goodwin and Milazzo's reference to Leave *campaigns*. We have seen that there is a view that it was mainly UKIP which had driven nativist populism of the previous period, when in reality Conservative contributions were also very important and closely intertwined with the smaller party's. Similarly, the view has become entrenched that it was the UKIP-linked Leave.EU, led by Farage and the businessman Arron Banks, which "led the xenophobic charge" in the referendum (Mulhall 2021: 38). Leave.EU was responsible for the notorious "racist" moment to which O'Leary referred: Farage's launch of the "Breaking Point" poster which used an image of Syrian refugees in Europe to represent the "threat" of immigration to the UK. The politics of this moment allowed the two campaigns to dramatize the division between them: Leave.EU actively sought the controversy around which it caused (Durrheim *et al.* 2018), while Michael Gove (2016) theatrically distanced Vote Leave – which as we have seen he led together with Johnson and Gisela Stuart – from the poster, saying that he "shuddered" when he saw it. This dispute followed "an often vicious internecine conflict" between the two campaigns for official recognition, which Vote Leave had won (Geoghegan 2020: 23) over Grassroots Out, an umbrella which Leave.EU, UKIP and other non-Tory groups had supported. Reflecting this antagonism, Leave.EU claimed that Vote Leave was not sufficiently emphasizing immigration, and many Remain leaders and commentators accepted at face value the opposition which the criticism suggested, viewing Leave.EU as the chief locus of racism in the campaign.

Although some people certainly noted that Vote Leave also pivoted to "migration, migration, migration" (Grant 2016: 3), afterwards many commentators accepted the idea that the two campaigns had differed significantly. Remain attacks on Vote Leave after the referendum often centred on its breaches of electoral law ("a scale and seriousness with no parallel in modern British politics", according to Gavin Millar QC, quoted by Geoghegan 2020: 30), and the deceit in its claim that the UK paid £350 million per week to the EU. Academic analysts often pursued a similar line. Eric Kaufmann (2018: 195) painted the alleged difference between the campaigns as a strategic split: "Vote Leave would concentrate on the waverers, often middle-class, who didn't want to be associated with UKIP 'racism', while Leave.EU fired up the anti-immigration base." Satnam Virdee and Brendan McGeever (2017: 1806), addressing the ideological contradictions analysed in Chapter 3, offered this narrative: "If the Vote Leave campaign was led by individuals like Boris Johnson who fantasized about re-establishing Britain as a global hegemon (i.e. Britain as the best in the world), many of the key leaders of Leave.EU articulated a narrative of British nationalism that was more insular and Powellite in tone (i.e. Britain for the British). At the centre of this perspective were concerns around immigration." A few years after the referendum, the consensus around a sharp difference between the campaigns could be stated as fact: for Adrian Favell (2020), Farage's poster "may have captured the median vote in the referendum" and its promoter was the principal victor; for Perry Anderson (2021), it was UKIP under Farage and Banks which "pulled no punches in the nativist operation it ran independently of Dominic Cummings's Vote Leave"; while Joe Mulhall (2021: 38–9) even attributed "a malicious poster that suggested that staying in the EU would result in 76 million Turks coming to the UK" to Leave.EU, although it was Vote Leave which had laboured that claim in broadcast, printed and online propaganda.

Leave.EU and Vote Leave

This interpretation, which protects the Johnson–Gove–Stuart operation from the charge of exploiting racism, fundamentally misunderstands the relationships between the two campaigns. Certainly, Leave.EU's pitch, while expressing the core sovereigntist case, was unambiguously Powellite. Its digital propaganda has not been made available for scrutiny (unlike Vote Leave's which was eventually published: DCMS 2018), but according to one of Banks' own employees quoted by Geoghegan (2020: 66), "some of these images were really horrible. The immigrants and refugee stuff." Leave.EU directly mobilized extreme right as well as UKIP support, with its advertisements "deliberately sent to supporters of the British National Party and Britain First", the group to which the murderer of Jo Cox MP was linked (Shipman 2016: 408). While on the surface extreme right groups played a low-key role (Smith & Colliver 2016), Thomas Davidson and Mabel Berezin (2018: 502) show that on social media, the BF connection could have been very important to the Leave.EU campaign: "in the week of the referendum, BF was far more active in promoting the cause on social media than UKIP, engaging nearly six times as many people. … Not only did BF have a larger audience than UKIP, it framed the issues of immigration and the EU in more extreme terms, in particular by connecting them to the issue of Islam." However, Banks' own online operation was also very extensive: "By the end of the referendum, Leave.EU was one of the largest British political sites on social media, with more than 800,000 Facebook followers" (Geoghegan 2020: 67).

Yet Vote Leave also mobilized immigration, and by no means everyone accepted Gove's attempt to distance his campaign from its rivals' racism. In the final televised debate of the campaign, Sadiq Khan, the pro-Remain Mayor of London, accused Johnson and his co-leaders of promoting "Project Hate" (Wright 2016). Charles Grant (2016: 3) noted that they "produced leaflets that were similar to those of Leave.EU, saying that Turkey was joining the EU (completely untrue, of course)". In fact, Vote Leave *combined* "Global Britain" with its own ruthless and (for the most part) Powellite propaganda. While Leave.EU flourished its anti-immigration credentials, Vote Leave was actually the more systematic producer of this type of sentiment. It strategically weaponized immigration on a massive scale, in ways which were both overtly and implicitly racist, and knowingly enabled hostility towards Europeans. Yet its more nuanced strategy persuaded some voters and commentators that it was not racist in the way that Leave.EU was. In reality, Shipman (2016: 36–56) demonstrates through his extensive interviews with participants that the differences between Vote Leave and Leave.EU concerned strategy and timing rather than the principle of mobilizing immigration. Cummings appears to have understood that while "sovereignty" attracted some middle-class Conservative voters who saw extracting the

UK from EU law and institutions as a value in its own right, this was regarded as important only by a minority. Similarly, the ability to make independent trade deals, which Conservative Europhobes saw as a potential gain of restored sovereignty, was a niche concern that was too abstract for many of the voters Leave needed in order to win.

Therefore Cummings "ignored members of his own board who wanted to push sunny visions of a buccaneering post-Brexit Britain, dismissing what he called 'go global' trade babble" (Geoghegan 2020: 38). He understood that the importance of immigration was not only that it engaged many who were uninterested in these concerns but also that it concretized sovereignty for many voters and could be blamed via freedom of movement on the EU. Therefore, the connection with immigration which UKIP had pioneered was indeed the method to win a wider, especially working-class and traditionally Labour, vote; yet because of Conservative hostility to UKIP and the need for a broad coalition of voters to win, this would best be constructed without Farage. Cummings agreed with Leave.EU that the campaign could not win without making immigration central, but he claims that his aim was to first establish its respectable credentials by focusing on sovereignty, before introducing immigration to widen Leave's appeal and concretize "taking back control". Therefore Cummings (2016) claims to have had a staged approach to the campaign, concluding: "Immigration was a baseball bat that just needed picking up at the right time and in the right way." Whether or not this gloss is true – Grant (2016: 3) believed there had been a change of approach as did Leave.EU's Richard Tice (2021: 7) in his later reflections – what is certain is that in the last month of the campaign, Vote Leave hit the immigration issue in a massive way. Cummings (2017) described the "key argument" of their whole campaign as: "Vote Leave to take back control of immigration policy. If we stay there will be more new countries like Turkey joining and you won't get a vote. Cameron says he wants to 'pave the road' from Turkey to here. That's dangerous. If we leave we can have democratic control and a system like Australia's. It's safer to take back control."

A key reason why commentators missed Vote Leave's aggressive anti-immigration propaganda is that they operated their campaign on two levels, one of which was partially invisible to people who inclined towards Remain. Although almost half of Johnson's speeches mentioned immigration, they did so in conjunction with "sovereignty", and it was secondary figures such as Priti Patel who focused even more on the issue (Moore & Ramsay 2017: 67–8). Geoghegan (2020: 36) claims that "unlike in traditional campaigns, Vote Leave's emotive images were not seen on posters and buses. They appeared privately, on people's social media feeds." This is partially correct, since Cummings put most of the campaign's money into targeted digital campaigning (Geoghegan 2020: 39), and his Facebook propaganda, in particular, was under the radar for the unsympathetic in 2016. However, the campaign relentlessly pushed its key argument through *all* the media at its disposal. Like most commentators, Geoghegan misses Vote Leave's official election broadcast, which was shown as the law required on all terrestrial public television channels and regularly repeated over the month between 23 May and polling day. This must have been by far the campaign's single most widely consumed item of propaganda, accessible to almost all the electorate including many, especially crucial, older voters who lacked access to social media. Better than individual advertisements from Vote Leave's Facebook portfolio, this broadcast exemplified how toxic the amalgam indicated by Cummings' "key argument" was in practice. Following lurid graphics representing the immigration threat of Turkey, Serbia, Albania, Macedonia and Montenegro joining the EU and the "£350 million a week" the UK was alleged to contribute, it climaxed with a split-screen video showing (staying in the EU) a surly foreign man elbowing a tearful elderly white woman out of the queue in an accident and emergency department, while (leaving the EU) the woman is contentedly treated without having to wait (Vote Leave 2016a).[1] This focus on a vulnerable old woman mimicked both the content and emotive appeal of Powell's 1968 speech and was similar to a campaign video of the right-wing Sweden Democrats, which "showed an elderly lady hobbling towards her pension, only to be overtaken why a crowd of burqa-clad women", although this was banned on television (Eatwell & Goodwin 2018: 37). While some leaflets pushed Johnson's case for a "fairer, safer immigration system" (Vote Leave 2016b), the broadcast's crude message was reflected in many others (Dranville 2016). Khan brandished one as he made his "Project Hate" accusation, and whistleblower Shahmir Sanni (2019) said that "[t]he campaign was always talking about Immigration. The most proud moment for many of Vote Leave's staff was how well the Turkey leaflet did." Tice (2021: 7) later claimed of the Turkey campaign, "We [Leave.EU] had never dreamt of going that far", and certainly Vote Leave, with its mainstream credentials, was able to get away with "Turkey" without the sort of opprobrium which was heaped on Farage's poster.

Nevertheless, Cummings (2016) was probably correct when he said that Vote Leave's huge, highly targeted Facebook campaign was the most influential strand of its propaganda, claiming that "in the official 10 week campaign we served about *one billion targeted digital adverts*, mostly via Facebook and strongly weighted to the period around postal voting and the last 10 days of the campaign" (emphasis in original). Since Vote Leave targeted only segments of the electorate, individual users could each have been presented with hundreds of advertisements. The Department of Culture, Media and Sport report (DCMS 2018) reproduces

---

1. The video had been removed from YouTube by 2018, unlike much Vote Leave material which was still online in 2021, but it is described in detail by Wheeler (2016).

the images, published after considerable pressure on Facebook to release them; although there is also non-immigration material, there are large overlaps in messaging, graphics and images with the broadcast, with clusters of ads focusing on immigration, Turkey and the £350 million. Immigration was presented both as an exemplar of "taking back control", with the overriding theme of sheer numbers of potential migrants, and as the threat of large numbers of migrants arriving from Turkey and four Balkan states. The Facebook material included a respectable, globalist element, featuring Johnson – who had previously been identified with a relatively liberal immigration stance but then adopted Farage's "Australia" proposal – with slogans such as "I'm pro-immigration, but above all I'm pro controlled immigration. In the EU the system has spun out of control. Join Me, Vote Leave" (DCMS 2018: 54). However, the dominant element of the Facebook propaganda echoed the broadcast, with even more lurid claims like: "5.23 MILLION MORE IMMIGRANTS ARE MOVING TO THE UK! GOOD NEWS???" (DCMS 2018: 45). The viewer was invited to press a "YES" or "NO" button; presumably "no" respondents were then targeted with further advertisements, since there were many variants which focused on each of the putative accession states and repeatedly on Turkey, while the poverty of potential immigrants was emphasized by images contrasting the countries' average incomes with the UK's.

The otherness of brown people from distant, Muslim-majority and/or little-known countries hardly needed to be laboured, and Cameron's memoirs (2019: 669) accused Johnson of mounting a racist campaign by focusing on Turkey and its possible accession: "It didn't take long to figure out Leave's obsession. Why focus on a country that wasn't an EU member? The answer was that it was a Muslim country, which piqued fears about Islamism, mass migration and the transformation of communities. It was blatant." He went on to evoke the notorious Smethwick slogan: "They might as well have said: 'If you want a Muslim for a neighbour, vote 'remain'." However, Cameron, who had allowed Crosby to use similar methods in the London election in the previous month, notably failed to criticize this propaganda in 2016, and it was justifiably said that he was only reaping what the Tories "had sowed since the mid-1960s when they had first begun to politicize immigration for electoral gain" (Bale 2016: 442). There was, moreover, almost certainly another reason why Vote Leave focused on the hypothetical "threat" of people from Turkey and other applicant states: it avoided directly targeting EU citizens already in the UK, who would have had the capacity to fight back and galvanize the Remain campaign to address the issue. Although Vote Leave's propaganda implicitly targeted Muslims, it directly implicated only small communities like the Turks and Albanians, not the majority of Muslims from the Indian subcontinent who represented a substantial part of the electorate. (The way in which Jewish organizations responded to Labour antisemitism in the 2016–19 period suggests that Cummings was wise to largely leave the large European population, many of whom would have had the capacity to fight back, alone.)

Vote Leave therefore had a double narrative, expressing both sides of the anti-immigration dilemma which the last chapter traced to Powell. The Johnson-centred advertisements represented a "rational" numerical appeal which did not reject immigration in principle but sought to "control" it, while the "FIVE MILLION", Turkey-centric advertisements contained both highly alarmist representations of numbers and implicit stereotyping of poor, Muslim and eastern European masses, effectively merging the principal racist themes of the previous decade. The hostility which the press and UKIP had whipped up meant that both narratives would have been easily understood. Yet for Cummings it was particularly important to develop a very direct populist appeal to motivate the substantial layer of people who did not normally vote, and so simple, emotive messages had a crucial role. Perhaps for this reason, Vote Leave did sometimes venture into attacks on existing EU migrants, for example in an advertisement labelled "Reason No. 8" to leave: "To stop convicted criminals from countries like Latvia and Romania coming to the UK" (DCMS 2018: 59). The implication that Latvians and Romanians were likely to be criminals appealed directly to voters with the crudest instincts. We cannot establish how the different elements of the propaganda were influential, as research into supporters' reception, discourse, "likes" and reposting is lacking. However, Vyacheslav Polonski (2016) argues that the emotive element was most significant: "the main Leave camp message was much more intuitive and straightforward [than Remain's], which is particularly important for social media campaigning. ... their message was also highly emotionally charged, which facilitated the viral spread of Leave ideas. There is evidence to suggest that high arousal emotions such as anger and irritation spread faster than messages focusing on rational or economic arguments, particularly on social media." Evaluating Vote Leave's propaganda, it appears as an attempt to arouse, if not hate, then fear of others, and compared to previous Tory election campaigns, it clearly represented a step-change in the strategic mobilization of racism. This was the first time that racism had been *the* central method of the right-wing side in a major national election.

Press hostility

However, the effectiveness of the Leave campaigns did not depend solely on their own propaganda. The striking complementarity of coverage in the pro-Brexit papers and their online offerings was probably almost as important. The right-wing press had, of course, played a large part in creating hostility to the EU (Rawlinson 2020) as well as to immigrants. For most of the Tory papers, the Leave campaign promised to fulfil the ambition of ending UK membership of the EU, which they had increasingly popularized over the previous quarter-century by exploiting the demand for immigration control which they had fostered for even longer. As "cultivation theory" in media research has proposed, the long-term, cumulative consequences of exposure to an essentially repetitive and stable system of messages are formidable (Morgan & Signorielli 1990). Although originally developed to account for the effects of television, this approach is also relevant to the tabloid press. Bianca Fox (2018) shows that readers' exposure to daily negative news stories about EU immigrants over a decade had already contributed strongly to negative attitudes towards them; Moore and Ramsay (2017: 136) argue that long-established press Euroscepticism "provides critical context for the campaign"; and Bob Berkeley, Omar Khan and Mohan Ambikaipaker (2005: 25) highlight the importance of the general tendency of the UK media always to "conduct the debate about immigration within the framework of immigration *control*" (emphasis added), which prepared the ground for Cummings' "Take Back Control" slogan.

Most previous evidence suggested, as Threadgold (2009: 1) summarized, "that political and policy discourses concerning immigration actually rule the media discourse, which in turn drives policy". However, during the referendum, the anti-EU newspapers shared a clear political objective with the Leave campaigns and acted simultaneously as amplifiers of their messages *and* as independent entrepreneurs of anti-immigration Europhobia. The content of the principal daily tabloids, the *Express, Mail, Sun* and *Star*, the broadsheet *Daily Telegraph* and their Sunday counterparts (with the exception, in this campaign, of the *Mail on Sunday*) reinforced longstanding Europhobic and anti-immigrant messaging. The extent of their commitment and the priority they gave to immigration are indicated by the fact that there were "seven times more front-page leads about immigration during the referendum campaign than during the 2015 general election", almost 80 per cent of which were in Leave-supporting tabloids (Moore & Ramsay 2016: 65). Moore and Ramsay (2016: 70, 72) show not only that pro-Brexit tabloid coverage "focused almost exclusively on claims by Leave leaders and covered their statements regularly, prominently and supportively" but also that many of the immigration articles were sourced from the Leave campaign. Coverage directly reflected Vote Leave's prime focus on Turkey's possible EU accession: there was an exceptionally high level of coverage of potential Turkish migration, as well as of Albania, another of Vote Leave's target countries. "12m Turks say they'll come to the UK", said the *Express* front page on 22 May 2016; "Albania is a hell-hole of corruption, exporting child prostitution, drugs, extortion, murder and money laundering", wrote the *Sun*'s political editor on 2 May 2016 (Moore & Ramsay 2016: 109). There was a "striking" level of negativity in this coverage, with 98 per cent of articles about Turks and 100 per cent of those about Albanians classified as negative. "Based on most definitions", Moore and Ramsay (165) conclude, "it is hard not to find their claims and coverage discriminatory." Tellingly, the theme of stresses on public services "tended to be associated with future immigration and therefore ... Turkey and Albania" (Moore & Ramsay 2016: 110) rather than with the existing eastern European member states, in line with Vote Leave's own approach.

However, Moore and Ramsay (2016: 73) also note that the Brexit press "went further than the campaign leaders in their reporting on immigration. Many of the negative news articles in the second half of the campaign were not prompted by the claims of the campaigns but resulted from the initiatives of newspapers." Thus, while Vote Leave largely eschewed direct attacks on migrants from existing eastern European member states, the Brexit press featured them, particularly targeting Poles, who were alleged to have "invaded" a small Derbyshire town, and Romanians, who were often associated with criminality. While Vote Leave, sensitive to the ethnic minority vote, mostly restricted its overt attacks to potential EU migrants, its press supporters often referred to a general immigration "problem", "migrant crisis" or "tidal wave"; and in this sense some of the newspapers were closer to Leave.EU in approach (the *Express* even used the same stock photo as Farage's poster). Moore and Ramsay remark on the "prominence, volume and persistence" of the immigration coverage, but also that (in step with Cummings' timetable) it increased sharply week-on-week: the final week saw more than 1,000 articles published about immigration (Moore & Ramsay 2016: 64, 65). Immigration also dominated coverage of the economic and health debates, in which they often echoed the connections which Vote Leave made. When not associated "with rape, murder or violence", migrants were "often characterized as job stealers or benefit tourists".

Overall, three metaphors were dominant: "migrants as water ('floodgates', 'waves'), as animals or insects ('flocking', 'swarming') and as an invading force" (Moore & Ramsay 2016: 77, 165). Immigration was central to these papers' coverage of Brexit as a whole, since although sovereignty was referred to frequently, this was "almost always in the context of other issues ... rather than being on an issue on its own"; by the end of the campaign, no fewer than two-thirds of all media articles which mentioned sovereignty also mentioned immigration (Moore & Ramsay 2016: 116, 120, 122). The impact of the tabloids also depended on their often sensational presentation and lurid vocabulary, which turned them into little more than propaganda machines for Leave and was all the more effective for delivering its appeal mixed in with news and supposedly journalistic comment. As much as the Leave campaigns, they stoked the referendum's populism, for example through devices like reporting Remain claims often in the context of Leavers' "fury" and "outrage" at their "lies", and by widely reproducing the Leave tropes which associated Remainers with "sneering", "grandees", "luvvies", "Hampstead liberals", "the Westminster elite", "experts", "the Establishment" and "Eurocrats" (Engesser *et al.* 2017). The effect of the attacks on the Remain "elite" is indicated by a poll showing that 46 per cent of Leave voters thought the vote would be rigged (Moore & Ramsay 2016: 156), anticipating the paranoia of MAGA (Make America Great Again) supporters whipped up by Trump in the 2016 and 2020 US elections.

Although by 2016 the circulations of the tabloids' print editions, as of newspapers as a whole, had long been in historic decline, they still played two very significant roles: these editions conveyed propaganda to the important minority of mainly older voters who were not online, while their online operations generated "much of the news that was liked and shared on social networks – indirectly influencing people through sharing and via online discussion" (Moore & Ramsay 2016: 166). Leave had the wholehearted support of the *Express, Mail, Sun* and *Telegraph*, giving it a strong overall preponderance (Levy, Aslan & Bironzo 2016). Although papers like the *Guardian, Independent* and *Financial Times* fulfilled similar functions for the other side, individually and collectively they had much smaller audiences, while the one Remain tabloid, the *Daily Mirror*, did not match the role played by the three principal Leave tabloids; not only did it have a much smaller circulation than theirs combined, but it also carried less referendum coverage (Moore & Ramsay 2016: 166). Overall, it is estimated that 41 per cent of newspaper articles were pro-Leave and only 22 per cent pro-Remain (Levy, Aslan & Bironzo 2016: 4).

In contrast to the press, television coverage was subject to a legal requirement for neutrality, provided debates on equal terms and – while it included some fact-checking of Leave claims – generally reflected the balance of the campaign; but this meant, of course, that it inevitably reproduced the relative coherence of the Leave side and the strategic failure of Remain. Moore and Ramsay (2016: 144) note that "even the BBC was using the [Leave trope 'Project Fear'] in its reporting". Partly because of Labour's relative abstention from the battle, the referendum on television was a "Tory story", polarized between Cameron/Osborne and Johnson/Gove, while the new "era of multi-party politics in the UK" was barely reflected in television coverage in England, although in Scotland the governing SNP were of course better covered; the pro-EU Liberal Democrats "were virtually invisible" (Deacon *et al.* 2016: 7, 2). An earlier analysis of immigration in the UK media had noted: "we know that the news agenda is very narrow at any one time across all media and that the television news follow the print media. TV … rarely covers stories that the print media have not covered" (Threadgold 2009: 11). Although we lack the depth of analysis which is available for the press in order to show in detail how far broadcasting coverage reproduced Leave narratives, it is certain that it offered no direct counterbalance to the Brexit tabloids' cohesive approach to immigration. Television channels also repeatedly showed Vote Leave's racist election broadcast without challenges from any of the broadcasting organizations regarding its content.

Hostile implications of the Leave campaigns for Europeans and Muslims

On television as in the press, migrants' and Europeans' own voices were rarely heard. Moore and Ramsay (2016: 111) note that, like the focus on criminality/illegality and the foregrounding of elite sources making critical statements about immigration, "the marginalization of individual immigrants in the campaign" reflected a common feature of UK immigration coverage. Both the Leave campaigns and media coverage had large, negative consequences for the groups that were directly and indirectly targeted, as well as for minorities more generally, but they were barely visible in the coverage. Certainly, as Moore and Ramsay (2016: 112–13) put it:

> It is not, nor will ever be, possible to show that inflammatory rhetoric was ever the cause of racist violence. ... [but] Leave leaders regularly and explicitly blamed migrants. ... The *Express, the Daily Mail*, and the *Sun* also blamed migrants ... then it should not be a surprise if some of their readers accepted their claims that migrants were to blame. Such acceptance would have necessarily increased resentment, intolerance and discrimination against migrants.

As Terry Threadgold (2009: 22) had remarked a little earlier, "media coverage [of immigration] does not simply mediate public understanding; it also mediates the lived experience of immigrants and their children. ... Members of ethnic and religious minority communities and their leaders ... knew they were unwelcome and tended to be associated with crimes and terrorism."

From a legal point of view too, Brexit was intrinsically threatening to Europeans in the UK. Although borders and bordering are fundamental features of modern society (Yuval-Davis, Wemyss & Cassidy 2019), and there were of course similar problems around the EU's external borders to those of other states, internally the EU largely "debordered" its 28 member states for its more than 500 million citizens if not for immigrants from outside the EU. As Adrian Favell (2019: 158) points out, "the essential point of EU freedom of movement was its revolutionary introduction of a regionally expansive non-discrimination by nationality, going well beyond established abstract notions of 'personhood' and human rights". The ending of EU citizenship in the UK therefore threatened "rebordering" (Yuval-Davis, Wemyss & Cassidy 2019: 1) for EU citizens, since they could lose their automatic rights to reside and work there. This danger of formal rebordering was accompanied by a deepening of the informal racialization of the European population, extending it from eastern Europeans, many of whom were concentrated in poorer suburbs, smaller towns and rural areas where they had widely experienced everyday racism, to many western Europeans, more of whom were educated professionals in London and other diverse cities, including many who had married and had children with British citizens. They had been more insulated from the hostility which eastern Europeans had faced, and for many, the referendum marked "a moment where [they found] themselves newly Othered" (Benson & Lewis 2019: 2213). Suddenly a major public vote centred on a threat to their taken-for-granted fundamental rights and way of life, and it appeared that half the electorate was prepared to sacrifice these. The threat was profoundly shocking, and many complained of "the deep uncertainty, the painful state of limbo" which they experienced (Remigi, Martin & Sykes 2017: xv). (A similar shock, but without the directly threatening political climate which Europeans faced in the UK, was experienced by British emigrants in other European states, whose rights were indirectly threatened.) Only a small minority of even long-term EU residents had taken out UK citizenship, since European citizenship – via the citizenship of another member state – guaranteed them virtually all the rights that UK citizens enjoyed. The principal right which they lacked was a vote in parliamentary elections, and parliament had voted down a proposal to accord them voting rights in the referendum. As a result, apart from Irish citizens (who had a distinct status in the UK which preceded and was separate from Ireland's EU accession), few who had come to the UK from other EU countries could vote in 2016.

The Leave campaigns' strategic ambiguity about the meaning of Brexit initially obscured the threat to Europeans, but it became more apparent as they brought immigration to the fore. Alarm among EU citizens could have posed a serious risk to Leave, and to head off a possible backlash, on 1 June 2016 Vote Leave issued a statement (Gove *et al.* 2016) which gave these specific assurances: "There will be no change for EU citizens already lawfully resident in the UK. EU citizens will automatically be granted indefinite leave to remain in the UK and will be treated no less favourably than they are at present." There was a clear deception here, in that although these Vote Leave leaders were members of Cameron's cabinet, they were neither speaking on its behalf nor putting themselves forwards as an alternative; there was no clear mechanism through which they could put their pledges into practice. Indeed, after the referendum the Conservative government, now under May's leadership, would fail to honour them, without protest from Johnson, Gove, Patel or the other Leavers who had joined her cabinet, or even from Stuart who was not a member of the Conservative Party. According to Amber Rudd (2021: 9), home secretary under

May, no one came to see her to ask for Vote Leave's pledge to be implemented. In 2016, however, these promises defused a potentially significant threat to the Leave cause.

As these developments unfolded, it was argued that the ending of EU citizenship rights involved the threat of EU citizens being formally subjected to the Conservative government's "hostile environment" policy alongside other migrants. Although up to this point Europeans had been protected from this policy, the referendum, Talaunt Guma and Rhys Dafydd Jones (2019: 2) argue, still "intensified an already hostile environment for (many) EU migrants. The campaign and its aftermath furthered a process of 'othering' and unsettling as manifest in increased attacks on people and property, anxieties and uncertainties around future rights, and complex tensions where belonging is contested through formal and informal practices and processes." The implicit and explicit hostility of the Leave campaigns and their press allies was matched by increasing popular hostility. In a post-referendum survey of younger eastern European migrants, half said racism towards them had increased, with 77 per cent having experienced it because of their nationality, accent or the way that they looked (Sime *et al.* 2017). The campaigns and press engendered a climate in which a threatening "othering" was practised both online and in the streets. By far the highest-profile physical attack was the assassination on 16 June 2016 of the Labour MP, Jo Cox, by Thomas Mair, who cried "Britain first" as he attacked her; he had connections to the eponymous far-right group but the cry also echoed the themes of Johnson, Farage and other Leave leaders. However, reports of violence and abuse against Europeans, often extending to members of other ethnic, religious and gender minorities, were growing in the late stages of the campaign. Police figures for politically and religiously motivated hate crime showed a sharp spike that peaked a week after the referendum and a continuing wave in the following two months (Corcoran & Smith 2016: 20). Overall, although there had been a general upward trend throughout the decade of increased right-wing campaigning, 2016–17 showed a larger annual increase than the preceding or succeeding years, and similar peaks occurred only around terror attacks (House of Commons Library 2019: 3). A study of eastern European migrants in semi-rural Lincolnshire reported that hostility, already routinized and normalized, "was exacerbated by Brexit which participants believed had further legitimized pre-existing community sentiments" (Lumsden, Goode & Black 2018: 179).

The principal Islamophobia monitoring group recorded one of the highest "spike points" for anti-Muslim hatred just after the referendum. Their examples included a Muslim woman being in a supermarket when two women told her to "leave the UK" and move to the EU instead as "we have left the EU now"; a man shouting, "Brexit, you P*ki", at a taxi driver and then assaulting him; and a Sikh radiographer who was reportedly told by a patient: "shouldn't you be on a plane back to Pakistan? We voted you out" (Tell MAMA 2017: 4, 7, 57, 158). Racist and gender hostility were linked: the LGBT+ anti-violence charity Galop recorded a 147 per cent increase in homophobic abuse in the three months following the vote. Researchers found relationships between Islamophobia, conspiracist beliefs and Leave voting and documented extensive anti-migrant hate speech from Leavers on Twitter (Swami *et al.* 2018). The reported abuse was certainly the tip of the iceberg, and while the perpetrators were probably a small minority of Leave voters, they were undoubtedly acting out the hostility of a much larger section. Nevertheless, while the referendum was underway, the Leave campaigns had an interest in avoiding physical harm to the Europeans, Muslims and others who they implicitly attacked. While both online and offline hostility must have been priced into their approach, Leave leaders will have seen highly visible man-ifestations of popular abuse, let alone violence, as a danger to their credibility. At the moment of Cox's murder, they feared that their momentum might have been reversed; high-profile cases of hostility to Europeans, Muslims or others could have had a similar effects. They may have watched with some nervousness the media reports of incidents like people being attacked for speaking foreign languages on the street, but Vote Leave's pledge to Europeans enabled them to deny responsibility.

Balancing ethnic minority and racist support

The role of ethnic minorities had a more general importance to Vote Leave's bal-ancing act as it mobilized its targeted, selective strategic racism. Unlike most EU citizens, people with the citizenship of Commonwealth countries could vote, as of course could Black, Asian and minority ethnic (BAME) UK citizens. These voters increasingly identified themselves as British rather than, or as well as, members of their families' nationalities of origin; on average they probably also possessed, because of their socio-economic positions as well as historic linkages to Commonwealth countries, fewer social and cultural connections with conti-nental Europe than the white British. While it was a bold pitch for Europhobes – most of whom had called for decades for reductions in Commonwealth im-migration – to reinvent themselves as campaigners for "fair" immigration rules for Commonwealth citizens, this approach potentially had an organic appeal to ethnic minority voters. This was an important secondary element of Vote Leave's strategy, and although for many minority voters, the Tories and UKIP who dominated the Leave campaigns were associated with racism, Cummings' separation of Vote Leave from Farage attempted to mitigate the damage. They aimed to persuade minority voters that in exiting Europe, the UK would reorient towards the Commonwealth, so that restricting EU immigration would benefit immigrants from its countries and especially family members of UK citizens. In a campaign leaflet, Vote Leave (2016b) claimed, alongside an image of a smiling young Black woman with a stethoscope, "[w]e'll be able to control numbers without having to turn away talented people from outside the EU who want to contribute". Although they suggested that "curry house workers" would find it easier to enter the UK once eastern Europeans could no longer come (MacShane 2018), they were in fact attempting to co-opt minority voters into removing Europeans' right to free movement without offering any new rights for non-EU migrants. In effect, they proposed to equalize the positions of European and non-European migrants by reducing the former to the latter's inferior status.

Nevertheless, Vote Leave's appeal to minorities, fronted by BAME Conservative MPs, may have helped Leave in gaining over 30 per cent of ethnic minority voters, a significant proportion even if much smaller than its clear majority among the white English and Welsh. Among minority voters just as among the white British, socio-economic indicators of disadvantage predicted greater support for Leave (Martin, Sobolewska & Begum 2019), and ethnic minority Leave voters were more likely to be male, older and foreign-born and less likely to have taken advantage of the ability to travel to, live or work in EU countries (Begum 2018). Ethnic minority Leavers raised concerns about the apparent ease with which Europeans could enter the UK, get work and access benefits, as well as increased pressures on public services and strained community relations. Among Hindus, who were much more pro-Leave than Muslims, Twitter analysis shows that transnational Islamophobia played a part in Brexit sentiment (Cheng Leidig 2019). For the Britons of colour living in other EU countries whom Michelle Benson and Chantelle Lewis (2019) studied after the referendum, racism was "not a Brexit story, but a life story", as they suffered both the "longstanding exclusionary operations of Britishness" and "levels of everyday racism in Europe that are equal to or more pronounced than what they had experienced" in the UK; indeed, some female Muslim Leave voters were concerned by the hijab and burkini bans in other member states (Martin, Sobolewska & Begum 2019).

For people of colour, Brexit could be seen as "unexceptional, located in the racial exclusions at the heart of British *and* European social formations" (Benson & Lewis 2019: 2211; emphasis added), so it is understandable that many ethnic minority voters in 2016 saw Leave less as an escalation of racism than as an option to be evaluated on the terms in which it was presented. However, the hostility which Leave and its press projected towards immigrants clearly cost it support: ethnic minority Remain voters were differentiated from their white equivalents, Neema Begum (2018) argues, by "the strength of their reaction to what they saw as the xenophobic and anti-immigrant tone of the Leave campaigns. In this sense, a Remain vote was more a vote against Leave than an endorsement of the EU. Many saw the referendum as unleashing a backlash against diversity that was directed against ethnic minorities." Slogans such as "take back control" and "make Britain great again" were unappealing to ethnic minority Remain voters, "who associated them with nostalgia for empire and a longing for a 'pre-immigration white era' on the part of the Leave campaign. Even the emphasis on sovereignty was interpreted by some as a cipher for post-colonial nostalgia." One of Benson and Lewis's respondents (2019: 2219) argued that Brexit "did not instigate racism and xenophobia, but brought it to the surface in a state-sanctioned way". Minority voters will also have been well aware that racists were not always very discriminating: a study of how non-Muslim men suffered Islamophobic hate crime after Brexit was entitled: "You All Look the Same" (Awan & Zempi 2018).

Vote Leave's pitch to ethnic minority voters and the prominence of some of its minority politicians may also have served to reassure white people that supporting Leave and wanting to restrict migration was not racist. Research shows, however, that many Leave voters opposed not only European immigration but immigration as such, and that Leave voting was significantly correlated with obviously racist attitudes. Having a stronger "Britishness identity" was associated with a large and positive effect on support for Brexit for minority and majority populations alike, but among white British, it was those who had a strong ethnic or racial identity who were more likely to support Leave (McAndrew, Surridge & Begum 2017: 18–19). Taken together with the evidence that those who identified more as English than British were more pro-Leave than others, this suggested that Englishness was the most "racialized" identity (McAndrew, Surridge & Begum 2017: 18), a finding supported by the linkage of English identity with the view that immigration "dilutes British culture" (Henderson & Wyn Jones 2021: table 4.4, 90).

For many white people with a strong ethnic identity, Anglo-Britishness was also linked with hostility to the Black and ethnic minority population. Maria Sobolewska and Rob Ford (2018: 22–3) argue that responses to the question of whether people thought equal opportunities for Black and Asian people had "gone too far" showed that many Brexit voters were concerned about "rapidly rising ethnic diversity caused by both recent and historic waves of immigration, and the sharp population growth among immigrant-origin minorities, including exponential growth in the mixed ethnicity population"; indeed, "about half the people who stated at the time of the referendum that immigration undermines British culture also thought that equal opportunities for ethnic minorities went too far". Although this attitude did not "correspond neatly to opinions on immigration", it was related to them, and the impact of both attitudes on the decision on how to vote in the EU referendum was statistically significant. Similarly, social-psychological research shows that individual predictors of prejudice

towards foreigners were independently related to the perceived threat of immigrants and, via this variable, to the Brexit vote (Golec de Zavala, Guerra & Simão
2017). There was a strong correlation of Leave voting with "authoritarian" views
(Curtice 2017), which are often linked to racism. Leave voters comprised a range
of views, which is why the differentiated messaging in Vote Leave's campaign
was so important, but Leave appears to have mobilized, as both Vote Leave and
Leave.EU intended, much of the consciously racist element in the electorate as
part of a wider coalition of voters opposed to immigration or (especially in the
case of ethnic minority voters) European immigration. Although the turnout
was only moderately above the average for general elections, analysis suggests
that 2.8 million habitual non-voters – those with minimal interest in politics and
to whom much of Cummings' late-stage racist messaging had been addressed
– voted, mostly for Leave (Singh 2016). A researcher comments on watching
when people swung to Leave in the British Election Study data: "the late swing
is predominantly people unenthused by classic Euroskepticism but super-duper
anti-immigrant (*Sun* readers rather than *Telegraph* readers)" (Richards 2020).

Remain's failure to challenge Leave's racism

Although some of Leave's opponents challenged its racist thrust, the policy of Britain Stronger In Europe, the official Remain campaign controlled by
Cameron, was to concentrate primarily on Brexit's economic threat and to avoid
the immigration issue, which they believed was Leave's territory. Certainly, concerted Remain opposition on this issue would have faced an uphill battle, since
Cameron's "tens of thousands" and "hostile environment" policies had strongly
reinforced the idea of an immigration "problem", and polls showed that many
Remain supporters shared Leavers' concerns. Yet immigration is the prime instance of the lack of a positive European message for which the Remain campaign was widely criticized. Stronger In did have a "script", circulated for use by
those appearing in the media, which "pitched free movement as a price worth
paying for access to the single market, and struck a positive tone on labour
movement"; but as Rafael Behr (2016) noted, this "was not the official position
of any of the parties involved" (Labour any more than the Tories) and "went
mostly unsaid". Instead Remain, "rather than seeking to argue for the benefits
of immigration to the UK or the positive cases for the movement of peoples,
first chose to play down the issue, then to emphasize their [own] proposals to
reduce migrant numbers" (Moore & Ramsay 2016: 165). Stronger In also failed
to push back when it became clear how strongly Vote Leave had promoted racist
messages, which as we have seen Cameron was fully aware of. They allowed
Leave leaders to label Remain "Project Fear" (the label the SNP had given to the

Unionist campaign in the Scottish referendum) while Leave's own attempts to arouse fear of foreigners went unopposed. These failures probably had significant electoral costs. First, they weakened Remain's mobilization among younger people, who were the most pro-European and antiracist and had most to benefit from freedom of movement, and who ultimately failed to vote in the same proportion as the older, more pro-Brexit age cohorts. Second, they inhibited Remain from gaining a larger majority of the ethnic minority vote, as it largely failed to counter Vote Leave's claim that reducing EU immigration would benefit non-EU migrants. These Remain failures reflected a broader failure to learn the lessons of Scottish voters' sharp turn to independence during the 2014 referendum – instead, Stronger In simply assumed that "Project Fear" had worked – and also of Cameron's own success in harnessing anti-Scottishness in 2015, which provided a template for Leave to mobilize racialized Europhobia. As Ailsa Henderson and Richard Wyn Jones (2021: 28) conclude, "it was as if campaign strategists were determined to pretend that the period between 19 September 2014 and 7 May 2015 had never happened".

The Conservative-led Stronger In's failings were mimicked by the Labour Party, which – ironically, since it campaigned separately for Remain because of a widespread view that it had been damaged by campaigning together with the Conservatives in the Scottish referendum – failed to develop a distinctive campaign. Like Stronger In, Labour focused on the economic and social costs of Brexit, while its trade union allies took "conscious decisions" to avoid immigration and "universally underestimated the impact of the migration issue on the campaign" (Fitzgerald, Beadle & Rowan 2020: 14). Indeed, leading Labour figures were divided on immigration: "Jeremy Corbyn, Gordon Brown and Hilary Benn wanted no controls on legal EU migration, while Yvette Cooper, Ed Balls and Tom Watson said that the EU's rules on free movement should be revised" (Grant 2016: 3). In any case, Corbyn, elected as party leader after the 2015 defeat, abdicated responsibility for Labour In for Britain to Alan Johnson, a former cabinet minister who was not part of the leadership, giving it a low profile; it produced, an academic observer noted, a "lacklustre campaign" (Hobolt 2016: 1264). This arrangement partly reflected Corbyn's own ambivalence about the referendum. Although a lifelong opponent of European integration who feared that the party's ability to implement a radical programme would be compromised by EU rules, as leader he could not join those Labour MPs and trade unions who actually backed Brexit, since clear majorities of the party's MPs, members and voters were pro-EU. Instead, the leadership's strategy was to avoid a high-profile commitment. Corbyn invested only modestly in Remain and – after even going on holiday during the campaign – avoided the television debates, limiting himself mostly to local Labour and union meetings. A study found that the leader of the opposition received less television coverage than Cameron or his Remain-backing chancellor, George Osborne, and less than Johnson, Farage, Gove and Duncan Smith, the four most reported Leavers (Centre for Research in Communication and Culture 2016: table 2.1). Labour mounted no real challenge to this marginalization. Corbyn "intuited that Brexit would win" (Pogrund & Macguire 2020: 19), in which case he would aim to steer it in a left-wing direction; had Remain won, he would have wanted Leavers to blame the Tories. It was more surprising, given Corbyn's reputation as an anti-racist, that he did little to counter Vote Leave's racism. It was almost as though the Labour leadership had not noticed their propaganda, rather as they were later accused of not recognizing antisemitism. Corbyn commented on the "well of hatred" which had caused Cox's killing, but he had done little to stop it being filled. On the pro-European left, the Another Europe is Possible campaign, with which Corbyn's ally John McDonnell had some involvement, defended freedom of movement but was too weak to seriously offset Labour's general failure.

A moment of deep, reactionary change

In this chapter, I have shown that racist anti-immigration politics, which in the previous decade had been mobilized mainly by the far right (even if earlier it had been driven by Conservatives), were used by the Johnson-led, official Vote Leave and their allied press in order to win the referendum, in a combined campaign which had no parallel in previous Tory general election campaigns. This account has shown that the widespread view that racism was only a secondary element of the vote, orchestrated mainly by the far right, is deeply mistaken, and that this view has contributed to a fundamental misunderstanding of what was at stake in Brexit. This was a moment of profound crisis in which far-right, racial-nationalist ideas were mainstreamed in a campaign led by Conservative ministers, producing an atmosphere of intimidation and even violence which was unprecedented in British elections since the Second World War. We shall see in Chapter 5 that the uglier side of the referendum did not disappear as the immediate shock wave of the result subsided; rather, in the aftermath it insinu-ated itself into the Conservative Party and government and through them into society, leading to three and a half further years of polarizing crisis and conflict, and afterwards to a far-right-leaning nationalist government. Indeed, the longer Brexit process produced a constitutional, social and geopolitical transformation of the United Kingdom which was more fundamental – and more threatening to Europeans and other minorities in the UK – than any since the world war itself.

5

EMBEDDED RACISM IN THE BREXIT CONFLICT

Let's state one thing loud and clear: we are not leaving the European Union only to give up control of immigration all over again.

Theresa May, 2016 (Seldon 2019: 131)

What we all know after the last 2½ years, and, more importantly, the EU knows it too, is that the single most important objective for the PM, which has dictated where the ZOPA [zone of possible agreement] has been, is ending free movement of people and having complete national control over which Europeans, not just which non-Europeans, get the right to settle here.

Sir Ivan Rogers (2019a: 21–2)

The referendum campaign had been "the UK's most divisive, hostile, negative and fear-provoking of the 21st century" (Moore & Ramsay 2017: 164) and indeed in living memory. The narrow result, perceived by many on the losing side as achieved through extensive dishonesty and abuse, provoked deep divisions both within parties and across society. These sharpened the cleavage between "open" or "liberal" and "closed" or "authoritarian" groups in parliament and the electorate, which now became known as "Leavers" and "Remainers". This would almost certainly have been the case whatever the 2016 outcome, since a narrow Remain win would have antagonized the emboldened Leave movement and electorate – and especially the more aggressive Leavers – probably leading to new conflict. Indeed, it is highly possible, given the climate which developed in the late stages of the referendum and its immediate aftermath, that with the Brexit press having paved the way for viewing a Remain win as illegitimate and almost half of Leavers believing that the vote would be rigged, this could have led to the kind of protest and violence which followed Trump's defeat in 2020. There would have been a temptation for the Brexit tabloids, Farage and some Tory Leavers to stoke this situation; extreme right groups, some of which leaned towards violence, would also have brought themselves to the fore. However, the Leave victory meant that open intimidation and violence, after initially surging, slowly dissipated and the climate which they created instead reshaped the political project as it passed into the hands of the Conservative government.

Brexit, for which there was no road map – let alone detailed plan – had to be implemented through unprecedented international negotiations. Unravelling the 45-year integration of the UK with EU law and institutions would inevitably have been a complex, lengthy and difficult process, inviting multiple proposals for its achievement and providing many occasions for conflict, so it was unsurprising that sharp divides shaped the politics of the negotiation period. The chief parliamentary battle was within the Conservative Party, between May and the Europhobes, who were mostly allied to Northern Ireland's Democratic Unionist Party (DUP). However, Remainer and "soft Brexit" forces (supporters of keeping the UK in the EEA), while initially marginalized, strengthened after a general election in June 2017. There was also a deep conflict between the Labour leadership, who conceded Brexit and the single market exit although they wanted to keep a customs union with the EU, and pro-European Labour MPs and supporters. Brexit's divisions and complexity splintered both main parties, leading to unprecedented numbers of MPs becoming independents and (in the cases of some Remainers) the creation of a new independent group which briefly became the party Change UK, with some joining the pro-EU Liberal Democrats. In 2018 and 2019 there was increasing resistance to the whole Brexit project from a large minority of opposition MPs and a strong new popular pro-European movement. The "Brexit conflict" – which in reality was a complex set of intersecting conflicts – continued until Johnson left May's government in mid-2018, becoming the chief figurehead of the Leave movement once more and winning the Tory leadership a year later, before going on to achieve a decisive victory in a further general election in December 2019.

The argument of this chapter is that the range of possible outcomes of the conflict, and the corresponding forms of Brexit, were decisively shaped by the anti-immigration meaning of the Leave victory, which made the ending of freedom of movement the key "red line" for the new prime minister in negotiations with the EU. This in turn excluded "soft" Brexit in the sense in which it was generally understood in 2016–17; although the understanding of this idea later became fuzzier, the exclusion of what it originally referred to remained. May understood the narrow result of the referendum as an absolute instruction to implement Brexit in a way which ended open EU immigration, reflecting how deeply embedded Leave's racism had become and how completely (as I explain below) the ruling Conservatives became a pro-Brexit party. Both May's proposed Brexit and the more radical version accomplished by Johnson in 2020 were decisively shaped by how the logic of the project had deepened during the referendum, although it radicalized further as a result of the conflict. This logic determined the central fault line and, to a considerable extent, the shape of post-Brexit politics.

Certainly, racism was not always *manifestly* central; over several years of increasingly intense political struggle, many additional dimensions – not only concerning the economic options for Brexit but also the roles of key public institutions, especially government, parliament, law and the courts, the press, broadcasting and social media – deepened the divisions between liberalism and illiberalism in the parties and society. If organized political racism was not as continuously manifest during this conflict as it had been during the referendum, this was partly because it appeared to have won, and as the battle switched from the ballot box to parliament first May and then Johnson were determined to force through, preferably by authoritarian means which were backed by the Tory press, versions of a withdrawal agreement which embedded it. Both supporters and opponents now mostly understood promises of increased immigration control to be baked into the very meaning of Brexit and the brands of its principal leaders. When Brexit went back to voters in 2019, in first the European Parliament election and then the general election, the main battle line was between the legitimacy of the referendum mandate and the demand for a second referendum, although Labour tried in vain to recomplicate the issue. This dilemma largely eclipsed immigration as an overt issue, but at critical points in the conflict, both May and Johnson made a point of emphasizing the centrality of ending freedom of movement in order to resignal the alignment of their Brexits with the racial nationalism of the Conservatives' Leaver base. Therefore, Johnson's 2019 election campaign would clearly revive Vote Leave's strategic racism, albeit not in such a dominant or decisive way as in 2016. Meanwhile, what was increasingly called a "culture war" swirled around and beyond the conflict. While this enveloped a much wider range of issues, accusations and denials of racism of all kinds, including colour racism, antisemitism and Islamophobia, were at its heart.

Clearly, Brexit was a dynamic process, and Chris Grey (2021: 18) is in principle correct to state that "the way events … unfolded was contingent rather than necessary: that is, with different decisions or different actions different outcomes were possible". However, many arguments about possible alternative outcomes overestimate the process's open-endedness and underestimate how once Brexit had become a dominant political reality, the ways in which it had developed over a number of years and particularly during the referendum imposed a certain frame of "necessity" on the actors. Thus, many arguments about possible alternative outcomes minimize what in fact were strong limitations on the possibilities. Grey, for example, repeatedly complains about Brexiters' irrationality and inability to recognize economic reality, as though they should have seen the need to soften Brexit; he does not always fully recognize the powerful rationality, in racist, anti-immigration terms, of a "hard" version. Likewise, Anand Menon and Jill Rutter (2020) suggest that Remainers were also irrational, because had they not staked all on defeating Brexit they could have achieved a significantly softer version of it. While touching on a real issue, they ignore the centrality of freedom of movement to Remainers and the incentive for pro-European MPs to defeat any Brexit that was fundamentally compromised on this antiracist issue. The conflict was certainly deeply exacerbated by the contingent effects of the 2017 election, which produced a "hung" parliament with no Conservative majority and no majority for any Brexit outcome, compounding the underlying difficulties of the issues and the weakness of May's majority. This clearly prolonged the stalemate, exposing even more fully than might otherwise have been the case the deep contradictions in society, the state and the country's democracy which Brexit brought to a head. Yet despite this broadening of the original issues, and a process which was always about much more than anti-immigrant racism, the conflict always centred on forms of Brexit which it had delimited. The following discussion shows how at all stages, Brexit provided much evidence of the structural impact of political racism, leading not only to predictably adverse conditions for the European minority in the UK but also to a much deeper constitutional and economic dislocation from the EU than would have been likely had racism not been so central.

The effect of anti-immigration politics on Brexit policy choices

The first major consequence of Leave's victory was the transformation of the Conservative Party. Although Vote Leave leaders were almost all Conservatives, three-quarters of the cabinet and well over half the parliamentary party had followed Cameron in supporting Remain. Even as the results came in, this was changing. I observed my local referendum count, where I was able to watch my local Tory MP, Neil Parish, a Cameron loyalist and the chief counting agent for Remain in the district, becoming less certain of his position by the minute as the results came in. Within days, he was nominating Johnson in the Tory leadership contest which followed Cameron's resignation, and soon after that, when Johnson dropped out, supported Andrea Leadsom, the hitherto minor politician who had been catapulted into the role of Leave standard-bearer as a result of her performance in the televised referendum debates. Parish's conversion was fairly typical but was less dramatic than it seems since before siding with Remain he had enthusiastically promoted the holding of a referendum in his 2015 election campaign; so this example underlines how the post-2016 transformation had been prepared by the overwhelmingly Eurosceptic climate among Tories. The majority's transition was, in effect, from Euroscepticism to a full acceptance of the Europhobic path which the referendum result dictated. Without the falling out between the Leave leaders during the leadership contest after Cameron resigned, it is likely that the transition would have been symbolically completed by a Leaver (Johnson) becoming prime minister in 2016, producing at that moment a version of the Vote Leave government which eventually took over three years later. Instead, Gove withdrew his support from Johnson, the latter withdrew from the contest and Leadsom's campaign imploded, with the result that May, formerly a nominal Remainer, became prime minister unopposed, and set about the task of delivering the referendum result.

While Leave leaders had led their supporters to believe that withdrawal from the EU would be straightforward, the referendum had decided only the principle of exit and left huge decisions about implementation for the government to make. May tried to exclude parliament from a significant role, using the executive's "Henry VIII powers" (named after England's tyrannical Tudor king), until she was forced by the Supreme Court to involve it, in a decision which provoked the *Daily Mail* to deliver one of its most notorious populist attacks, when it labelled the judges "enemies of the people" (Breeze 2018). (This was an approach which Johnson would revive in 2019–20, producing further historic legal conflicts.) In theory, May could have acknowledged the narrowness of the vote and reassured the 48.1 per cent Remain minority by seeking consensus around a "soft" version of Brexit, replacing the UK's semi-detached position within the EU with a more detached position formally outside it. This would have been consistent with the long-held Eurosceptic position that economic integration was acceptable but that the UK should reject increasing political union, or "federalism" as they called it. As we have seen, the few Leavers who researched the UK's post-Brexit options had been sufficiently impressed by the complexities and economic risks to have recommended a more or less off-the-shelf option based on membership of the EEA. Such a route (the "Norway option") would have kept the UK within the single market although without participating in setting its rules, and possibly without membership of the EU's customs union, although several permutations could have been possible. Given the UK's size and the complexity of its integration in the EU, such a status would still have still entailed elaborate negotiations, but there is no doubt that EU leaders would have been prepared to explore it. If the government had also honoured Vote Leave's pledge to unilaterally guarantee EU citizens' rights, this would also have reassured both the EU and Remainers, many of whom were in a state of profound shock and not yet capable of reviving their opposition. In late 2016 and early 2017, few directly challenged the legitimacy of implementing the referendum result, which was fully accepted by Labour, the main parliamentary opposition.

In reality, May's government showed no inclination to explore these options. As early as August 2016, the cabinet had agreed that restricting immigration would be at the heart of any Brexit deal (Asthana 2016) and she told the Conservative conference in October 2016, "let's state one thing loud and clear: we are not leaving the European Union only to give up control of immigration all over again" (Seldon 2019: 131). In her Lancaster House speech of January 2017, May made it clear that she aimed for a "hard" Brexit defined by ending freedom of movement, and for this reason excluded any form of continuing membership of the single market. As Anthony Seldon (2019: 132) concludes, "both Remainers and 'soft' Brexiters had been roundly defeated". It was her position which "meant that the EU never seriously considered what, if any, compromises it could make on free movement" but simply insisted that this was one of the four pillars of the single market (Portes 2020). Moreover, May also refused to unilaterally guarantee the rights of EU citizens already living in the UK.

These have sometimes been represented as the weak choices of an "over-compensating Remainer" (Rutter & Menon 2020) or because of May's personal antipathy to immigration evident in the "hostile environment" policy that she had implemented as home secretary; her chancellor, Philip Hammond (2021), later claimed that her conference speech was "almost a coup". In reality, however, the priority for restricting immigration was dictated by the centrality of this aim to Conservative policy over a considerable period (the "tens of thousands" idea, after all, came from Cameron not May) and above all by the way in which Leave had won. It is very difficult to imagine any possible Conservative prime minister in late 2016 – and certainly Johnson or Leadsom, who joined May's cabinet and did not dissent, or Gove, who was initially outside it but remained equally silent – *not* prioritizing this goal. There were, certainly, additional measures which the UK government could have used to mitigate migration within single market rules but had not previously bothered to; but Vote Leave had moved the politics of the issue beyond them. Had May not rejected the single market and freedom of movement, she would have aroused the opposition of Leavers in the cabinet, parliament and the wider Tory Party, while Farage and the extreme right could have mobilized on the streets in protest. Whereas a soft, consensual approach would have divided the Conservatives and revived UKIP, a hard Brexit offered May the opportunity to unite her party as a pro-Brexit force (with the exception of a few persistent Remainers), marginalize UKIP and divide Labour. Following this logic, May turned herself into a caricature of a Leaver, doubling down on her own and the party's new identity by repeating the mantra "Brexit means Brexit" and insisting that "no deal" with the EU was "better than a bad deal". She not only used her conference speech to attack Remainers as "citizens of nowhere" – applying to them an anti-cosmopolitan trope generally associated with antisemitism – but also obliged two other ex-Remainer ministers, Jeremy Hunt and Amber Rudd, to announce policies which discriminated against EU citizens in the public services. The woman once known for urging the Tories in

2002 to stop being the "nasty party" was now leading its retoxification after the partial liberalization of the Cameron years.

Although some later argued that during May's premiership, Remainers missed crucial opportunities to agree a compromise soft Brexit, in late 2016 and early 2017 her "red lines" were generally accepted to have paved the way for a hard departure; Remainers had not rejected a soft option because it was not on offer. Indeed, May maintained this core position throughout her premiership, even if she moderated its interpretation a little as the problems became clear. Rogers (2019a: 21–2) summed up the situation: "What we all know after the last 2½ years, and, more importantly, the EU knows it too, is that the single most important objective for the PM, which has dictated where the ZOPA has been, is ending free movement of people and having complete national control over which Europeans, not just which non-Europeans, get the right to settle here." Indeed, it was not just future freedom of movement which was denied; May was also determined to use the position of EU citizens already in the UK as a "negotiating tool" (Seldon 2019: 342). This is perhaps the most striking confirmation that a logic of hostility to Europeans in the UK was built into the government's position. As Tanja Bueltmann (2020: 5) comments, all those "affected by a potential change in status due to Brexit were to spend well over three years in limbo", and for many that would last much longer. As noted above, Johnson and other Vote Leave cabinet ministers abandoned their original promise without a protest, as did Leave MPs outside the government: even Gisela Stuart, who had chaired British Future's (2016) review which recommended the unilateral policy.

May's confidence that her approach would pay political dividends was confirmed by its effects on Labour. Having allowed the Conservative factions to monopolize the referendum and failed to challenge Vote Leave's racism, the Labour leadership was keen to see Brexit implemented so as to move politics back to social and economic issues (Corbyn even called naively for the immediate triggering of the Article 50 process the day after the 2016 vote). Yet Brexit would, except partially during the 2017 election, prevent any such movement; instead it further complicated the party's already profound left–right divisions throughout the following years. Although many MPs contested Corbyn's leadership, much of Labour's centre-right agreed with his left-wing faction in supporting the implementation of the referendum result, and in the new situation he accepted its anti-immigration meaning, including ending freedom of movement. The small, mainly right-wing minority who had supported Leave in the referendum went even further, remaining actively pro-Brexit; some of these would support the Conservatives in the 2019 election and were awarded peerages by Johnson over the following year. However, since large majorities of Labour's MPs, members and voters still supported Remain, Corbyn also opposed May's proposals for the withdrawal agreement and the future economic relationship with the EU, insisting that Labour could deliver a "jobs-first Brexit" which would remain close to, but not inside, the single market, agree a UK–EU customs union and retain its standards for workers', consumers' and environmental rights. Ironically, as Labour invoked these rights – which could only be threatened by a post-Brexit choice of the British government – it supported the removal of the principal workers' right which was directly threatened by Brexit: the freedom of British workers to seek work in other EU countries. In 2017, the Labour leader even adopted an anti-eastern European stance, when he said that a Labour Brexit would not allow "the wholesale importation of underpaid workers from central Europe in order to destroy conditions, particularly in the construction industry" (Lewis 2017). While Corbyn easily defeated a direct leadership challenge by the pro-European Owen Smith in late 2016, Labour's Remainers gained momentum as popular Europeanism grew. The pro-EU minority of MPs, spanning the non-Corbynite left and sections of the centre-right, increasingly challenged the leadership, boxed Corbyn further into opposing May's Brexit and built parliamentary alliances with the SNP, Liberal Democrats and the sole Green MP.

The hung parliament, the Irish backstop and radicalization of the conflict

May's immigration-driven "red line" against the single market left her without a clear model of the UK's future economic relationship with the EU and weakened her hand in the negotiations. It is important to emphasize that in 2016 her government was hardly better informed than the Leave leaders had been about the huge structural transformation of the UK's international and domestic relationships which Brexit would involve. According to a senior civil servant quoted by Shipman (2018: 22), it was "not possible to underestimate the level of knowledge in the cabinet at that point", and in any case they lacked a meaningful civil service infrastructure to handle the task, which was simply unprecedented. Despite May's red line, the cabinet included a considerable range of opinion, and the lack of an obvious pathway increased the scope for division. When she eventually triggered Article 50 in October 2016, the government was still unclear about its strategy and would often be described over the next two years as negotiating more with itself and its party than with the EU. As Rogers (2019b: 38) explains, her 2016–17 speeches, made "largely for domestic consumption", united the other 27 EU states against the UK's position, gave them time to take control of the negotiating process and committed the UK to a timetable in which it barely had time to work out its objectives let alone secure them. The UK conceded to the EU's insistence on concluding the withdrawal agreement before beginning trade talks, and the first phase of discussions confirmed that May had exacerbated the UK's inferior structural position as both the applicant state and the economically more dependent party. It also appears to have gradually become clear to May that despite her initial rhetoric, the UK economy – which all studies showed would be negatively affected by any form of Brexit and especially single market withdrawal – could not afford a deep breach, let alone a "no deal" exit. The government would need to make compromises which the hard-Brexiter element, especially the European Research Group (ERG), would resist. Deceived by polling which showed the Conservatives with a commanding lead, May therefore called the general election for 8 June 2017 in the hope of winning a larger majority which would enable her to override the ultras.

May did not campaign strongly on immigration, which "faded from view" as the Tories had no new proposals; Labour too "were fighting on their most restrictionist immigration policy for decades" (Cowley & Kavanagh 2018: 424), and figures released during the campaign showed that net immigration was falling, mainly because EU nationals were leaving (Brooks 2017). However, the low salience of the immigration issue did not signify a weakening of the racism which the referendum had brought to the fore. Amnesty International UK (2017) tracked 25,688 abusive tweets sent to women MPs in the first six months of 2017: 31 per cent of the total were directed at one MP, the shadow home secretary Diane Abbott, Labour's most prominent Black female figure, and this rose to 45 per cent during the six weeks before the election. Despite a poor campaign, May increased the Tory share of the Leave vote, making inroads into working-class support for Labour, while Remainers switched to Labour. Although the overall result has been widely understood as a positive vote for Corbyn's socio-economic policies, research shows this was indeed "a Brexit election" in which votes were "heavily influenced" by Brexit preferences (Mellon *et al.* 2018: 719). However, as the gap between the two parties almost closed, May was denied an overall majority, and far from marginalizing the hard Brexiters she now became hostage to both the ERG, some of whose members were given ministerial posts, and the DUP, whose support she literally bought with £1 billion extra funding for Northern Ireland. At the same time, the "hung" parliament offered opportunities for the opposition and Remain forces to seriously constrain the government's Brexit position. Indeed parliament, far from being sidelined as May had intended, would now enter a period of influence unprecedented in a century, while a mass Remainer movement began to emerge online and on the streets, sensing the possibility of moderating or even frustrating the Brexit project.

After the election, there was again, as there had been in mid-2016, a theoretical opportunity for May to compromise. Indeed, she seems to have tried to abandon talk of "no deal" and move towards "a softening of her stance on immigration to pave the way for a closer economic relationship with the EU", but the cabinet blocked this (Seldon 2019: 286–7). "Instead of saying, 'Let's look at this again', we made the red lines even redder", May's chief whip, Julian Smith, concluded (Seldon 2019: 299). As in the previous year, May's priority was party unity, and that now meant on the right's terms, which largely ruled out an opening to Labour. In any case, as Gabriel Pogrund and Patrick Maguire (2020: 34) argue, Labour was divided, Corbyn was "instinctively uncomfortable about dealing with the Tories" and "the inconvenient truth was that Labour did not yet know what it wanted from Brexit". When Labour Remainers pressed the leadership to support remaining in the single market, it was not only Corbyn who resisted; the party's Brexit spokesman, Keir Starmer, would not support the move, and some MPs from Leave-voting areas "would not have let him go there even if he had wanted to. To accept membership of the single market was to accept freedom of movement, and their constituents would not wear it, as the likes of John Mann and Gareth Snell reminded their colleagues" (Pogrund & Maguire 2020: 129). May hoped to peel off this anti-immigrant element from Labour, to compensate for the small numbers of Remainer and soft Brexit Tories, while rallying the pro-Brexit mainstream of her party around a withdrawal agreement. Yet the election result weakened her position in the EU negotiations, and she was forced to agree to the EU's demands on financial contributions, while she agreed in September 2017 to write a guarantee of rights into the withdrawal agreement but only through a scheme which forced EU citizens to apply to remain, rather than the promised unilateral guarantee: a compromise which, it would become increasingly evident, threatened the security of many Europeans in the UK.

This left arrangements for the land border between Northern Ireland and the Irish Republic as the decisive issue, and this proved intractable. The site of continuous violence during three decades of low-level war between the British Army and the Provisional IRA, the border had been neutralized largely through the UK's and Ireland's common membership of the EU and the single market, which had been crucial prerequisites of the 1999 Good Friday Agreement. The danger of Brexit to the peace settlement had been raised during the referendum in both parts of Ireland and by former British prime ministers involved in the peace process, but their concerns had been dismissed by Leave leaders and ignored by English voters, although in Northern Ireland itself 56 per cent voted Remain, including two-fifths of Unionists. Now the effect of Vote Leave's anti-immigration campaign, which effectively locked the UK out of the single market, would be felt at the heart of the withdrawal negotiations. Caught between this red line and her commitment not to introduce a "hard border" between the two parts of Ireland – which would threaten the peace and disrupt local economies – in December 2017 May agreed to a "backdrop" arrangement whereby Northern Ireland would remain in the single market and customs union, unless or until arrangements were agreed which would render border controls unnecessary.

When the DUP furiously rejected this proposal, which they saw as weakening the union of Northern Ireland with Great Britain, the government (including Johnson) agreed a revised "backstop" in which, to avoid a hard border, the UK as a whole would remain in a customs arrangement with the EU, which represented a major concession by the EU. Despite UK single market membership remaining firmly excluded – because of its implications for immigration, May and the Europhobes "both believed it would be a repudiation of the referendum result" (Seldon 2019: 428) – when May developed her withdrawal plan further in the direction of a compromise with the EU, at Chequers in July 2018, Johnson and David Davis resigned from the government. This signalled the beginning of deep conflict within the Conservative Party, with Johnson saying that May's plan was "a big turd" and it was vital for Britain not to "surrender" on immigration or money (Seldon 2019: 435) The following week, Trump visited the UK and openly touted Johnson as an alternative prime minister. In turn Johnson veered politically in Trump's direction, suggesting that the UK might emulate his aggressive negotiating tactics, in a speech which Trump's adviser, Steve Bannon, claimed to have helped write (Cadwalladr 2019).

After the publication of the draft withdrawal agreement in November 2018, it was rejected in parliament three times in six months, as Brexiters including Johnson, for whom the backdrop had become anathema, combined with the anti-government forces (the Scottish and Welsh nationalists, Liberal Democrats, Greens, the majority of Labour and a handful of Conservative Remainers) against loyalist Tories and the small number of pro-Brexit Labour and ex-Labour MPs. The prolonged crisis led to two extensions of the withdrawal deadline, before each of which the government hyped the danger of "no deal" and spent billions preparing to mitigate the damage which its own policies would have provoked. In this situation, the Brexit conflict deepened further in both parliament and society. As Rogers (2019b: 46–7) comments, although "for decades, some of the staunchest standard bearers of the case for leaving the post-Maastricht EU [had] made the case for staying in the so-called Single Market, remaining a signatory to the EEA agreement but leaving the institutions of political and juridical integration of the Union"; now the Europhobes represented this as "Brexit in Name Only". The ERG, Brexit newspapers, Farage and their social media followers increasingly advocated "no deal", the culmination, Rogers (2019b: 49) suggests, of "Brexitism as a revolutionary phenomenon, which radicalized as time went on and was now devouring its children".

The ERG's aim was to ensure a Brexit "with a minimal role for the EU in British affairs and maximum flexibility to deregulate and sign free trade deals around the world" (Geoghegan 2020: 110), and they were in contact with Farage (Tice 2021: 12), who had left UKIP and formed a Leave Means Leave campaign. The pro-Brexit Institute of Economic Affairs proposed that, instead of shadowing the

EU, the UK should dispense with a range of tariffs, quotas and regulations, environmental protections should be loosened and the NHS should be opened up to international competition: "It was a none-too-subtle pitch for a free trade deal with the United States" (Geoghegan 2020: 168). Rogers (2019b: 41) described the Brexiters' widely disseminated narrative of betrayal by a "Remainer elite" as "the emerging British equivalent of the *Dolchstosslegende* – the stab in the back myth – which, post Versailles, the German military, Hindenburg and others, propagated to blame the Weimar civilian elite for having betrayed a supposedly undefeated army". While members of the ERG were the parliamentary frontmen for the extreme Brexiters, Leave.EU had not gone away. Arron Banks used "the social media muscle he'd built with Leave.EU to push the Conservatives to adopt a hardline interpretation of the Brexit vote", with its Facebook page instructing its almost million-strong following to join the Tory Party as a part of an entrist "blue wave", and he bought adverts against the remaining liberal Conservative MPs. Of the 29 targeted by Banks, 20 did not stand for the party in the 2019 general election (Geoghegan 2020: 70), many of them after Johnson expelled them.

On the pro-European side, the 2016–17 willingness to compromise had evaporated when it became obvious that May's "was going to be a Conservative Brexit and a hard Brexit" (Seldon 2019: 225). The perception that the government had proceeded to implement the narrow referendum majority without taking into account the strength of Remain opinion motivated opposition. While a small number of Tory and Labour MPs continue to advocate the "Norway option", in 2018–19 Remainers inside and outside parliament increasingly focused on the demand for a second referendum on the terms of Brexit, with an option for the UK to remain in the EU. The new mass, extra-parliamentary, pro-European movement, with a determined activist base mobilizing repeated million-strong demonstrations in central London, increasingly challenged the legitimacy of the referendum result, citing among other reasons that only 37 per cent of the electorate had supported it; the denial of a vote to EU citizens; the deceitful claim that the UK paid £350 million per week to the EU; and Vote Leave's infractions of electoral law, which – had the referendum been legally binding rather than advisory – could have invalidated it. Leave's racism was not an overt theme in the Europeans' campaign, but it was a powerful underlying belief which delegitimized Brexit. Likewise, freedom of movement was their most important positive symbol of the EU, and their attachment to it was perhaps the deepest obstacle to any compromise with May's policy.

Without this conflict, Britain "would almost certainly have left the European Union as planned at the end of March 2019 with the agreement negotiated by Theresa May" (Geoghegan 2020: 121). Instead, Johnson finally achieved a version of her deal but only by reintroducing the customs border in the Irish Sea that had been anathema to him and other Brexiters a year earlier. The significance of this was that, while it conceded the continuing application of single market rules in Northern Ireland and sacrificed his erstwhile DUP allies, it "kept alive the ERG's vision of a deregulated 'Global Britain'" (Geoghegan 2020: 222), although by 2020 hopes for an early US trade deal were fading. If Remainers and Labour had supported May, they could ultimately have had a somewhat "softer" trade deal with the EU than that which Johnson delivered (Menon & Rutter 2020); but they would not have saved freedom of movement or kept the UK in the single market, the original meaning of "soft Brexit", because for May controlling immigration and avoiding a deep split in the Conservative Party were always the highest priorities.

From political to social and legal Europhobia

This polarizing crisis aroused widespread anti-Europeanism as well as hostilities towards specific nationalities such as Germans, always the core European enemy. The increasingly central role of Ireland also reawakened traditional British anti-Irish sentiment among Brexiters, who had hardly contemplated that their indifference to the problems which Brexit caused for Ireland would cause them serious difficulties. Even pro-EU experts had believed, as Michael Dougan (2017: 71) put it, that "the interests of Northern Ireland [would] hardly play a decisive role" in "a complex and multifaceted set of multinational negotiations". Yet, since the interests of the EU and Ireland coincided, this may have been, Rogers (2019b: 19) notes, "the first Anglo-Irish negotiation in history where the greater leverage [was] not on London's side of the table. And the vituperation aimed at Dublin politicians tells one just how well that has gone down with the politicians and apparatchiks who had not bothered to work out that this was no longer just a bilateral business, and are now appalled to find they are cornered." Brexiters and their press did not conceal their contempt for those who dared to make the peace and prosperity of the island of Ireland prevail over the British nationalist project. Priti Patel even urged using the threat of food shortages to bring Ireland to heel; reported as a threat to "starve Ireland", it could not have been better calculated to insult a country whose worst historic memory of British oppression was the famine of 1845–52. Unsurprisingly, anti-Irish sentiments were also widely expressed by Brexit's grassroots supporters.

Meanwhile, as Europeans continued to experience abuse in local settings and online, popular Europhobia had its counterpart in the government's treatment of Europeans in the UK. During the long period in which May's government used EU citizens as "bargaining chips", many applied to the UK's existing complicated and expensive systems for non-citizens to gain permanent residence and citizenship, often experiencing frustration and rejection, particularly because of a new requirement for private health insurance (Yeo 2020: 186–7). Only on 1 March 2019, 33 months after the referendum, did the state finally launch a new scheme through which resident EU, EEA and Swiss citizens could apply for "settled status". By June 2021, over 6 million applications had been made, but many were duplicates or from people not currently resident in the UK; the Office of National Statistics estimated that 3.5 million EU citizens lived in the UK in mid-2020. By 2021, 2.75 million had been offered settled status, but 2.28 million had been offered only temporary "pre-settled" status and so would have to apply again, creating an individual cliff edge for each of them at a later date. Thousands had been refused, disproportionately among people who made paper applications, who were mostly women and included those from non-European countries who had derivative rights through an EU state (Barnard & Costello 2021). In addition, grants of status were made electronically so that EU citizens received no physical proof, a decision which Johnson's government refused to change even when it was shown to put individuals at risk of discrimination in situations when lettings agencies, landlords, councils, banks, GP surgeries, hospitals, schools, border control, etc., asked them to prove their settled status. Failures to automatically confirm residence rights also created situations in which applicants would become illegal residents after 30 June 2021.

Even on that date, a significant number of Europeans were still not aware that the scheme existed, or if they were aware that they needed to apply; applications proved more difficult for people who already faced social exclusion or whose independence or autonomy was reduced; some people would struggle to navigate an application because of difficulties accessing the app; some would lack evidence proving their eligibility; and others would fail to convert from pre-settled to settled status (Migration Observatory 2020a). Children and the elderly were particularly left behind (Skandachanmugarasan, Devine & Hopkins 2019), as were people from outside the EU such as the East Timorese community whose right to residency depended on the citizenship of Portugal, an EU state (Webster 2021). A Home Office minister, Brandon Lewis, notoriously stated that these people could then be "deported", and although his comment was withdrawn, the risk that some Europeans would meet the fate of the "Windrush" victims was built into the process. Indeed, the risks for Europeans who failed to gain settled status were in principle greater than they were for "Windrush" people, since they would not have a legal right to remain (Yeo, Sigona & Godin 2019: 3).

The referendum had repelled EU citizens moving to the UK for work, leading for example to a 96 per cent reduction in the numbers of EU nurses registering to work in the UK nine months later (Siddique 2017) and a moderate downward trend in EU immigration during the rest of the decade (Migration Observatory 2020d). EU citizens who had made their lives in the UK widely confirmed feelings of victimization as their previously secure status in society was eroded by changes in attitudes as well as policy. As the UK left the EU, polling showed that a majority of Leavers supported the government's insistence that EU citizens apply for the right to stay in the UK, rather than having their rights confirmed as Vote Leave had originally proposed (Deltapoll 2020), while almost half said they were "bothered" by people from non-English-speaking countries talking to each other in their own language (YouGov 2020). On the other side, a survey of Europeans conducted by the3million showed that "even respondents granted a status, while relieved, ... remained anxious ... . Ultimately, their experience tells a story not of feeling friendship and a sense of protection, but one of the erosion of trust and disintegration. Rather than making [European] citizens feel ... settled, 'unsettling status' would be a much more appropriate name for the scheme" (Bueltmann 2020: 3). Many saw this whole period as one of profound alienation; having moved to the UK and established themselves in work, community, family and personal relationships, they had taken for granted the equal rights which EU citizenship gave them. The3million argued that overall, there had been "a process of disintegration since the EU referendum vote that cuts across the nation, communities and even individual families. There is an erosion of trust; an erosion of well-being; and an erosion of the sense of belonging" (Bueltmann 2020: 42). For many, there was also "a real shift" in their sense of identity, with a strengthening European identity and a declining confidence in what had been, in many cases, a developing British identity. The problem, the3million argued, was that the trigger for this Europeanism had been the experience of "othering" through Brexit (Bueltmann 2020: 33). Europeans in the UK underwent a similar process to that of many historic victims of group discrimination, finding a new meaning in a collective identity which had previously been less important. At the same time, many British Remainers also felt more European as a result of Brexit, and polling found them less tolerant of Leavers than the latter were of them (Ipsos MORI 2020).

This story was one in which official and popular hostility towards Europeans combined to disintegrate British society in a broader sense, just as the hostile environment had long spread insecurity from non-European migrants to larger ethnic minority communities. It was, the3million argued, "not just a story about EU/EEA and Swiss citizens, but also many British citizens, be they family members or those connected in other ways. Consequently, [this] is, in many ways, about the very fabric of relationships and communities throughout the UK rather than just about EU/EEA and Swiss citizens" (Bueltmann 2020: 42). Prior to Brexit, those who depended on EU citizenship for their rights had enjoyed a form of citizenship in the UK, with almost all the rights of UK citizens themselves; in the aftermath, the majority were reduced to a type of permanent residency which compromised those rights, and this was exacerbated by the refusal to provide documentation; the large "pre-settled" minority had gained temporary residency but faced uncertainty about its continuation; and a smaller but significant minority had effectively been forced into a situation which could entail their losing rights to work, rent or access the NHS and even forcible removal from the UK. Even before the scheme deadline, the Home Office was carrying out deportation flights of EU citizens found guilty of offences; local authorities were engaging in informal deportations of homeless and other marginalized Europeans, euphemistically described as "reconnection" to countries of origin (Barnard & Costello 2020); and the number of EU citizens detained at the UK border increased dramatically. The overall effect of these changes was to hugely expand the non-citizen population with limited rights, with EU citizens representing over 5 per cent of the total population and two-thirds of those who were not UK citizens. In some London boroughs EU citizens made up more than a third of the population, and in several towns and cities in eastern England they were more than a fifth (de Quetteville 2021). Nor did these residents have a straightforward option of gaining UK citizenship, since the government, possibly with an eye to the electoral implications for the Conservatives of these local concentrations, made it even more difficult than previously for EU citizens to apply for citizenship.

By the early 2020s, therefore, hostility to Europeans was being consolidated in the UK. It encompassed a number of strands, old as well as new, mobilizing historic wartime hostility towards Germans, the old British racialization of the Irish, racialized class resentments against eastern Europeans and general anti-immigrant xenophobia, and it was expressed at both popular and policy levels. Whiteness may have meant that many Europeans, especially if they were embedded in protective professional and social environments, still existed in a less regularly threatening situation than most people of colour. Indeed socially, even elite Brexiters accommodated a degree of Europhilia, with prominent figures like Farage married to Europeans. However, the dynamic of the Europhobic project drove Brexiters and their press to constantly renew aggressive nationalism towards the EU, which together with the problems of citizenship and street-level and online hostility inevitably created an experience of threat, stress and harassment for the European minority. The3million reported that even "well meaning, Remain-voting friends seem surprised at the level of isolation and insecurity this has caused" (Bueltmann 2020: 42). Little attention has been given to the short- and long-term effects on children who suddenly found their British identity questioned, an experience which could result in lasting harm, since research by the Migration Observatory (2020b) showed that adult children of migrants born in the UK were twice as likely to feel discriminated against because of their race, ethnicity, nationality, language, accent or religion compared to the foreign-born. Another factor which has been little remarked on is that where previously most Europeans had been content to be politically semi-detached,

Brexit had "sparked a new awareness of public discourse [and] led to the emergence of new political and discursive attitudes and strategies, as well as persuasive reflexivity and incipient activism on the part of EU nationals" (Vathi & Trandafoiu 2020). Applications for citizenship grew slowly, despite their costs and complexity, alongside the demand for settled status. These developments may, in turn, have further hardened Conservative determination to deny EU citizens voting rights, since their widespread electoral participation would almost certainly constitute a threat to Tory majorities. All these developments confirmed that 2016's racialization of Europeans in general, which had been implicit in the hostility of the Leave campaigns and explicit in that of many of their supporters, had been deepened by the Brexit process and conflict. We shall see in Chapter 6 that in the final stages of this crisis, as Johnson fought for and won power and then governed in campaigning mode, anti-Europeanism was combined with repeated evocations of hostility to Muslims, immigrants and asylum seekers, and calibrated with a "culture war" campaign against antiracism, in the nationalist Conservatives' determination to consolidate their Brexit base.

6

JOHNSON'S VICTORY AND THE NATIONALIST TORY REGIME

We have seen that there was a sense on all sides of the post-referendum conflict that immigration control was intrinsic to Brexit, and rejection of freedom of movement was common ground across the Conservative Party and much of Labour. The Labour and Tory MPs who continued to pursue the Norway option highlighted its economic benefits rather than movement rights, and freedom of movement was explicitly defended only by the European movement, for whom it was the core of European citizenship. Immigration declined rapidly in polling salience after 2016; while this was sometimes attributed to the reduced numbers of new European immigrants, it was much more likely to have been because of the fact that Brexiters – having won the principle of ending freedom of movement and being focused instead on blocking May's deal – no longer felt the need to campaign on these numbers, while many of their supporters believed that they were actually being controlled. Even Farage, when he launched his Brexit Party for the 2019 European elections, did not campaign on immigration. Followers who had attended one of his rallies boasted to me on Twitter that he had not mentioned it in his speech; it was so central to Farage's brand that he did not need to emphasize it at every twist and turn, since when he talked of the "betrayal" of Brexit his supporters would have understood that immigration control was part of what he was complaining about. The position of Conservative leaders, in contrast, was more ambiguous, and whenever they appealed to the public or their party membership over the heads of parliament, political racism came into the open. When May wrote an "open letter" to the public on 25 November 2018 in an attempt to get support for her agreement, her first point was: "It will honour the result of the referendum. We will take back control of our borders, by putting an end to the free movement of people once and for all" (BBC News 2018a), and official advertisements reinforced this message.

The extreme right, Farage and Johnson in the crisis

By this point, May's project was in deep crisis and this represented Johnson's opportunity. Within weeks of resigning from her government in July 2018, so that he could openly challenge her for the premiership, he oriented towards Trump (who was popular with Brexiters) and published his notorious *Telegraph* column likening burqa-wearing Muslim women to "letterboxes". While these comments were widely minimized as "casual", the timing suggested that the anti-Muslim message was anything but accidental, leading the chairman of the Conservative Muslim Forum, Mohammed Amin, to protest that the article was "anti-Muslim" and would "whip up hatred of women who wear the niqab and burqa"; he rightly commented that "Johnson is a master of the English language – he must understand exactly what effect his language will have" (BBC News 2018b). Following these comments, Tell MAMA (2018: 3) reported a short-term 375 per cent increase in Islamophobic incidents, the largest spike during 2018, with many of them against burqa-wearers; almost half of the perpetrators directly referenced Johnson or his language. As Matthew D'Ancona (2019) suggests, Steve Bannon – with whom Johnson was in touch in this period and maintained a discreet channel even after he became prime minister – "had not provided the precise script. But he had undoubtedly urged Johnson, who was floundering at the time, to go out and make some noise, to get the plaster falling off the ceiling." D'Ancona adds that this was "a crucial moment of self-definition in which Johnson completed his transition from *popularity* (Wodehouse-quoting, loveable cyclist) to *populism* (divisive champion of Brexit, foe of elites and dog-whistling nativist)" (emphases in original). Although this glosses over how far he had already moved in this direction through Vote Leave in 2016, his article undoubtedly showed a new determination to use racism as a political method in his campaign for the Conservative leadership. Even the idea that Johnson's comments were a "dog whistle", which recognizes his intention to connect with voter racism, underestimates their significance by implying that it was merely a tactical intervention. In context, it was an indication that he was reviving the strategic approach which he had fronted for Vote Leave.

To achieve power through an ERG-style Brexit and a secure parliamentary majority, Johnson needed to place himself in the leadership not only of the Conservative Party but of the wider Leave movement, with its strong racist tendencies, and to deepen his connection with the Tories' increasingly racial-nationalist electorate. Brexiters included many who were not natural Tories and had supported not only UKIP but also the BNP and other far-right groups. We saw that many Leave supporters had lashed out at people from ethnic, racial and gender minorities after the referendum; judging by widely reported comments, they believed that the UK had voted to remove all "immigrants", among whom they often included people of colour in general. As we have seen, the extreme right had played a significant social media role during the referendum, merging into the Leave.EU campaign, and the post-2016 situation offered them new opportunities (Smith & Colliver 2016). Although right-wing antisemitism was growing (Community Security Trust 2020), Joe Mulhall (2019: 1) notes that on the surface the organized extreme right were toning down their traditional mix of "explicit racism, broad anti-immigrant politics and vitriolic homophobia", adopting "a more mainstream platform that allows them to circumvent the traditional *cordon sanitaire* that has marginalized them for decades". The 2017–19 stalemate offered them, as well as Johnson and Farage, the chance to channel Brexiters' resentment at the failure of May's government to deliver on what both Leave campaigns had assured them was the simple and straightforward choice to leave the EU. Mulhall (2019: 1), analysing the rhetoric espoused at a series of extreme Brexit events during 2018 and comparing it to polling, argued that "it becomes evident that large parts of the contemporary far-right's platform – namely anti-Muslim politics, co-option of the free speech debate and an anti-elite populism – has widespread public support". The extreme right leader Stephen Yaxley-Lennon (aka Tommy Robinson) gained a new notoriety by presenting himself as a "martyr" on the back of contrived legal battles; lionized by the US and international far right, through which he raised significant funds, he increasingly mobilized on the streets. In 2018–19, the far right descended on the capital in numbers not seen in decades, with one demonstration estimated at 50,000, and Yaxley-Lennon claimed, "We couldn't have done this 3 years ago. We couldn't have done this 4 years ago", with Mulhall (2019: 1) noting, "many have asked whether the far right has now become acceptable and perhaps entered the mainstream in the UK". Indeed, when "Tommy Robinson" mobilized the angriest elements on the streets, he also counter-balanced the televisual impact of the pro-European demonstrations for the benefit of the Brexit movement as a whole, even though the Europeans had much larger numbers. His appointment as an adviser by UKIP's new leader, Gerald Batten, was another indication of the porous boundaries between the extreme and radical right groups.

As D'Ancona (2019) commented, "the old partitions that separated respectable institutions – including mainstream political parties – from fringe opinion are being torn down. Network politics means that all right-wing messaging exists on a continuum. One part of the network can say what another cannot. Which is not to say that the degree of co-ordination is high or even especially significant. What matters is that each part of the network performs its role – governing, campaigning or mobilizing street support." While the extreme right itself had not fully entered the mainstream, as Mulhall speculated it might, it was on the edges of the "new network politics" of the radicalized wider right.

Bannon, an adviser to Johnson and Farage, also admired Robinson, but the latter's semi-incorporation into UKIP was used by Farage (who had resigned the leadership after the referendum) as a reason for resigning from the party altogether, helping him to emphasize the gap between his personal brand and the extreme right. As UKIP faded into electoral insignificance, Farage's new Brexit Party had, as its funder Arron Banks put it, "a tightly controlled central structure, almost a dictatorship at the centre" (Geoghegan 2020: 230). Even more than the pre-2016 UKIP, it appealed to Brexiters across the board, gaining the support of a large swathe of Conservative voters, members, councillors and probably MPs in the May 2019 European elections. Farage played his traditional role of the challenger forcing the Tories to tack to the right more successfully than ever, winning the largest share of the vote and reducing the Tories to 9 per cent of the vote, their lowest ever in a national election.

Farage's success, on top of the ERG's parliamentary opposition, finally led to May's resignation on 24 May 2019, creating the opening for Johnson to take the leadership. When Johnson attacked Muslims in 2018 – and the signal was predictably amplified by media coverage and antiracist protest – his ploy had cut through to its intended audiences. In the Conservative leadership election, he doubled down on the comments, saying that "it is vital that we as politicians remember that one of the reasons why the public feels alienated now from us all as a breed is because we are muffling and veiling our language. We don't speak as we find and cover it up in bureaucratic language when what they want to hear is what we really think" (Mairs 2019). In a televised debate, he was challenged by an imam and said he apologized for any offence caused by his burqa remarks but not for their substance. He was also bounced by one of his rivals, Sajid Javid, the only Muslim in the highest level of the Conservative leadership, into endorsing an inquiry into Islamophobia in the party. This was the only occasion on which the party's Islamophobia issue was taken up by a member of the leadership; Lady Sayeeda Warsi, a former party chair, had repeatedly raised the issue, but by 2019 she was a marginal figure. Javid's challenge was embarrassing for Johnson, but the public reminder of his anti-Muslim prejudice almost certainly did him little harm with the Tory selectorate. According to a survey conducted the same week for Hope Not Hate (2019), only 8 per cent of Conservative members agreed that the party had "a problem of Islamophobia or racism towards Muslims", while 79 per cent disagreed, although large proportions simultaneously endorsed a range of anti-Muslim sentiments. At the very moment that Javid was standing for the leadership, only 8 per cent agreed with the statement that "I would be proud of Britain if we were to elect a Muslim as our Prime Minister", while 43 per cent agreed that "I would prefer to not have the country led by a Muslim". Tory MPs eliminated Javid from the contest before the membership vote, and Johnson won it with a large majority and postponed the Islamophobia enquiry. Certainly, the dominant issue in the Tory leadership race was Brexit itself, rather than Muslims or immigration, but this episode confirmed the extent to which anti-Muslim racism was baked into the pro-Brexit Conservative Party, and that Johnson's alignment with it benefited more than it harmed him.

"Racism became a central election issue for the first time"

The first months of Johnson's premiership were also dominated by the final phases of the battle over Brexit, and issues of immigration, Muslims and Europeans' rights were overtaken by struggles over the measures which he took to try to force it through, especially the "prorogation" (suspension) of parliament at the end of August, which was ruled unlawful by the Supreme Court on 24 September 2019. Following this defeat, Johnson manoeuvred to hold a general election in which he would achieve a parliamentary majority to replace the minority position he had inherited. His main theme, greatly amplified by the Tory press, was that Remainers, the opposition parties and the courts were blocking the Brexit for which the referendum had voted. Johnson repetitively used emotive, threatening language about "surrender" and "betrayal" in a strategic manner; Amber Rudd, resigning from his cabinet, even accused him of "legitimizing violence" (Walker 2019). Consolidating his authoritarian direction, a number of Conservative MPs who refused to support his machinations, including senior ex-ministers from May's government, were summarily expelled from the party and prevented from standing for it again.

When Johnson finally achieved the election, held on 12 December 2019, political racism was widely evident but not dominant as in 2016. His campaign, as Peter Geoghegan (2020: 41, 209) summarizes, was "a ramped up reprise of Vote Leave. There were dubious claims and disinformation, anonymous adverts on social media and incessant lying", and the Tories were assisted by an almost invisible network of hyper-partisan websites as well as "astroturf" or fake grassroots groups. The party ran what commentators credited as a sophisticated, highly targeted online operation; in what was called a "post-truth election", a study showed that 88 per cent of Conservative advertisements featured misleading claims (Geoghegan 2020: 199–202). Johnson's slogan "Get Brexit Done" cleverly appealed both to frustrated Brexiters and to middle-ground opinion exhausted by the three and a half years of political and legal conflict, and his campaign was tailored to former Labour voters in "red wall" Leave-majority seats in the north and Midlands (Cooper & Cooper 2020).

Hostility towards immigrants was woven into the campaign at many levels, although it also included headline retail offers (more hospitals, nurses and police). At the outset it was reported that, if the party's lead fell below 10 per cent in the polls, Cummings and another ex-Vote Leave staffer in Johnson's office planned to "revisit some of their greatest hits from the referendum campaign, including 'Turkey week' in which they highlighted the potential for Turkish accession to the EU. This time it would involve drawing attention to the policy passed at Labour conference", which the Tories would represent as one of "open borders" (Shipman & Wheeler 2019). Eight days later, Michael Gove (2019) claimed that "Labour is now explicitly in favour of unlimited and uncontrolled immigration", and the same day the Conservatives began to pump out similar propaganda on Twitter and Facebook: "Under Corbyn's Labour, immigration would surge", "Corbyn's plan for unlimited and unrestricted immigration is the biggest threat to our public services including our NHS", etc. In an indication of the continuing synergies between different sections of the right, the ground had already been prepared by Leave.EU, which continued to have a huge presence on Facebook; an analysis of their September–October 2019 posts found "multiple untrue claims that Labour planned to 'abandon immigration controls altogether'" (Skopeliti 2019).

A week after his immigration pitch, Gove homed in on Europeans in the UK, using a tabloid article to falsely claim that it was "unfair" that EU citizens had "preferential access to free NHS care … without paying in" (O'Carroll 2019), and a little later Johnson, promising to "bear down" on immigration, said – to outrage from European and migrant organizations – that "over the last couple of decades or more … we've seen quite a large numbers of people coming in from the whole of the EU [...] able to treat the UK basically as though it's part of their own country" (Bulman 2019). The3million conducted a national survey of Europeans in the UK during the election, and reported these responses: "Yes we treat UK as our home because most of us, after years of working and paying taxes in this country [... we have] homes and a family here and going back to our own country it is not an option anymore"; "I avoid any contact with British people for the fear of them being Brexit supporters; I had many unfortunate encounters and I don't deal with it too well" (Bueltmann 2020: 43–4). In terms of hostile content, therefore, the 2019 election continued where the referendum had left off, but the open attacks on European residents suggested that Johnson, Gove and the Vote Leave element had been emboldened since 2016 when, as we saw in Chapter 4, they focused mainly on prospective migrants from Turkey and Albania. Open hostility to Europeans in the UK, which they had made efforts to neutralize during the referendum, had been normalized in the intervening years as the Conservatives' ideological Europhobia deepened. Likewise, building on the Tory approach in the 2016 London election, in 2019 they also played (in conjunction with India's ruling nationalist party, the BJP) the sectarian card to appeal to Hindu voters, presenting Labour as "anti-Hindu" and using Kashmir to evoke anti-Muslim sentiments (Hundal 2019; Saddique 2020).

However, political racism did not play the same role that it had in the referendum. There is no evidence that anti-immigrant messaging approached the same scale, and hostility to migrants and Europeans appeared to be a secondary means of reviving the spirit of 2016 and discrediting Labour in a campaign dominated by the delivery of Brexit. Yet the election still saw the most explicit and influential debate about racism which has ever taken place in a British general election, but focused overwhelmingly on Labour's antisemitism crisis, with some left-wingers pushing back over Tory Islamophobia. On the surface both of these issues were about members' and supporters' racist comments, which the parties failed to suppress, but the party leaders were also compromised, Corbyn by loose historic associations with antisemitic figures and failures to recognize antisemitism, Johnson by his history of racist comments. However, Labour's crisis was far more politically potent, both for structural reasons (the party's antiracist ethos, the historic role of Jewish Labour members, opposition to Corbyn within the party) and because a highly public internal conflict over antisemitism had reached an advanced stage, the leadership had run out of excuses and support for Labour among Jews had almost disappeared. Two weeks before polling day, the UK chief rabbi, Ephraim Mirvis, made a declaration on behalf of the Jewish community that Corbyn was "unfit for high office" (Barclay 2019), and he was supported by other faith leaders. The Tories and others used this to brand Labour racist, while Labour did not make a campaign issue of Tory Islamophobia, which had only limited public airings; the Muslim Council of Britain complained that it was still "hard to get Islamophobia on the agenda" (Versi 2019). The Tories' strategic anti-immigrant and anti-European interventions were not even mentioned in this debate, while accusations that Tory candidates shared antisemitic conspiracy theories on social media (Geoghegan 2020: 282) also gained little attention. Lady Warsi commented that Black and Muslim voters would "question how racism became a central election issue for the first time, but with little reference to the ways racism affects them, the structural and institutional form of racism faced by people of colour seeming to have less traction in the public imagination" (Murphy 2019).

The Conservatives' amalgam of Brexit, anti-immigrant and anti-European themes with selective antiracism, all faithfully reinforced by their press allies, helped them to consolidate the racial-nationalist electorate. Johnson's discreet relationship with Farage was also crucial, as the latter withdrew over half his candidates in favour of the Tories, claiming, with some justification, "What we did in a sense was to create Boris Johnson" (Ewen 2019: 117), although his remaining candidates, it has been estimated, "may have cost the Conservatives around 25 of the seats that Labour managed to retain" (Curtice, Fisher & English 2021: 473). On the other side, Corbyn's Brexit ambiguity and antisemitism failures divided liberal and left opinion, which split between Labour, the Liberal

Democrats and the Greens in ways which were mutually damaging under the first-past-the-post system. The Tories gained an 80-seat majority over all other parties with 43.6 per cent of the vote, although the left, centre and nationalist parties which opposed Johnson's Brexit solution together had 52 per cent. After the election, for the first time a majority of both Tory MPs and ministers were "original" Leavers who had voted Leave in 2016, rather than former Remain voters (Lynch 2020). A post-election summary by election scholars (Cutts *et al.* 2020: 20), acknowledging that Brexit had "accelerated a longer-term realignment in British politics and reshaped the country's political geography", commented that this "owes much to how political parties have mobilized the issue, with Nigel Farage, UKIP and then later the Brexit Party, playing an important role in politicizing the question of EU membership, and also merging it with immigration – and then the Conservatives building directly on this". Some of Johnson's supporters also interpreted his election triumph through a racial lens: a Twitter user reported, "Girlfriend's just called me. She's British-Indian. Told me when she left work last night some drunken lads shouted 'Time you fucked off back to your own country now you P*ki c**t!' at her. This in her hometown where she was born and raised" (Anon 2019). A Cabinet Office briefing confirmed that "police tracked increases in Brexit-related hate crime in March 2019 and the end of that year – two other periods of intensive political and public focus on leaving the EU" (Graham-Harrison & Cadwalladr 2020), underlining the continuing link between the Brexit mobilization and abusive behaviour.

Labour antisemitism as a case of political racism

Labour's antisemitism crisis, the most prominent racism issue in the 2019 election, is worthy of further discussion, because while it is different from the right-wing racial nationalism which is the main subject of this book, it exemplifies general issues of political racism. Racism always involves fantastical assumptions about power as well as inferiority, but antisemitism has always been very distinctive in ascribing major economic power to wealthy Jews as well as producing discrimination against poorer Jews. It was part of the repertoire of sections of the left in the nineteenth century, when it was named "the socialism of fools", before it became the core of Nazism's wide-ranging project of racial-national domination. After the extermination of European Jews, antisemitism came to be regarded as the archetypal right-wing racism, as a new international consensus was reflected in UN instruments such as the International Declaration of Human Rights and the Genocide Convention. Certainly, antisemitism remained central to the ideology of far-right movements, but left-wing forms also continued, for example in communist states during the Cold War.

In the early twenty-first century, some analysts and campaigners renewed the claim (first made decades earlier) that hostility to Israel had produced a "new antisemitism", a form of hostility to Jews which was implicit in anti-Zionism and manifested itself in some forms of opposition to Israel, especially to its existence as a Jewish state (Hirsh 2017; Rich 2018). In principle, the idea of a "new antisemitism" makes sense; it would be curious if antisemitism was frozen in what the sociologist Keith Kahn-Harris (2019) calls "consensus antisemitism", that is, historic sentiments which all could agree were anti-Jewish, in the context of the radically altered geopolitical situation of Jewish communities after the foundation of the state of Israel. It would also be strange, since we know that racialization of enemies is a persistent tendency in nationalist conflicts, if the struggle between rival nationalisms over Israel–Palestine had *not* stimulated new racisms; indeed, anti-Arab racism in Israel is also clearly such an outcome (Shaw 2015). Yet exactly which criticisms of Israel are legitimate and which antisemitic is highly contested. For many anti-Zionists, the destruction of Palestinian society during the establishment of the state of Israel in 1948, together with ongoing Israeli repression and dispossession of Palestinians in the occupied West Bank, Jerusalem and Gaza, makes its very existence as a Jewish state a matter of legitimate criticism, leading for example to calls for a single, secular, bi-communal state in Israel–Palestine. For many supporters of Israel, however, fundamental questioning of the state conjures up the threats of some Palestinian organizations and their supporters such as the Iranian regime to "destroy" Israel and drive Jews out of Palestine, if not "into the sea".

The difficulties are illustrated by the International Holocaust Remembrance Alliance (IHRA) working definition of antisemitism, which is advocated by Jewish communal organizations and the Johnson government as a desirable legal and policy definition. This gives the statement that "Israel is a racist *endeavour*" (emphasis added) as an example of antisemitism, because it implies that the very idea of a Jewish state is racist; this is seen as discriminatory because it denies Jews the right to national self-determination. However, this idea has been confused with the different claim that actually existing Israel is a racist (or apartheid) *state*, which implies that it is systematically racist in its treatment of the Palestinians. This second idea is not inherently antisemitic, but the IHRA definition does not mention it, and because of this and other vagueness has been criticized for allowing legitimate criticisms of Israel to be judged antisemitic (Feldman 2016; Renton 2021: 20–25). It will be evident that the identification of antisemitism in political opposition to Israel depends greatly on context. Where criticism of Israel as a racist state is accompanied by calls for Palestinian-Jewish cooperation, respecting human rights and the collective identities of both communities, it can hardly be regarded as racist; where it supports or is ambiguous towards the destruction of Israel and its Jewish community, it is obviously discriminatory.

Although, as we have noted, there is still much right-wing antisemitism, Western mainstream and even far-right parties are mostly pro-Israeli and the charge of "new antisemitism" is made against the left. The election in 2015 of Jeremy Corbyn, a high-profile anti-Zionist, as Labour leader, brought these issues to the fore in the party, in which Jews had always been well represented. Although his stance was not widely regarded as antisemitic, it came to be seen as stimulating antisemitism among some Labour members and supporters – primarily but not only on social media (Community Security Trust 2019) – creating a crisis in which the party's failure to control them led to its being represented as racist. Changing the Israel–Palestine situation was certainly a political aspiration for Corbyn, but it was not a goal for which Labour mobilized strategically in the electoral arena, nor did it propagate antisemitic ideas to its supporters. That antisemitism spread in party milieux in the absence of a strategic intention to mobilize, fuelled by the interventions of some national figures like former London mayor Ken Livingstone, illustrates the potential for "ordinary" supporters' activism to generate political dynamics around a type of racism.

The case also illustrates the interrelationships between different types of racist attitudes which we have also seen in Brexit: although Labour antisemitism increased in tandem with Corbyn-inspired opposition to Israel, accusations of "new antisemitism" gave way to simpler arguments that classical antisemitism had become widespread. The Community Security Trust (2020) shows that, unlike right-wing antisemitism, left-wing antisemitism peaked around political crises, but Ben Gidley, Brendan McGeever and David Feldman (2020) argue that it also drew on the existing "reservoir" of hostility towards Jews in Britain, while David Renton (2021: 28) – agreeing that politically motivated Labour controversy degenerated, as prominent figures and their supporters doubled down on dubious claims, into blatant "old" antisemitism – argues that it *deepened* that reservoir. Labour's failure to suppress its supporters' antisemitism was viewed as an acceptance of it by many British Jews, feeding insecurity and fear linked to their long history of victimization and persecution. Unlike stereotypical racist victims, most British Jews were not underprivileged, and the hostility they experienced was partly because attachment to Israel had become an important part of their identity.

These characteristics, interestingly, are similar to those of western Europeans in the UK, who are threatened – despite many of them being relatively prosperous – because of their links to the hated EU (even if Brexiter criticisms of the EU are very different to anti-Zionist criticisms of Israel). This paradox appears to have been implicated in Corbyn's failure to recognize the depth of the problem, as one of his collaborators points out: "He's very empathetic, Jeremy, but he's empathetic with the poor, the disadvantaged, the migrant, the people of the bottom of the heap. Happily, that is not the Jewish community in Britain today" (Andrew Murray, quoted in Pogrund & Maguire 2020: 120–21). Nor, of course, was it Israel or the Israelis, who were in a powerful position vis-à-vis the Palestinians; yet many British Jews still felt deeply threatened by the hostility towards the Jewish state. This antisemitism was not always recognized as a form of racism because of its failure to fit the frozen historical concept, but, as Kahn-Harris (2019: 163) comments, the idea "that there is a clear dividing line between political ideology and group identity is naive at best". Indeed, on the other side, anti-Zionism had become an important part of many secular socialist, political Islamist and Muslim identities, and the victimization of Palestinians was often represented as an example of hostility towards Muslims. This case emphasizes features we have seen in the transformation of anti-EU politics into anti-European racism: how national conflicts, involving hostility towards states, can inform political and social hostility towards groups, and how political attachments can become a part of social identities so that threats related to them are experienced as racism. In the 2019 election, however, Labour's antisemitism crisis was also a gift to the Conservatives, enabling them to indulge in a selective antiracism which protected their own racist positions.

"New" immigration policy, old politics

When the UK formally left the EU on 31 January 2020, Johnson (2020) celebrated with a flowery speech about "Global Britain" at Greenwich, but in Ipswich signs appeared saying "It's OK to be white", the "Queens English is the spoken tongue here", hailing the moment "we finally get our great country back", and telling those unwilling to speak English to leave the UK: "You won't have long till our government will implement rules that will put British first. So, best evolve or leave" (Tidman 2020). The contrast highlighted the ambiguity in the new dominant Conservatism, which Ken Spours (2020) characterized as "an eclectic mix of populist English nationalism and nativism; neoliberal deregulation together with a mild Keynesianism" which was "capable of being steered in differing directions at the same time". The Tories' "lack of ideological anchoring, Johnson's adaptability and the Party's desire to both secure power and extend its political bloc" all made shape-shifting "both possible and inevitable". Interpretations of the new regime's immigration dilemmas chimed with this view; despite Johnson's racially compromised record, the expert contributors to Steve Ballinger's collection (2020) saw his election victory as a potential "reset moment" for immigration policy. Much of their case rested on polling which showed that voters were both less concerned about immigration and more positive about its impacts, and some "softening" of Leave–Remain differences on the issue. Such "sustained positive changes", Jonathan Portes (2020) argued, were "well embedded", and it was "against this background that the government will have to work out its post-Brexit policy". It was plausible, he reasoned, that while immigration had not fallen very much, "many perceive that it has fallen, or believe that Brexit means that it will fall considerably in future. It may also be that the prospect of the end of free movement, and hence the increase in the UK's ability to control migration flows (and move towards a more skill-focused system), may be generating more positive attitudes, even if overall numbers do not reduce significantly; in other words it is the perception of 'control', rather than numbers *per se*, that matters." A study suggested that the accusations of racism made against the Leave campaign may also have caused some to soften their attitudes, although this effect was stronger among Remainer than Leaver opponents of immigration (Schwartz *et al.* 2020).

Portes (2020) also remarked on "a marked shift in both the volume and tone of media coverage since the referendum, with considerably fewer negative or 'scare' stories", although he failed to make the obvious link with the ending of sustained right-wing campaigning on the issue. Portes believed that immigration policy was "already heading in a more liberal direction" which could benefit some of the non-EU migrants applying to enter the UK, even if EU migrants faced more restrictive conditions, being in principle no longer able to gain entry to lower-skilled and lower-paid occupations, while those who qualified would have significantly fewer rights, pay large fees and need prospective employers to apply on their behalf. A decision to offer a visa route for British national (overseas) passport holders from Hong Kong to come to the UK, in the event that the Chinese regime implemented its proposed security law there, was also invoked to support the "liberalizing" interpretation. This represented a change when compared to the late 1960s and early 1970s, when the arrival of eastern African Asians (who also held a form of British citizenship without the right to residence in Britain) was widely opposed on explicitly racist grounds. According to Portes (2020), with this commitment Johnson had associated himself "with the legacy of Ted Heath – who did allow entry to Ugandan Asians in 1972 – rather than that of Enoch Powell, Norman Tebbit, and Margaret Thatcher". Similarly optimistically, some pointed to greater ethnic diversity in parliament (although this resulted mostly from an increased proportion of ethnic minority Labour MPs), and that in July 2019 Johnson appointed a minority MP, Javid, as chancellor of the exchequer, the second office of state, replacing him with another minority MP, Rishi Sunak, in 2020; while in Priti Patel he had a home secretary, whose parents were Ugandan Asians, unveiling policies that would reduce immigration. One Conservative glossed this: "We're not just saying, 'You don't have to be racist to think immigration is too high', we're living those values" (Bush 2020).

However, such liberal assessments underestimated the constraints on Johnson's immigration choices as a result of the Brexit realignment of British politics, rather as arguments that May could have "chosen" to keep the UK in the single market had done. The decline in the salience of immigration occurred against an overall backdrop of societal differences on the issue which remained sufficiently strong that the Migration Observatory (2020c) suggested that they could have become the major "point of political cleavage in Britain". Analysis showed that modest *policy* convergence between the views of Leavers and Remainers belied continuing polarization of *emotional* attachments (Duffy *et al.* 2019); voting had further aligned with Brexit identities in the 2019 election compared to 2017 (Surridge 2020); and party polarization over relationships with Europe amounted to "affective polarization" between what were "effectively two tribes", Conservatives and Brexit Party supporters on the one hand, and Labour, Liberal Democrat, SNP and Green voters on the other (Bale & Webb 2020). Even polling interpreted as showing "softening", with sentiment "becoming more positive after the 2016 EU referendum and sustaining at that level ever since", actually showed plenty of signs of continuing opposition: 42 per cent agreed that "we don't talk about immigration enough" while 45 per cent would still prefer reductions in immigration (far more than those who took the opposite views), indicating a strong constituency for anti-immigration politics even after five years in which it had been less prominent (Rolfe, Katwala & Ballinger 2021: 3–4). The conclusion that Johnson's dropping of the numerical target was "an opportunity to move the debate on" belied the probability that the greater preference for "control" over lower numbers registered the continuing resonance of the Vote Leave campaign. Indeed, there was evidence of support for a hard line towards Europeans: BSA polling which asked if EU migrants should have to apply to come and live in the UK found that even half of Remainers agreed. British Social Attitudes analysts interpreted this as "widespread support for ending freedom of movement with the EU" (NatCen 2020: 1–2); however, respondents had not been asked if they agreed with UK citizens also losing rights as a result of this change, which unsurprisingly fewer supported in earlier surveys. In this light, the finding were adapted to not only the continuing anti-immigration consensus but also how academic pollsters reflected the new political climate.

Johnson had won by restoring the Conservatives' hold over the right-wing electorate after their searing experience of losing heavily to Farage in the European elections, and he clearly believed that he needed to keep reminding this base of his alignment with racial nationalism. It was implausible, therefore, to think that immigration policy could be separated from this kind of electoral politics, even if labour shortages might result in tweaks to policy and hostility was refocused away from the numerical goal. The racism of Brexit, Johnson's leadership campaign and the general election could not simply be abandoned once he was secure in power, in the manner of the mythical right-wing social democrat quietly ditching his socialist-sounding rhetoric. Just as increased cabinet diversity acted as a cover for avoiding action to address deep-seated racial inequalities, limited changes to immigration policy were combined with a continuation of the hostile environment for most poor, non-white immigrants, as well as the increasing absorption of Europeans into it. They were also accompanied by serial racist theatre: unlike Trump, who performed his populism on Twitter, Johnson himself did not engage so directly with his electorate, but his regime governed in campaigning mode, with a propaganda operation celebrating the cruelties of the immigration system. Just two months after the election, the government resumed deportation flights to Jamaica, which had been suspended following the Windrush scandal. The February 2020 flight, intended to include some who had lived in the UK since early childhood (but had served prison sentences, in some cases for minor offences), was likely to separate over 40 children from their fathers. It provoked outrage from migrant charities and the opposition, but when interventions saved half those designated from being deported, they prompted Johnson's press secretary to say that "certain parts of Westminster still haven't learned the lessons of the 2019 election" (Proctor & Quinn 2020).

A series of issues confirmed that these "lessons" were central to the regime's propaganda. In early 2020, Farage, who had passed control of his party, soon renamed Reform, to his collaborator Richard Tice, put himself to the fore again with a campaign, quickly supported by the Brexit press, to prevent small boats from France carrying desperate Syrian refugees and others from landing on southern English shores. The numbers involved were small, but Patel was not to be outdone and gave the head of the UK's Maritime Security Centre the grandiose title of "clandestine channel threat commander", while her department looked at the possibility of physically blockading the boats in the English Channel; by 2021, it was reported that they were practising such operations and that the French were collaborating by firing rubber bullets at migrants to prevent them embarking. On social media, official Home Office accounts, as well as those of Johnson, Patel and the party, were used to represent the highly vulnerable migrants only as victims of traffickers. This continued even after 16-year-old Abdulfatah Hamdallah drowned while crossing in an inflatable dinghy, using shovels for oars, in a journey in which no trafficker had been involved. The regime lost no opportunity to remind its racial-nationalist base of its achievements in countering undesirable immigrants, boasting of migrant returns and further deportation flights, while in 2021 it introduced a Nationality and Borders Bill – dubbed the "anti-refugee bill" by organizations which worked with asylum seekers – which (in breach of the Refugee Convention) denied the obligation to assist those who had not come directly from a country where their life or freedom was threatened, provided powers for their offshore detention and criminalized assistance to them even for humanitarian reasons (like saving them from drowning).[1] Promoting the bill, Patel (2021) tweeted an advertisement which linked "failed asylum seekers" with "dangerous foreign criminals" as targets of removal. Similarly, the UK–EU endgame in late 2020 was accompanied by high-powered anti-European aggression in ministerial speeches, social media and the Brexit press, as the government sought to cancel through domestic legislation some of the Northern Ireland elements of the international agreement which it had signed with the EU less than a year previously. When finally a thin trade agreement was struck and the UK left the single market on 31 December 2020, it was the ending of freedom of movement which was the great triumph of this moment for Patel (2020), as she proclaimed that "[a]fter many years of campaigning ... [w]e are delivering on the will of the British people".

The political direction from which the government approached immigration remained, therefore, that of 2016. Despite Johnson's and Patel's boasts of a "fairer" immigration system, the abolition of freedom of movement and denial of the rights to many existing EU citizen residents had no corollary in a general expansion of rights for non-EU migrants (nor, as we saw in Chapter 4, had it ever been intended to). Overall, the government's new proposals represented, as Yeo (2020: 11) put it, "relatively minor amendments to the existing system". The offer to Hong Kongers was certainly a liberal move if considered in isolation, but, as Michaela Benson (2021: 25–6) argues, "the rhetoric of exceptionality" which depicted Hong Kongers as "'good migrants' for 'global Britain'" concealed colonial logics which had long racialized the city's population, as well as the utility of the "exception" for the general presentation of Brexit immigration policy. Government announcements about the scheme recycled "longstanding stereotypes that present the Hong Kong Chinese as hardworking and entrepreneurial, a ready-made model minority who should be welcomed with open arms", infusing new meaning into "an anachronistic and ambiguous legal status, an afterlife of empire that until now had been glaringly empty of significance for its holders". The offer only looked non-racist through a frozen prism; taken together with the hostile environment and the new regime for EU migrants, it represented a selective racism typical of Britain's colonial past. Hong Kong residents, deemed to embody the UK's loyalty to its erstwhile subjects, were worthy migrants; Europeans, linked to the despised EU – and especially eastern Europeans whom Iain Duncan Smith (2021) called "very low-value, low-skilled

---

1. When the West's defeat by the Taliban in Afghanistan in 2021 exposed those who had worked for the UK government and non-governmental organizations to extreme threats, the government had to be pushed by some of its backbenchers into allowing even 5,000 Afghans to come to the UK over the following 12 months; the Home Office had been deporting asylum seekers to Afghanistan, arguing the country was safe, until two weeks earlier.

people" – were unworthy. The idea that Hong Kongers might, unlike Europeans, be induced to show gratitude by voting Conservative, as the party's favourite Jewish and Hindu minorities were increasingly doing, could also have been part of the calculation.

Patel used a Zoom meeting with Jewish leaders to blame travellers for crime (Travellers Times 2020); Jews were a worthy minority, travellers not. At the same time, Johnson showed his attitude to the Tories' least favourite group, Muslims, by postponing the proposed Islamophobia inquiry until after a general commission of racism organized by Munira Mirza, a member of his staff who had been critical of ideas like structural racism and Islamophobia. The need for a new general racism inquiry was unclear: the Stuart Hall Foundation showed that 375 recommendations from previous inquiries lay unimplemented (Ashe 2021: 2). Nevertheless, the Commission on Race and Ethnic Disparities (2021), which had only one token white member, usefully rejected the idea that "institutional racism" was prevalent in the UK, while in his introduction, its chair, Tony Sewell, even managed a revisionist gloss on slavery, which he eventually had to withdraw. The report's inadequacies were widely ridiculed by experts and antiracist campaigners, but it probably served its purpose, as its central ideas were reproduced in the pro-government press, reported largely uncritically on television and recycled on social media. Afterwards, the report on Islamophobia in the Conservative Party (Singh Investigation 2021) was finally published – although the party was not acknowledged as its publisher – and recognized anti-Muslim incidents but not the evidence of widespread anti-Muslim sentiment. It judged Johnson's remarks about Muslim women to be "provocative" but only a minority of the commissioners found them "offensive" or that he had breached the party's code of conduct. Likewise, it exonerated Zac Goldsmith, the 2016 mayoral candidate whose campaign had mobilized Islamophobia. Johnson told the enquiry that as prime minister, he would use different language; having banked the political capital from "burqagate" and defused the threat of serious investigation, he could afford to strike a conciliatory pose.

Although Cummings resigned from Johnson's office 11 months after the 2019 election, immigration remained at the heart of a Vote Leave-style propaganda approach across a range of slick party and government social media operations which no longer depended on his initiative. Indeed, it was not Cummings but Isaac Levido – a protégé of Crosby who had pioneered the undercover racist propaganda approach for Goldsmith – who had run the election campaign. There were strong reasons to believe that this orientation had become central to the Tories' relationship to their electorate. Sobolewska and Ford (2019) warned that, despite the lower salience of immigration as an issue, Britain risked "a heated and divisive argument over immigration and diversity, with substantial electorates holding divisive views on both sides"; while British citizens were "more flexible and pragmatic on the specifics of migration than they are in the abstract", the "complex and politically consequential racial attitudes driven by [the] identity attachments" of many white voters made "playing the race card a continuing electoral temptation". Even if conflict over migration eased, they suggested, "other political conflicts between identity conservatives and identity liberals [were] likely to replace it", risking a general "culture war".

Events in 2020 seemed to confirm this prediction, as the survey by Peter Mitchell (2021: 61–97) shows. When Black Lives Matters protests broke out across the UK, Johnson paid lip service to their concerns but was quick to claim that demonstrations had been "subverted by thuggery" and to embrace a range of symbolic issues from a "culture war" perspective. After protesters in Bristol tore down a statue of the slaver Edward Colston, Johnson hyped a "threat" to statues of Winston Churchill; when the BBC decided to perform an orchestral-only version of "Rule Britannia" at the Last Night of the Proms because the words were widely seen as celebrating slavery, he pronounced this an affront to national tradition; and when vacancies arose on the Equality and Human Rights Commission, he appointed the writer David Goodhart, who had defended the "hostile environment" and together with Eric Kaufmann had developed the idea that "racial self-interest" was not racism. Meanwhile, although there was no election in the offing, the Tories ran a targeted anti-immigration Facebook campaign against Labour MPs in marginal seats (Stone 2020), while nearly 60 Tory MPs formed a group to "ensure that institutional guardians of history and heritage, tasked with safeguarding and celebrating British values, are not tarnished by cultural Marxist dogma, colloquially known as the 'woke agenda'" – although the idea of "cultural Marxism", popularized by the US alt-right, was widely regarded as antisemitic (Mortimer 2020). This group published a book in which the chapter on immigration by Nick Fletcher MP reported, in an account with uncanny echoes of Smethwick, Powell and Farage, that a constituent he spoke to was obliged to live next door to six eastern European men and was therefore "naturally concerned because he could see his community being withered away before his eyes, and his daughter no longer had friends on her street to play with". Citing the man's ritual "I'm not racist, though, Nick", Fletcher added, "[t]his is what decades of the left's rhetoric have done. It has made those who have legitimate concerns scared of being tarnished with words which could cost them friends, a career and a future" (Common Sense Group 2021: 97). Meanwhile, Patel deployed her own experiences to gaslight Black people complaining about the structural racism they experienced in the UK (Sodha 2020). On the extreme right, a new more openly racist, antisemitic organization, Patriotic Alternative, sought to capitalize on the "All Lives Matter" reaction to Black Lives Matter (Murdoch 2020).

The continuing centrality of race was also apparent in response to the Covid-19 pandemic, which began just as the UK formally accomplished Brexit

in January 2020, and which in the course of two years would make vaccine resistance a potent new source of far-right sentiment. Despite the Brexiter mantra
of "controlling borders" and the trade barriers which the UK's exit was about to
create, Johnson's (2020) celebratory speech attacked "bizarre autarkic rhetoric,
when barriers are going up" as a result of the virus. Accordingly his government failed for almost a year to institute anything resembling serious border
controls; it appeared that these were to be used only against "migrants", not the
visitors and returning British citizens who were introducing infection. As the
UK saw the highest death rates in Europe, the government was also reluctant
to acknowledge the structural racism exposed by the disproportionate death
toll among Black and ethnic minority people (Public Health England 2020).
Hate crimes against Chinese people increased, some Tory MPs echoed Trump's
talk of the "China virus" and social media were filled with anti-Chinese abuse
and conspiracy theories, fanned by the extreme right (Hacked Off 2020). As
pandemic policy failures and Brexit disruption undermined the regime's popularity, it had few incentives to abandon the racial-nationalist frame which
had served it so well, and one observer soon commented, "[w]hen levelling up
proves to be impossible, and when the rift in its electoral coalition opens, the
Conservative Party will return to immigration in desperation. It will have to.
With no European Union to act as a receptacle for grievance, immigration will
have to be made more salient again" (Collins 2021). This rather assumed that the
Tories had ceased to pursue immigration themes, which as we have seen was far
from the case. It also assumed that the thin agreements with the EU would stave
off conflict rather than providing new occasions for the regime and its press to
ratchet up Europhobic sentiment. But the point was well made: whether or not
Johnson remained prime minister, "immigration", the core issue of nativist racial
nationalism, would probably return with a vengeance if the Tories' situation became critical. Indeed, by the time of the May 2021 local elections, Johnson was
sending "gunboats" to Jersey to counter French fishermen, and a few months
later, when Brexit's driving away of international lorry drivers resulted in serious shortages, his transport minister gaslighted the Europeans its policies had
driven away, blaming "importing European, often Eastern European, labour un-
dercutting the domestic market" (Sweney 2021), and Johnson (2021) reiterated
that "the way forward for our country is not to just pull the big lever marked
'uncontrolled immigration'".

The fractures in the British union, which Brexit had deepened, also provided
fertile ground for Tory nationalism and raised the danger of renewed racialization. The Conservatives had shown a willingness to subordinate the unity
of the UK's four nations to the overriding demands of leaving the EU, polls
showed their members were willing to sacrifice Northern Ireland and Scotland
to this goal (Smith 2020) and Johnson had joined them when, in order to

secure the withdrawal agreement, he abandoned Northern Ireland Unionists by agreeing to the customs border in the Irish Sea. This reflected a trend in the Conservative Party towards what Michael Kenny and Jack Sheldon (2020) call "a resurgence in the 2016–2019 period of an older belief in a unitarist state, and a new form of pro-Union activism in policy terms". Against commentators who depicted Britain's Conservatives "as having abandoned their unionist vocation", they identified "the coalescence of a more assertive and activist strain of unionist sentiment" in reaction to Scottish and Irish nationalism. In turn, under Johnson's premiership, this assertiveness stimulated further support for Scottish independence and Irish reunification, while even in Wales an independence movement made headway. Support for the non-English nationalisms was magnified by the prominence of the devolved administrations during the pandemic, since they were perceived as having performed better than Johnson's government had in England. Elections for the Scottish Parliament in 2021 returned a majority committed to a second independence referendum, which would probably be refused by the UK government. In this case observers widely foresaw a new Scottish crisis, in which English nationalism could be the "wild card" (Sobolewska & Ford 2020: 341); although Anthony Barnett (2021), arguing for a "certainty" of eventual independence which observers increasingly credited, believed it could release a new progressive English national project, in the short term it looked more likely to provide new scope for the regressive Anglo-British nationalism which Brexit had strengthened. It would be logical for the Conservatives to emphasize the English character of their project, even as their Scottish party pressed a more conventional Unionist case; renewed conflict with the SNP, including perhaps the incipient racialization of 2015, would also have the advantage of squeezing out Labour once more and boosting the Tories' chances of retaining power through the decade.

Despite these incentives for the Brexit Tory regime to maintain the ethos of 2016, it was also possible that its weaker international position, after its ally Trump was defeated in 2020, would inhibit its nationalist extravagance, especially in relation to Ireland with which the incoming Democratic administration had special links. Trump's defeat delivered a final blow to the already failing Brexiter fantasy that a close relationship with him would deliver a favourable early trade deal with the USA to replace (at least in their propaganda) the single market. His exit was also symbolically damaging in a more general sense; Johnson had behaved sycophantically towards Trump, and members of the Biden administration had expressed contempt for both Brexit and the Tory leader. The situation worsened for Johnson after the failed insurrection of 6 January 2021, which was a cue for sustained protestations by his acolytes that he was not, after all, Britain's Trump. At this moment Matthew Goodwin, having joined the right-wing think tank the Legatum Institute, was quick to protest that "Johnson is socially liberal at heart, Trump is authoritarian. Johnson is instinctive free trader, Trump is protectionist. Johnson is pro-migration at heart, Trump is xenophobe" (Goodwin 2021). The reader will surely be sceptical and note the reliance on assertions about a "heart" which, when it came to politics, many doubted that Johnson possessed. As this book has emphasized, terms like "xenophobe" and "authoritarian" do not describe heart or soul so much as behaviour. On this criterion, Johnson had done as much as anyone to bring racism, migration barriers and authoritarianism (and for that matter protectionism, with the erection of extensive barriers to European trade) to the very centre of British politics. If Trump was a US Johnson, Farage and Tommy Robinson rolled into one, Johnson *was* his partial British equivalent, who had reconciled Conservativism with Faragism, even if he lacked Trump's tendency to openly embrace the street-level extreme right.

Johnson had been central to the Brexiters' referendum and election victories, but by the end of 2021 was turning into an electoral liability. His chaotic, opportunist governing style damaged his credibility, and the Tories' polling weakened, including among Leavers and in the "red wall" areas which had helped provide their majority. Johnson faced an attempt to remove him by some of his backbenchers, and although he fought to hold on to office – offering culture-war "red meat", including the use of the Royal Navy against refugee dinghies in the English Channel – many believed that he would be ousted in 2022 or before the next election which was due by 2024. A new prime minister (who might even be one of the ethnic-minority figures that Johnson had promoted) might project greater competence, but they were unlikely to change the regime's politics. All the possible candidates were Brexiters and supported the three major repressive laws going through parliament as the premiership crisis erupted, which restricted the rights to vote and protest as well as refugee rights. Although majority public support for Brexit itself had disappeared, the Conservatives' electoral base was still drawn overwhelmingly from the large pro-Brexit minority, and a racial-nationalist approach to immigration and the European Union was likely to remain *de rigueur* for any new leader.

CONCLUSION

Political Racism has shown how distinctive forms of right-wing agency to which political racism was central helped to produce, in the UK between 2016 and 2021, fundamental – but regressive – constitutional, economic, political and social change. As the Introduction made clear, there is no suggestion that these forces provide a complete explanation of Brexit and its aftermath, but the book has demonstrated that they made important contributions to the emergence of new structures in the UK's relations with the EU, with major effects on its economy, society and wider international relations as well as its party system and electoral patterns. The study's core idea has been used to simultaneously highlight political action as a distinctive component of contemporary racism and distinctive new forms of racism as a key element in the stronger nationalist trend in mainstream right-wing politics. In these ways the book has contributed, the author hopes, to studies of both racism and right-wing politics, as well as to the analysis of Brexit and its aftermath, in ways which I summarize below.

Political racism in global and comparative perspective

This book has shown that in an age where open racism is frowned upon, political actors are more central than ever to its persistence, and that they are more than ever innovative in actively stirring and renewing racist ideas. While ruthlessly exploiting its potentials for immediate goals, they covertly rekindle old hatreds, construct new racialized targets and help to resediment racial sentiments in society. The political actors who mobilize racism are not only organized parties and their leaders (which I have broadly categorized as mainstream, radical and extreme right, while stressing the networking between them and the tendency for mainstream right parties to be transformed in a far-right direction), ad hoc campaigns (like the Leave organizations), networks and movements but also mass media, social media actors ("ordinary" users as well as public figures) and street-level actors (both organized and unorganized). The study has focused on campaigning around electoral contests, in which established actors and media tend to be dominant, but it has also shown how the loci of racist action are transformed as mainstreaming develops, and how political campaigning interacts with popular and policy racism, which also independently affect social relations and especially the lives and experiences of minorities.

The discussion has also focused on specific ways in which political actors have moved racism on, for example by consolidating the racializations of the ideas of immigrant and asylum seeker, looking to express these in apparently neutral, inferentially racist numerical terms, and extending racism's specific targets, notably in the directions of Muslims (an internationally widespread phenomenon) and Europeans (a peculiarity of British nationalist racism). In a global perspective, whiteness clearly remains racism's anchoring concept, people of colour are its main targets and nativism is its prime contemporary expression; but we have seen that far-right racism, especially but not only in its mainstreamed form, has shown a great capacity for flexible or what I have called "pick 'n' mix" enemy construction, favouring some old minorities, even those of colour, while intensifying hostility to new others, including some white people. It does this in order both to construct political coalitions and to obfuscate and deflect antiracist resistance. In a sense, racism is always selective, but the refinement of selective racism and its increasing combination with selective antiracism are striking features of the British case which have general relevance.

The concept of political racism evidently has wide applicability. Forms of it could be traced to the population policies of historic as well as recent empires and found in totalitarian and authoritarian regimes earlier in the modern period. However, the forms that I have discussed are most developed in contemporary democracies and democratizing states, even if they also have echoes in fully authoritarian states like China and pseudo-democracies like Russia. Their new importance is part of the global trend for the rise of authoritarian nationalism and the increasingly transnational right wing which is feeding this. This trend includes reactions to the globalization of economy and society, to the internationalization of state power (of which the EU is a uniquely developed form), to a rule-based international order and to cosmopolitan ideas of social justice, environmental action, democracy and (we have seen in the Covid-19 pandemic) public health. However, the instantiation of these trends is, as always, highly specific to national contexts. States, societies and political cultures have distinct histories, and traditions of political racism vary greatly, as do their contemporary modes, which is why this study has had a particular national focus.

In this context, the Brexit reaction against regional integration is a very specific instance of the general trend against internationalization, which is unique (to date) in its extraction of a major state from a developed, complex international union, just as the EU is a unique example of such a union. Brexit also grew out of historic specificities of the UK – its imperial and military histories, its distinctive multinational character, its largely unreformed state and electoral institutions – as well as the specific political crises of the twenty-first century which this book has analysed. In these senses, the British case may not provide a close model for analysing developments in other states. The USA appears to be the closest comparator, not least because of the co-incidence of Brexit and Trump, the extensive links between Brexiters and the US right and the similarly anachronistic electoral institutions which enable minority rule. Yet, comparing the two quickly leads us to important differences, such as the higher profile of the extreme right and the more widespread resort to violence in the USA, which partly reflect its more extreme domestic (rather than imperial) history of racism. Similar points could be made in a comparison of Britain and India, where the anti-Muslim racism of the Hindu nationalist regime has developed with brutal-ity and violence on a scale not seen in the UK. In the European context, political racism has been part of a widespread trend towards the rise of radical right parties, leading to transformations of mainstream right parties in a far-right di-rection, although (as of 2021) these have mostly not gone as far as in the UK except in Hungary and Poland.

The British case also raises questions about the relationships of racism, na-tionalism and secessionism. This discussion has shown that, while nativism itself involves an ideological fusion of racism and nationalism, its political mobiliza-tion became most effective when it was recombined with the British nationalist project, which itself depended on this recombination for its success. This in turn led to the broadening and deepening of racism, which in turn fed the nationalist movement and regime. There were, therefore, dynamic interrelationships be-tween racism and nationalism, despite the extent to which they were co-defined from the outset. The case also raises the specific role of secessionist conflict in the authoritarian, political-racist transformation of the right. We will never know whether a far-right tendency would have achieved dominance in the UK through political racism alone, without the project of seceding from the EU, but in reality Johnson achieved his premiership through it and his regime's charac-ter reflected this. The case appears to demonstrate that while political racism can be a powerful multiplier of anti-internationalization secessionism, giving its nationalism a hard edge and a sustained campaigning focus, secession can also be an important multiplier of political racism and far-right politics. It is surely interesting that in the aftermath of this secession, the UK was the only western European state in which a radically transformed mainstream party re-mained in power. On the face of it, this kind of effect seems unlikely in cases of "small-country" secessionism within major states, although a racist big-nation reaction to regional secessionism, which was an incipient feature in the UK, could also be seen in Spain, where the stalemated Catalan conflict helped fuel the rise of the far-right Vox party, with tendencies among some supporters on both sides of the conflict to racialize the other. Political racism has certainly played a central role in other countries without secessionism – indeed, Salvini made the Lega a more powerful racial-nationalist force while abandoning northern secession from Italy – but secessionist conflict can provide incentives to mobilize it. Varieties of constitutional politics have also been combined with political racism in the rise of the US right, from electoral and Supreme Court gerrymandering to Trump's "stolen election" claims, and in Modi's rule, through discriminatory citizenship legislation against Muslims. It can be argued that divisive and intractable constitutional issues are likely to play roles in future cases, as secessionist ideas become more influential in the USA (Walt 2021) and elsewhere.

While the distinctiveness of the Brexit experience should lead us to emphasize its limitations as a general model of political racism, making obvious the need to examine the variations in its contexts, scope and forms, the techniques through which Brexit was achieved are more likely to be comparable across cases, given the ease with which ideas and practices circulate across borders and the transnational character of the right-wing universe. In this context, the expertise which the British right has developed in exploiting and obfuscating racism could prove of wider importance. Leaders like Farage and Johnson have found that even occasional forays into targeted hostility go a long way in cultivating racial-nationalist audiences who understand the constraints of political correctness under which they operate. Vote Leave showed that when blatant racism cannot be elaborated extensively in leaders' speeches, it can still be spewed out on an industrial scale in social media propaganda, which is even more effective for stimulating user-authored content. False reassurances can be offered to threatened minorities, which may serve to deflect opposition, at least for the duration of an electoral campaign. Some minorities can be partially co-opted into political-racist projects in order to similarly confuse, and vigorous complaints about the racism which they suffer may serve to mask the right's own more extensive strategic racism and its lack of interest in addressing structural racism. The weaponization of opposition to political correctness, repackaged as "anti-wokeness", can be used as a means of attacking antiracism, and anti-antiracism has now become a key method of sustaining racist support. None of these methods are original or exclusive to Brexit politics, but they have been extensively honed not only by its politicians and journalists but also by its organic social media intellectuals as they verse themselves in the ideological finer points, all of them making distinctive British contributions to the increasingly global arena of racist ideas and practice.

This book has argued that for organized actors, and especially for radicalized mainstream right parties, political racism is a strategic method more than it is an ideological commitment. This was obvious, in the case of Brexit, in the way that Boris Johnson prevaricated over which side to support in the referendum before choosing Leave. For him, as a consummate political opportunist, this was primarily a career decision; his overriding goal was to achieve the premiership and, through some ups and downs, he used Brexit to achieve that. However, he has continued to be regarded as a shape-shifter and is regarded as having partially set aside some Conservative orthodoxy, for example in economics, in his drive to maintain power. However, this book has shown that, despite some liberal optimism, there have been definite limits to the flexibility which he has shown around immigration. The conclusion we can draw from this is that while the use of political-racist methods may be a choice for leaders and parties, that choice has consequences, narrowing their further options in a path-dependent way. In the case of a radical, nationally transformative movement like Brexit, this may transform parties' and leaders' core interests and electorates, pulling them further into the racial-nationalist ideological corner and, because of the resistance to the radical policies which they are forced to pursue, lead them more towards authoritarian means. In this way, this study could point to deepening connections between racial nationalism and authoritarianism in the contemporary right.

Understanding racism in Brexit and the nationalist Tory regime

As I stressed in the Introduction, the book's focus on organized political racism as a major driver is distinctive in the field of Brexit analysis, which typically avoids the very concept of racism and largely distinguishes immigration politics from it. The book has demonstrated how this dominant approach, which I argue involves denial even when not accompanied by apologetics, has been damaging both empirically and analytically, and I have presented an alternative narrative which has led to conclusions which alter the way in which Brexit and its consequences are grasped.

The book has shown that Brexiters, who since 2016 have included almost the whole of the ruling Conservative Party, have themselves understood anti-immigration politics as a principal meaning behind their project and in particular as central to relationships with their electorate. Their triumph over European migration has arguably been the most striking single policy success ever achieved by the political-racist tradition in the Conservative Party and the far right – since it has undermined the basis of around half of the UK's immigration as well as the status of millions of people in British society – and in this sense it can be seen as a culmination of its whole history from Powell to Farage and Johnson which was discussed in Chapter 2. Throughout the whole period, certainly, this politics had reproduced policy racism over immigration and citizenship, alongside the growing normative and legal antiracism to which it has had to adapt, but this was mostly the result of defensive strategic decisions by Conservative and Labour governments which reacted to or anticipated the right's demands for stricter control. During 2016–21, in contrast, proactive political racism finally came into its own, achieving the huge symbolic and practical victory of ending free movement. To express the argument in a nutshell: 23 June 2016 was an even more important racist moment in modern British politics than 20 April 1968 when Powell spoke in Wolverhampton. This study has shown that like his speech, but unlike any of the Conservative (or even UKIP) general election campaigns of the previous half-century, the racism-charged referendum electrified politics, stirred popular aggression and sent shockwaves through the political elite. However, we have seen that its implementation was more organized and its effects ultimately more concentrated and decisive than the post-Powell outcomes. Powell failed in his manifest aims of drastically limiting and reversing migration and his lack of a coherent political strategy led to his marginalization, despite his great impact on popular racism, his indirect impacts on policy racism and the inspiration he has provided for generations of rightists. Successive Tory leaders learned from this outcome – and the polarization which his extreme right acolytes produced as they were countered by the first mass antiracist movement – that in exploiting his legacy, they should nevertheless avoid his overt, emotive racist appeal. We have seen therefore that in no general election between 1968 and 2016 (not even in 2015, barely 12 months before the EU referendum) did the Tories ever campaign primarily on immigration, let alone in such a massive, concentrated, emotive and aggressive way; nor could the secondary elements of racial politics in their campaigns be argued to have delivered them victory. Likewise, when Conservatives, the new radical right UKIP and the extreme right revived anti-immigrant racism from the 1990s onwards, we have seen that they did so chiefly in the euphemistic, inferentially racist language that I have called "numerical racism", albeit combined with sufficient attention to specific targets to arouse their voters. Farage was certainly the most effective strategic racist after Powell, as he popularized the fusion of anti-immigration politics and Europhobia, but even he only laid some of the foundations for the referendum victory, which occurred only when Johnson, Gove and other mainstream Conservative leaders took up the mantle and allowed Cummings to go all-out on immigration.

A central contribution of the book has therefore been to show precisely why 23 June 2016 had such profound effects. It has demonstrated that, building on Farage's methods and the momentum he had helped to create (but with the man himself outside Johnson's main Vote Leave camp), during the referendum the Leave campaign and its allied press campaigns orchestrated a coalition of anti-immigration and nationalist opinion to win. Because they carried this out through an exceptional mobilization of extreme propaganda in what was in any case a highly consequential contest, they helped arouse a climate of aggression and intimidation which deepened its polarizing effects. The styles and tropes of the propaganda and press coverage were not new – they had been used by the same or similar actors over the previous half-century, as the mimicking of Powell underlined – but here they were used with unprecedented scale, intensity and concentration, taking full advantage of the new opportunities created by social media.

This book has therefore argued that this represented a historic step-change in the political mobilization of racism compared to the election campaigns of the previous half-century, with almost certainly decisive consequences not only for the immediate electoral outcome but also for the types of Brexit, Conservative regime and policy environment which emerged in its aftermath. Having demonstrated, I hope conclusively, that the widespread perception of Farage as the referendum's prime racemonger does not survive a serious examination of the evidence, we are left with the reality that racism was not a fringe or secondary feature but rather a central factor in Leave's success. If this part of the argument is accepted, then it is unconvincing to treat the rest of the Brexit crisis merely as the playing out of constitutional and economic conflicts. I have shown that, not only for May and Johnson but also for Corbyn and much of the Labour right, the ending of free movement (the goal in which immigration control was crystallized) became an immovable "red line" which fundamentally limited the scope of the domestic conflict and therefore also the international negotiations over these wider issues and in the end proved the decisive frame within which their outcomes were structured.

This is not, of course, to say that nothing could have been different. The margin in 2016 itself was close enough that several factors, individually or in combination, could have changed the result, although I have argued that a narrow Remain victory would have triggered different forms of the same polarization. After the referendum, something like May's late 2018 agreement with the EU could have been agreed, and while it would still have been a racist, no-free-movement Brexit, it would have been less "hard" in other respects than Johnson's 2019 version. However, too much commentary has been overly influenced by these secondary issues, and also by polling showing how the salience of and hardness of attitudes to immigration declined after 2016, into believing that the lesser visibility of racism meant that it became less significant over the next few years. On the contrary, this book has argued, the changes in the salience and invisibility of immigration largely reflected the fact that organized racism had won and was perceived to have done so: freedom of movement was ending, fewer Europeans were coming to the UK and more were leaving and immigration was seen as being "controlled" by the politicians who had promised to control it. The racist campaigning that had accelerated in the decade beforehand and especially during the referendum rapidly decelerated after its victory; the correlation of its absence with the "softening" over immigration is surely *prima facie* negative evidence that organized political racism makes a very significant contribution to anti-immigration attitudes. Moreover, Leave voters widely understood the main demand for immigration control as embedded in the direction that Brexit was taking and the politics of the new regime, even if opposition politicians and commentators with other interests have too often contrived to gloss over this. I have also demonstrated that in order for Tory nationalists to take power, consolidate it and rule into the 2020s, their regime repeatedly returned to campaigning mode against migrants, refugees and selected minorities while deepening and institutionally embedding the hostility to Europeans that the Europhobes had promoted. If the 2019 general election did not involve an all-out or decisively racist campaign like 2016's, this was because it did not need to: politics had already changed, racism was baked into the "oven-ready" Brexit which just needed to be "done" and overt racist campaigning required no more than a secondary role. If 2016 was a fundamental step-change in political racism, 2019 was certainly a stepping down but one which kept the earlier campaign very much in focus.

There are questions about the British experience which this book raises but has not answered except in indirect ways. Why did Brexit's opponents fail to prevent its victory despite its racist thrust, and what does this failure mean for the future, especially for the large sections of society which continue to regard Brexit as illegitimate, for Europeans whose position has fundamentally deteriorated and for migrants and people of colour who are the targets of the nationalist Tory regime's wider anti-immigrant, racist and anti-antiracist policies? Obviously these are very large issues which cannot be fully addressed in a few concluding remarks. I have alluded to the gradual strengthening of antiracism since the late twentieth century, but clearly this did little to slow the Europhobic, anti-immigrant momentum in the decade before Brexit. I examined the strategic failures of the Stronger In and Labour/union campaigns in 2016 and their general avoidance of direct confrontation with their opponents' racist approach, and I showed how these largely carried over into the 2016–19 debates, in which supporters of freedom of movement were a minority even among opposition MPs. Although there were pro-European organizations in the UK before 2016, popular Europeanism was weak, and the Remain campaigns did not seriously try to arouse it. This situation certainly changed when a very large pro-European movement developed in 2018–19, but it ultimately failed to shift public opinion more than marginally and subsided after Johnson's election win, even if it helped sediment a strong Remainer identity which shows signs of having lasting legacies. Likewise, no general community of the many Europeans of different nationalities in the UK existed in 2016, as previously there was little that required them to recognize common interests; Brexit's apparently sudden threat to them was insufficient to galvanize a movement in the course of a few weeks, especially since Vote Leave sought to pre-empt criticism on the issue. Within the post-2016 pro-European movement, Europeans in the UK themselves developed strong new organizations; unlike those of the wider movement, these have continued closer to scale because they have had to deal with the huge fallout of Brexit for millions of people.

A big problem is that although Europeanism, among both Britons and EU citizens, has been strongly inflected with antiracism, it has not always been strongly connected with organized antiracism; it has largely been a movement of the white centre-left and has not engaged strongly with communities of colour, even if established pro-migrant organizations have taken up the cause of newly vulnerable EU citizens. Similarly, while supporters of the growing antiracist movement are overwhelmingly opposed to Brexit, it has not featured strongly in their campaigns, which have focused on injustices to people of colour as well as more fundamental historical and institutional decolonization. Finally, although opposition to both racism and Brexit are overwhelmingly majority positions among Labour members and voters, one of the few continuities in its leaderships' positions in recent years has been a reluctance to openly challenge anti-immigrant politics at key moments. The new leadership elected in 2020 maintained this orientation, focusing on regaining the older electorate in so-called "red wall" seats, that is, majority-Leaver constituencies in the north of England, even at the expense of its largely Remainer voting base. Yet as Tarik Abou-Chadi, Reto Mitteregger and Cas Mudde (2021) argue, current transformations of the working class offer social-democratic parties a viable route to create pluralist coalitions rather than condemning them to chase the mainstreamed far right for the racial-nationalist vote. In short, the linkages of political racism with Brexit and Tory nationalism which I have analysed in this book have also not been fully recognized in oppositional discourses in the UK, and paradoxically, a simplistic version of the idea of structural racism could also be playing a role in this failure, obscuring the role of organized racist agency in reproducing structures of race. The antiracist forces in society will need to recognize and confront the powerful structures which political racism has created if this deeply regressive phase in British history is to come to an end.

BIBLIOGRAPHY

Abou-Chadi, T., R. Mitteregger & C. Mudde 2021. *Left behind by the Working Class? Social Democracy's Electoral Crisis and the Rise of the Radical Right*. Berlin: Friedrich Ebert Stiftung.

Ahmed, S. 2010. "Feminist killjoys (and other willful subjects)". *S&F Online* 8(3), http://sfonline.barnard.edu/polyphonic/print_ahmed.htm.

Albrecht, S., M. Fielitz & N. Thurston 2019. "Introduction". In M. Fielitz & S. Albrecht (eds), *Post-digital Cultures of the Far Right*, 7–22. Bielefeld: Transcript Verlag.

Amnesty International UK 2017. "Black and Asian women MPs abused more online". https://www.amnesty.org.uk/online-violence-women-mps.

Anderson, P. 2004. "A flag of convenience? Discourse and motivations of the London-based Eurosceptic press". In R. Harmsen & M. Spiering (eds), *Euroscepticism: Party Politics, National Identity and European Integration*, 151–70. Amsterdam: Rodopi.

Anderson, P. 2021. "The Breakaway". *London Review of Books*, 21 January.

Anon (@MaidenSarah1) 2019. Tweet, 16 December. https://twitter.com/maidensarah1/status/1206516628286005248?s=12.

Anthias, F. & N. Yuval-Davis 1983. "Contextualizing feminism: ethnic, gender and class divisions". *Feminist Review* 15(1): 62–75.

Ashe, S. 2021. *SHF Race Report: 40 Years of Tackling Racial Inequality in Britain*. London: Stuart Hall Foundation.

Asthana, A. 2016. "Restricting immigration will be at heart of Brexit deal, Theresa May says". *The Guardian*, 31 August.

Awan, I. & I. Zempi 2018. "'You all look the same': Non-Muslim men who suffer Islamophobic hate crime in the post-Brexit era". *European Journal of Criminology* 17(5): 585–602.

Bale, T. 2013. "More and more restrictive – but not always populist: explaining variation in the British Conservative Party's stance on immigration and asylum". *Journal of Contemporary European Studies*. https://doi.org/10.1080/14782804.2013.766474.

Bale, T. 2016. *The Conservative Party from Thatcher to Cameron*. Second edition. Cambridge: Polity.

Bale, T. *et al.* 2017. "Who leads and who follows? The symbiotic relationship between UKIP and the Conservatives – and populism and Euroscepticism". *Politics* 38(3): 378–90.

Bale, T. & C. Kaltwasser (eds) 2021. *Riding the Populist Wave: Europe's Mainstream Right in Crisis.* Cambridge: Cambridge University Press.

Bale, T. & P. Webb 2020. "Research with party members offers an important clue about how to heal Brexit divisions". The Conversation. https://theconversation.com/brexit-and-migration-our-new-research-highlights-fact-free-news-coverage-109309.

Ballinger, S. (ed.) 2020. *The Reset Moment: Immigration in the New Parliament.* London: British Future/King's College Institute for Policy Studies.

Barclay, A. 2019. "The Chief Rabbi's extraordinary intervention and the collapse of Labour's Jewish support". Blog, 9 November. https://blogs.lse.ac.uk/religionglobalsociety/2019/11/the-chief-rabbis-extraordinary-intervention-and-the-collapse-of-labours-jewish-support.

Barnard, C. & F. Costello 2020. "Deportation and 'reconnection' of homeless EU nationals in the UK". London: UK in a Changing Europe.

Barnard, C. & F. Costello 2021. "EUSS: paper applications to a digital scheme". London: UK in a Changing Europe.

Barnett, A. 2021. "Introduction: 'Tom Nairn is the one'". In T. Nairn, *The Break-up of Britain.* Third edition, ix–xxiii. London: Verso.

BBC News 2018a. "Brexit: Theresa May's 'letter to the nation' in full". 25 November. https://www.bbc.co.uk/news/uk-politics-46333338.

BBC News 2018b. "Boris Johnson faces criticism over burka 'letter box' jibe". 6 August. https://www.bbc.co.uk/news/uk-politics-45083275.

Begum, N. 2018. "Minority ethnic attitudes and the 2016 EU Referendum". London: UK in a Changing Europe.

Behr, R. 2016. "How remain failed: the inside story of a doomed campaign". *The Guardian,* 5 July.

Bell, D. 2011. *The Idea of Greater Britain: Empire and the Future of World Order, 1860–1900.* Princeton, NJ: Princeton University Press.

Bell, D. 2020. *Dreamworlds of Race: Empire and the Utopian Destiny of Anglo-America.* Cambridge: Cambridge University Press.

Bell, D. & S. Vucetic 2019. "Brexit, CANZUK, and the legacy of empire". *British Journal of Politics and International Relations* 21(2): 367–82.

Benson, M. 2020. "Brexit and the class politics of bordering: the British in France and European belongings". *Sociology* 54(3): 501–17.

Benson, M. 2021. "Hong Kongers and the coloniality of British citizenship from decolonization to Brexit and the foundation of 'Global Britain'". http://www.research.lancs.ac.uk/portal/en/publications/-(64c16bfa-b231-4bab-a96e-181a882c0bc7).

Benson, M. & C. Lewis 2019. "Brexit, British people of colour in the EU-27 and everyday racism in Britain and Europe". *Ethnic and Racial Studies* 42(13): 2211–28.

Berkeley, B., O. Khan & M. Ambikaipaker 2005. *What's New about the New Immigrants?* York: Joseph Rowntree Foundation.

Bhambra, G. 2017. "Brexit, Trump, and 'methodological whiteness': on the misrecognition of race and class". *British Journal of Sociology* 68(S1): S214–32.

Breeze, R. 2018. "'Enemies of the people': populist performances in the *Daily Mail* reporting of the Article 50 case". *Discourse, Context & Media* 25: 60–67.

British Future 2016. Report of the Inquiry into Securing the Status of EEA+ Nationals in the UK. London: British Future.

Brooks, T. 2017. "Why immigration faded from view in election 2017". In E. Thorsen, D. Jackson & D. Lilleker (eds), *UK Election Analysis 2017: Media, Voters and the Campaign*. Bournemouth: Centre for the Study of Journalism, Culture and Community.

Bueltmann, T. 2020. Experiences and Impact of the EU Settlement Scheme: Report on the3million Settled Status Survey. Newcastle: the3million/Northumbria University.

Bulat, A. 2017. "'We are not tolerant as a nation, but we want others to tolerate us': Romanians' experiences of discrimination and their attitudes towards British people". *Euxeinos: Governance and Culture in the Black Sea Region* 22: 25–43.

Bulman, M. 2019. "Boris Johnson faces backlash and claims of racism after saying migrants should not 'treat UK as their own'". *The Independent*, 9 December.

Burke, M. 2019. *Colorblind Racism*. Cambridge: Polity.

Bush, S. 2020. "There is growing unease in the Tory party but while it's directed at Dominic Cummings, the PM is safe". *New Statesman*, 26 February.

Cadwalladr, C. 2019. "Video reveals Steve Bannon links to Boris Johnson". *The Observer*, 22 June.

Cameron, D. 2019. *For the Record*. London: William Collins.

Carmichael, S. & C. Hamilton 1967. *Black Power: The Politics of Liberation*. New York: Vintage.

Centre for Research in Communication and Culture 2016. *Media Coverage of the EU Referendum (Report 5)*. Loughborough: CRCC.

Centre for Social Investigation 2018. "CSI Brexit 4: people's stated reasons for voting leave or remain". Oxford: Nuffield College.

Chakelian, A. 2016. "The racial politics of Zac Goldsmith's London mayoral campaign". *New Statesman*, 6 April.

Cheng Leidig, E. 2019. "Immigrant, nationalist and proud: a Twitter analysis of Indian diaspora supporters for Brexit and Trump". *Media and Communication* 7(1): 77–89.

Collins, P. 2021. "Why Boris Johnson's Tories will want to keep immigration in the spotlight". *New Statesman*, 6 January.

Commission on Race and Ethnic Disparities 2021. *Commission on Race and Ethnic Disparities: The Report*. London: HM Government.

Common Sense Group 2021. *Common Sense: Conservative Thinking for a Post-liberal Age*. London.

Community Security Trust 2019. *Engine of Hate: The Online Networks behind the Labour Party's Antisemitism Crisis*. London.

Community Security Trust 2020. *Antisemitic Incidents Report 2019*. London: Community Security Trust.

Conboy, M. 2006. *Tabloid Britain: Constructing a Community through Language*. London: Routledge.

Cooper, L. 2021. *Authoritarian Contagion: The Global Threat to Democracy*. Bristol: Bristol University Press.

Cooper, L. & C. Cooper 2020. "Get Brexit done: the new political divides of England and Wales at the 2019 election". *Political Quarterly* 91(4): 751–61.

Copsey, N. *et al.* 2013. *Anti-Muslim Hate Crime and the Far Right.* Middlesbrough: Teesside University Centre for Fascist, Anti-Fascist and Post-Fascist Studies.

Corcoran, H. & K. Smith 2016. *Hate Crime, England and Wales, 2015/16.* London: Home Office.

Cousins, G. & R. Fine 2012. "A common cause: reconnecting the study of racism and antisemitism". *European Societies* 14(2): 166–85.

Cowley, J. 2017. "Nigel Farage: the arsonist in exile". *New Statesman*, 8 December.

Cowley, P. & D. Kavanagh 2018. *The British General Election of 2017.* London: Palgrave Macmillan.

Cummings, D. 2016. "On the referendum #20: the campaign, physics and data science. Vote Leave's 'Voter Intention Collection System' (VICS) now available for all". https://dominiccummings.com/2016/10/29/on-the-referendum-20-the-campaign-physics-and-data-science-vote-leaves-voter-intention-collection-system-vics-now-available-for-all.

Cummings, D. 2017. "On the referendum #21: Branching histories of the 2016 referendum and 'the frogs before the storm'". https://dominiccummings.wordpress.com/2017/01/09/on-the-referendum-21-branching-histories-of-the-2016-referendum-and-the-frogs-before-the-storm-2.

Curtice, J. 2017. "The vote to leave the EU: litmus test or lightning rod?". In E. Clery, J. Curtice & R. Harding (eds), *British Social Attitudes 34*, 157–80. London: NatCen Social Research.

Curtice, J., S. Fisher & P. English 2021. "The geography of a Brexit election: how constituency context and the electoral system shaped the outcome". In R. Ford, T. Bale, W. Jennings & P. Surridge (eds), *The British General Election of 2019*, 461–94. London: Palgrave Macmillan.

Cutts, D., R. Ford & M. Goodwin 2011. "Anti-immigrant, politically disaffected or still racist after all? Examining the attitudinal drivers of extreme right support in Britain in the 2009 European elections". *European Journal of Political Research* 50(3): 418–40.

Cutts, D. *et al.* 2020. "Brexit, the 2019 general election and the realignment of British politics". *Political Quarterly* 91(1): 7–23.

Dathan, M. 2015. "Nigel Farage: some Muslims want to kill us". *The Independent*, 12 March.

Davidson, T. & M. Berezin 2018. "Britain first and the UK Independence Party: social media and movement-party dynamics". *Mobilization: An International Quarterly* 23(4): 485–510.

Davis, A. 2018. *India and the Anglosphere: Race, Identity and Hierarchy in International Relations.* London: Routledge.

D'Ancona, M. 2019. "Bannon's Britain: Boris Johnson, Nigel Farage and Tommy Robinson are enmeshed in the new network politics of the Right". https://members.tortoisemedia.com/2019/09/28/bannons-britain/content.html?

DCMS (Department of Culture, Media and Sport) 2018. *Vote Leave/50 Million Ads.* London: DCMS.

De Quetteville, H. 2021. "EU citizens make up a third of the population of some British towns". *Daily Telegraph*, 25 June.

Deacon, D. & D. Wring 2016. "The UK Independence Party, populism and the British news media: competition, collaboration or containment?" *European Journal of Communication* 31(2): 169–84.

Deacon, D. *et al.* 2016. *UK News Coverage of the 2016 EU Referendum: Report 1 (6–18 May 2016).* Loughborough: Centre for Research in Communications and Culture.

Deltapoll 2020. Survey Results. http://www.deltapoll.co.uk/wp-content/uploads/2020/02/Deltapoll-Immigration200130.pdf.

Dougan, M. 2017. "The 'Brexit' threat to the Northern Irish border: clarifying the constitutional framework". In M. Dougan (ed.), *The UK after Brexit: Legal and Policy Challenges.* London: Intersentia.

Dranville, R. 2016. "The visual propaganda of the Brexit leave campaign". https://hyperallergic.com/310631/the-visual-propaganda-of-the-brexit-leave-campaign.

Duffy, B. *et al.* 2019. *Divided Britain? Polarisation and Fragmentation Trends in the UK.* London: The Policy Institute.

Duncan Smith, I. 2021. Interview, BBC *Newsnight*, 31 December 2020. *The London Economic*, 1 January.

Durrheim, K. *et al.* 2018. "How racism discourse can mobilise right-wing populism: the construction of identity and alliance in reactions to UKIP's Brexit 'Breaking Point' campaign". *Journal of Community and Applied Social Psychology* 28: 385–405.

Eatwell, R. & M. Goodwin 2018. *National Populism: The Revolt against Liberal Democracy.* London: Pelican.

Eddo-Lodge, R. 2017. *Why I'm No Longer Talking to White People about Race.* London: Bloomsbury.

Edgerton, D. 2018. "Preface to the paperback edition". In *The Rise and Fall of the British Nation: A Twentieth-century History.* London: Penguin.

Edgerton, D. 2020. "Britain's persistent racism cannot simply be explained by its imperial history". *The Guardian*, 24 June.

El-Enany, N. 2020. *Bordering Britain: Law, Race and Empire.* Manchester: Manchester University Press.

Elahi, F. & O. Khan 2017. "Introduction: what is Islamophobia?" In Elahi & Khan (eds) *Islamophobia: Still a Challenge for Us All*, 5–13. London: Runnymede Trust.

Engesser, S. *et al.* 2017. "Populism and social media: how politicians spread a fragmented ideology". *Information, Communication and Society* 20(8): 1109–26.

Essed, P. 1991. *Understanding Everyday Racism: An Interdisciplinary Theory.* London: Sage.

Evans, G. & J. Mellon 2019. "Immigration, Euroscepticism, and the rise and fall of UKIP". *Party Politics* 25(1): 76–87.

Ewen, N. 2019. "Creating Boris: Nigel Farage and the 2019 election". In D. Jackson *et al.* (eds), *UK Election Analysis 2019: Media, Voters and the Campaign.* Bournemouth: Centre for Comparative Politics and Media Research.

Favell, A. 2008. "The new face of east–west migration in Europe". *Journal of Ethnic and Migration Studies* 34(5): 701–16.

Favell, A. 2019. "Brexit: a requiem for the post-national society?" *Global Discourse* 9(1): 157–68.

Favell, A. 2020. "Crossing the race line: 'No Polish, No Blacks, No Dogs' in Brexit Britain? or, the Great British Brexit Swindle". *Research in Political Sociology* 27: 103–30.

Feldman, D. 2016. "Will Britain's new definition of antisemitism help Jewish people?" *The Guardian*, 28 December.

Fitzgerald, I., R. Beadle & K. Rowan 2020. "Trade unions and the 2016 UK European Union referendum". *Economic and Industrial Democracy*. https://doi.org/10.1177/0143831X19899483.

Foot, P. 1965. *Immigration and Race in British Politics*. Harmondsworth: Penguin.

Ford, R. 2014. "The decline of racial prejudice in Britain". http://blog.policy.manchester.ac.uk/featured/2014/08/the-decline-of-racial-prejudice-in-britain.

Ford, R. & M. Goodwin 2010. "Angry white men: individual and contextual predictors of support for the British National Party". *Political Studies* 58: 1–25.

Ford, R. & M. Goodwin 2014. *Revolt on the Right: Explaining Support for the Radical Right in Britain*. London: Routledge.

Ford, R., M. Goodwin & D. Cutts 2012. "Strategic Eurosceptics and polite xenophobes: support for the UK Independence Party (UKIP) in the 2009 European Parliament elections". *European Journal of Political Research* 51(2): 204–34.

Foster, P. 2021. "Inside the Brexit deal: the agreement and the aftermath". *Financial Times*, 22 January.

Fox, B. 2018. "Making the headlines: EU immigration to the UK and the wave of new racism after Brexit". In B. Ecaterina & V. Marinescu (eds), *Migration and Crime: Realities and Media Representations*, 87–107. London: Palgrave Macmillan.

Fox, J. & M. Mogilnicka 2017. "Pathological integration, or how east Europeans use racism to become British". *British Journal of Sociology* 70(1): 5–23.

Fox, J., L. Morosanu & E. Szilassy 2012. "The racialization of the new European migration to the UK". *Sociology* 46(4): 680–95.

Garner, S. 2007. "The European Union and the racialization of immigration, 1985–2006". *Race/Ethnicity* 1(1): 61–87.

Gentleman, A. 2019. *The Windrush Betrayal: Exposing the Hostile Environment*. London: Faber.

Geoghegan, P. 2020. *Democracy for Sale*. London: Head of Zeus.

Gerbaudo, P. 2019. *The Digital Party: Political Organisation and Online Democracy*. London: Pluto.

Gidley, B., B. McGeever & D. Feldman 2020. "Labour and antisemitism: a crisis misunderstood". *Political Quarterly* 91(2): 413–21.

Gilroy, P. 1987. *There Ain't No Black in the Union Jack*. London: Hutchinson.

Gilroy, P. 2004. *After Empire: Melancholia or Convivial Culture*. London: Routledge.

Gilroy, P. 2019. "Refusing race and salvaging the human". *New Frame*, 22 June. https://www.newframe.com/long-read-refusing-race-and-salvaging-the-human.

Goldberg, D. 2002. *The Racial State*. London: Wiley.

Golec de Zavala, A., R. Guerra & C. Simão 2017. "The relationship between the Brexit vote and individual predictors of prejudice: collective narcissism, right-wing authoritarianism, social dominance orientation". *Frontiers in Psychology*. https://doi.org/10.3389/fpsyg.2017.02023.

Goodfellow, M. 2019. *Hostile Environment*. London: Verso.

Goodhart, D. 2014. "Racism: less is more". *Political Quarterly* 85(3): 251–8.

Goodhart, D. 2017. *The Road to Somewhere: The Populist Revolt and the Future of Politics*. London: Hurst.

Goodwin, M. 2021. Tweet, 7 January. https://twitter.com/GoodwinMJ/status/1347311 073565827073.

Goodwin, M. & J. Evans 2012. *From Voting to Violence? Far Right Extremism in Britain*. London: Hope Not Hate.

Goodwin, M. & O. Heath 2016. "The 2016 referendum, Brexit and the left behind: an aggregate-level analysis of the result". *Political Studies* 87(3): 323–32.

Goodwin, M. & C. Milazzo 2017. "Taking back control? Investigating the role of immigration in the 2016 vote for Brexit". *British Journal of Politics and International Relations* 19(3): 450–64.

Gopal, P. 2019. *Insurgent Empire: Anticolonial Resistance and British Dissent*. London: Verso.

Gove, M. 2016. "I shuddered when I saw Farage's anti-migrant poster". Video. *The Guardian*, 19 June.

Gove, M. 2019. "Buy Jeremy Corbyn, get a second leader free". *The Times*, 11 November.

Gove, M. *et al.* 2016. *Restoring Public Trust in Immigration Policy: A Points-based Non-discriminatory Immigration System*. London: Vote Leave.

Graham-Harrison, E. & C. Cadwalladr 2020. "UK facing risk of 'systemic economic crisis', official paper says". *The Guardian*, 24 November.

Gramsci, A. 2011. *The Prison Notebooks*, Volume 2. Trans. J. Buttigieg. New York: Columbia University Press.

Grant, C. 2016. *How Leave Outgunned Remain: The Battle of the "Five Ms"*. London: Centre for European Reform.

Grey, C. 2021. *Brexit Unfolded: How No One Got What They Wanted and Why They Were Never Going To*. London: Biteback.

Guéron-Gabrielle, J. 2020. Interview with Priyamvada Global. *Varsity*, 15 November.

Guma, T. & R. Jones 2019. "'Where are we going to go now?' European Union migrants' experiences of hostility, anxiety, and (non-)belonging during Brexit". *Population, Space and Place* 25(1). https://doi.org/10.1002/psp.2198.

Hacked Off 2020. *Covid Press Coverage: Part One*. London: Hacked Off.

Hage, G. 2017. *Is Racism an Environmental Threat?* Cambridge: Polity.

Hall, S. 1983. "The great moving right show". In S. Hall & M. Jacques (eds), *The Politics of Thatcherism*, 20–33. London: Lawrence & Wishart.

Hall, S. 1995. "The whites of their eyes: racist ideologies and the media". In G. Dines & J. Humez (eds), *Gender, Race and Class in Media*, 18–22. London: Sage.

Hall, S. 1997. "Race, the floating signifier". Northampton, MA: Media Education Foundation. https://www.mediaed.org/transcripts/Stuart-Hall-Race-the-Floating-Signifier-Transcript.pdf.

Hall, S. *et al.* 1978. *Policing the Crisis: Mugging, the State and Law and Order*. London: Macmillan.

Hammond, P. 2021. Interview. Brexit Witness Archive. London: UK in a Changing Europe.

Hansen, R. 2000. *Citizenship and Immigration in Post-War Britain.* Oxford: Oxford University Press.

Harmsen, R. & M. Spiering 2004. "Introduction: Euroscepticism and the evolution of European political debate". In R. Harmsen & M. Spiering (eds), *Euroscepticism: Party Politics, National Identity and European Integration,* 13–35. Leiden: Brill.

Henderson, A. & R. Wyn Jones 2021. *Englishness: The Political Force Transforming Britain.* Oxford: Oxford University Press.

Hinton, J. 1989. *Protests and Visions: Peace Politics in Twentieth-century Britain.* London: Radius.

Hirsh, D. 201. *Contemporary Left Antisemitism.* London: Routledge.

Hobolt, S. 2016. "The Brexit vote: a divided nation, a divided continent". *Journal of European Public Policy* 23(9): 1259–77.

Hobolt, S., T. Leeper & J. Tilley 2020. "Divided by the vote: affective polarization in the wake of the Brexit referendum". *British Journal of Political Science* 51(4): 1476–93.

Hobsbawm, E. & T. Ranger (eds) 1983. *The Invention of Tradition.* Cambridge: Cambridge University Press.

Holland, J. 2020. *Selling War and Peace: Syria and the Anglosphere.* Cambridge: Cambridge University Press.

Holland, J. 2021. *Race, War and AUKUS.* London: UK in a Changing Europe.

Holloway, L. 2018. "Racism: intending not to discriminate isn't enough". Runnymede Trust, 23 April. https://www.runnymedetrust.org/blog/intending-not-to-discriminate-isnt-enough.

Home Office 1999. The Stephen Lawrence Inquiry: Report of an Inquiry by Sir William MacPherson of Cluny. London: Home Office.

Hope Not Hate 2019. *The Conservative Crisis over Islamophobia.* London: Hope Not Hate.

House of Commons Foreign Affairs Committee 2018. *Global Britain.* London: House of Commons. https://publications.parliament.uk/pa/cm201719/cmselect/cmfaff/780/780.pdf.

House of Commons Library 2019. *Hate Crime Statistics.* Briefing paper 8537. London: House of Commons Library.

Howard, P. 2015. *Pax Technica: How the Internet of Things May Set Us Free or Lock Us Up.* New Haven, CT: Yale University Press.

Hundal, S. 2019. "Concerns over 'foreign interference' as India-linked Hindu nationalist group targets Labour candidates". *Open Democracy,* 6 November. https://www.open democracy.net/en/opendemocracyuk/concerns-over-foreign-interference-as-india-linked-hindu-nationalist-group-targets-labour-candidates.

Hussein, S. 2017. "British Muslims: an overview". In F. Elahi & O. Khan (eds), *Islamophobia: Still a Challenge for Us All.* London: Runnymede Trust.

Ipsos MORI 2020. "Tolerance across the values divide?" London: Ipsos MORI.

Jaffrelot, C. 2009. "The militias of Hindutva: communal violence, terrorism and cultural policing". In L. Gayer & C. Jaffrelot (eds), *Armed Militias of South Asia: Fundamentalist, Maoists and Separatists,* 199–236. New York: Columbia University Press.

Johnson, B. 2020. "PM speech in Greenwich: 3 February 2020". https://www.gov.uk/government/speeches/pm-speech-in-greenwich-3-february-2020.

Johnson, B. 2021. Interview with Andrew Marr. BBC1, *The Andrew Marr Show*, 3 October.

Juan-Torres, M., T. Dixon & A. Kimaram 2020. *Britain's Choice: Common Ground and Division in 2020s Britain*. London: More in Common.

Kahn-Harris, K. 2019. *Strange Hate: Antisemitism, Racism and the Limits of Diversity*. London: Repeater.

Kaldor, M. 1991. *Europe from Below: An East–West Dialogue*. London: Verso.

Kaufmann, E. 2017. *"Racial Self-interest" is not Racism*. London: Policy Exchange.

Kaufmann, E. 2018. *Whiteshift: Populism, Immigration and the Future of White Majorities*. London: Allen Lane.

Keane, J. 2020. *The New Despotism*. Cambridge, MA: Harvard University Press.

Kelley, N., O. Khan & S. Sharrock 2017. *Racial Prejudice in Britain Today*. London: NatCen Social Research.

Kenny, M. 2014. *The Politics of English Nationhood*. Oxford: Oxford University Press.

Kenny, M & N. Pearce 2018. *Shadows of Empire: The Anglosphere in British Politics*. Cambridge: Polity

Kenny, M. & J. Sheldon 2020. "When planets collide: the British Conservative Party and the discordant goals of delivering Brexit and preserving the domestic Union, 2016–2019". *Political Studies*. https://doi.org/10.1177/0032321720930986.

Knott, K. 2009. "Becoming a 'faith community': British Hindus, identity, and the politics of representation". *Journal of Religion in Europe* 2(2): 85–114.

Kopecký, P. & C. Mudde 2002. "The two sides of Euroscepticism: party positions on European integration in east central Europe". *European Union Politics* 3(2): 297–326.

Kwarteng, K. et al. 2012. *Britannia Unchained: Global Lessons for Growth and Prosperity*. London: Palgrave Macmillan.

Lancaster, C. 2019. "Not so radical after all: ideological diversity among radical right supporters and its implications". *Political Studies* 68(3): 600–16.

Leconte, C. 2010. *Understanding Euroscepticism*. London: Macmillan.

Lentin, A. 2016. "Racism in public or public racism: doing antiracism in 'postracial' times". *Ethnic and Racial Studies* 39(1): 33–48.

Lentin, A. 2020. *Why Race Still Matters*. Cambridge: Polity.

Levy, D., B. Aslan & D. Bironzo 2016. "UK press coverage of the EU referendum". Oxford: Reuters Institute for the Study of Journalism.

Lewis, H. 2017. "Jeremy Corbyn: 'wholesale' EU immigration has destroyed conditions for British workers". *New Statesman*, 23 July.

Lumsden, K., J. Goode & A. Black 2018. "I will not be thrown out of the country because I'm an immigrant: eastern European migrants' responses to hate crime in a semi-rural context in the wake of Brexit". *Sociological Research Online* 24(2): 167–84.

Lynch, O. 2015. "Suspicion, exclusion and othering since 9/11: the victimisation of Muslim youth". In J. Argomaniz & O. Lynch (eds), *International Perspectives on Terrorist Victimisation: An Interdisciplinary Approach*, 173–200. London: Palgrave Macmillan.

Lynch, P. 2020. "The Conservative Party". In A. Menon (ed.), *Parliament and Brexit*, 11–14. London: UK in a Changing Europe.

Mason, R. 2016. "Top Conservatives condemn Zac Goldsmith's 'disgusting' mayoral campaign". *The Guardian*, 7 May.

McAndrew, S., P. Surridge & N. Begum 2017. "Social identity, personality and connectedness: probing the identity and community divides behind Brexit". *SocArXiv.* https://doi.org/10.31235/osf.io/w95xa.

McKenzie, R. & A. Silver 1968. *Angels in Marble: Working Class Conservatives in Urban England.* Chicago, IL: University of Chicago Press.

Macintosh, I., D. Sim & D. Roberttson 2004. "'We hate the English, except for you, cos you're our pal': identification of the 'English' in Scotland". *Sociology* 38(1): 43–59.

MacShane, D. 2018. "Brexiters' British curry house betrayal". https://infacts.org/brexiters-british-curry-house-betrayal.

Mădroane, A. 2018. "Romanian immigration in the British newspapers: engaging audiences during the Brexit referendum campaign". In C. Beciu *et al.* (eds), *Debating Migration as a Public Problem: National Publics and Transnational Fields*, 139–71. Oxford: Peter Lang.

Mairs, N. 2019. "Boris Johnson insists he will continue to speak his mind despite burka row if he becomes PM". https://www.politicshome.com/news/article/boris-johnson-insists-he-will-continue-to-speak-his-mind-despite-burka-row-if-he-becomes-pm.

Malik, K. 2020. "The uncomfortable truths about Roger Scruton's conservatism". *The Observer*, 19 January.

Mann, M. 1993. *The Sources of Social Power*, Volume 2. Cambridge: Cambridge University Press.

Mann, M. 2005. *The Dark Side of Democracy: Understanding Ethnic Cleansing.* Cambridge: Cambridge University Press.

Manolova, P. 2017. "Editorial – looking beyond the public discourses on migration: experiences of Bulgarians and Romanians in the UK". *Euxeinos: Governance and Culture in the Black Sea Region* 22(4): 3–7.

Margetts, H. *et al.* 2016. *Political Turbulence: How Social Media Shape Collective Action.* Princeton, NJ: Princeton University Press.

Martin, N., M. Sobolewska & N. Begum 2019. "Left out of the left behind: ethnic minority support for Brexit". University of Manchester Working Paper.

Mazower, M. 1998. *Dark Continent: Europe's Twentieth Century.* Harmondsworth: Penguin.

Mellon, J. & G. Evans 2016. "Are leave voters mainly UKIP?" British Election Study. britishelectionstudy.com/bes-impact/are-leave-voters-mainly-ukip-by-jonathan-mellon-and-geoffrey-evans/.

Mellon, J. *et al.* 2018. "Brexit or Corbyn? Campaign and inter-election vote switching in the 2017 UK general election". *Parliamentary Affairs* 71(4): 719–37.

Menon, A. 2021. "We still don't know what or who Brexit is actually for". *The Independent*, 3 June.

Menon, A. & J. Rutter 2020. "As we close in on a Brexit that pleases next to nobody, how did we end up here?" *The Observer*, 6 December.

Migration Observatory 2020a. *Unsettled Status – 2020: Which EU Citizens are at Risk of Failing to Secure their Rights after Brexit?* Oxford: Migration Observatory.

Migration Observatory 2020b. *Migrants and Discrimination in the UK.* Oxford: Migration Observatory.

Migration Observatory 2020c. *UK Public Opinion Toward Immigration: Overall Attitudes*. Oxford: Migration Observatory.

Migration Observatory 2020d. *EU Migration to and from the UK*. Oxford: Migration Observatory .

Migration Watch 2018. www.migrationwatchuk.org.

Mitchell, P. 2021. *Imperial Nostalgia*. Manchester: Manchester University Press.

Modood, T. 2005. *Multicultural Politics: Racism, Ethnicity and Muslims in Britain*. Edinburgh: Edinburgh University Press.

Moore, M. & G. Ramsay 2017. *UK Media Coverage of the 2016 EU Referendum Campaign*. London: King's College London Policy Institute.

Morgan, M. & N. Signorielli (eds) 1990. *Cultivation Analysis: New Directions in Media Effects Research*. London: Sage.

Mortimer, J. 2020. "Leading Tories challenged for using phrase linked to 'anti-Semitic dog-whistle'". *Left Foot Forward*. https://leftfootforward.org/2020/11/why-are-leading-tories-using-a-phrase-linked-to-an-anti-semitic-dog-whistle.

Moses, A. 2002. "Conceptual blockages and definitional dilemmas in the 'racial century': genocides of indigenous peoples and the Holocaust". *Patterns of Prejudice* 36(4): 7–36.

Mudde, C. 2007. *Populist Radical Right Parties in Europe*. Cambridge: Cambridge University Press.

Mudde, C. 2010. "The populist radical right: a pathological normalcy". *West European Politics* 33(6): 1167–86.

Mudde, C. 2012. *The Relation between Immigration and Nativism in Europe and North America*. Washington, DC: Migration Policy Institute.

Mudde, C. 2019. *The Far Right Today*. Cambridge: Polity.

Mulhall, J. 2019. *Modernizing and Mainstreaming: The Contemporary British Far Right*. London: Hope Not Hate.

Mulhall, J. 2021. *Drums in the Distance: Journeys into the Global Far Right*. London: Icon.

Murdoch, S. 2020. *Patriotic Alternative: Uniting the Fascist Right?* London: Hope Not Hate.

Murphy, P. 2018. *The Empire's New Clothes: The Myth of the Commonwealth*. Oxford: Oxford University Press.

Murphy, S. 2019. "Lady Warsi says Tories still failing to tackle 'racism at every level'". *The Guardian*, 13 November.

Nairn, T. 2021. *The Break-up of Britain*. Third edition. London: Verso.

NatCen 2020. "Post-Brexit public policy". *British Social Attitudes 37*. London: NatCen.

Newth, G. 2021. "Rethinking 'nativism': beyond the ideational approach". *Identities*. https://doi.org/10.1080/1070289X.2021.1969161.

North, R. & R. Oulds 2016. *Flexcit: Flexible Exit and Continuous Development*. Epsom: Bretwalda.

Office of National Statistics 2016a. Internal Migration, England and Wales: Year Ending June 2015. London: ONS.

Office of National Statistics 2016b. Population Estimates for UK, England and Wales, Scotland and Northern Ireland: mid-2016. London: ONS.

O'Carroll, L. 2019. "Gove 'lying' about EU citizens' NHS rights to gain votes". *The Guardian*, 17 November.

O'Neill, B. 2017. "Voting 'leave' meant leaving the single market – and most voters knew it". *Spectator* blog. http://blogs.spectator.co.uk/2017/01/voting-leave-meant-leaving-single-market-voters-knew.

O'Toole, F. 2018. *Heroic Failure: Brexit and the Politics of Pain*. London: Head of Zeus.

Parekh, B. (ed.) 2010. *The Future of Multi-ethnic Britain: A Report*. London: Runnymede Trust.

Patel, P. 2020. Tweet, 9 November. https://twitter.com/pritipatel/status/1325828317665177600?lang=en.

Patel, P. 2021. Tweet, 6 July. https://twitter.com/pritipatel/status/141232144634126745 8?lang=en.

Paul, K. 1997. *Whitewashing Britain: Race and Citizenship in the Postwar Era*. Ithaca, NY: Cornell University Press.

Pertwee, E. 2017. "Islamophobia across borders". In F. Elahi & O. Khan (eds), *Islamophobia: Still a Challenge for Us All*. London: Runnymede Trust.

Pogrund, G. & P. Macguire 2020. *Left Out: The Inside Story of Labour under Corbyn*. London: Bodley Head.

Polonski, V. 2016. "Impact of social media on the outcome of the EU referendum". In D. Jackson, E. Thorsen & D. Wring (eds), *EU Referendum Analysis: Media, Voters and the Campaign*. Bournemouth: Centre for the Study of Journalism, Culture and Community.

Pomerantsev, P. 2019. *This Is Not Propaganda: Adventures in the War against Reality*. London: Faber.

Portes, J. 2020. *Immigration between the Referendum and Brexit*. London: UK in a Changing Europe.

Proctor, K. & B. Quinn 2020. "Deportation flight concerns coming from 'Westminster bubble', says No 10". *The Guardian*, 11 February.

Prosser, C., J. Mellon & J. Green 2016. "What mattered most to you when deciding how to vote in the EU referendum?". British Election Study internet panel, London, 11 July.

Public Health England 2020. *Disparities in the Risk and Outcomes of COVID-19*. London: Public Health England.

Rawlinson, F. 2020. *How Press Propaganda Paved the Way to Brexit*. Brussels: Council of the European Union.

Remigi, E., V. Martin & T. Sykes (eds) 2017. *In Limbo: Brexit Testimonies from EU Citizens in the UK*. London: In Limbo.

Renton, D. 2021. *Labour's Antisemitism Crisis: What the Left Got Wrong and How to Learn from It*. London: Routledge.

Rich, D. 2018. *The Left's Jewish Problem*. London: Biteback.

Richards, M. 2020. Tweet, 7 December. https://twitter.com/MariosRichards/status/1336041246293372928.

Richardson, J. 2009. "'Get shot of the lot of them': election reporting of Muslims in British newspapers". *Patterns of Prejudice* 43(3/4): 355–77.

Rogers, I. 2017. "The history and origins of Brexit". Speech at University of Glasgow, 16 October. https://policyscotland.gla.ac.uk/blog-sir-ivan-rogers-brexit-speech-text-in-full-october-2017.

Rogers, I. 2019a. "Where did Brexit come from and where is it going to take the UK?" Lecture at UCL European Institute, 22 January. https://www.ucl.ac.uk/european-institute/sites/european-institute/files/sir_ivan_rogers_lecture_ucl_22012019.pdf.

Rogers, I. 2019b. *Nine Lessons in Brexit*. London: Short Books.

Rolfe, H., S. Katwala & S. Ballinger 2021. *Immigration: A Changing Debate*. London: British Future.

Roudijnn, M. 2019. "State of the field: how to study populism and adjacent topics? A plea for both more and less focus". *European Journal of Political Research* 58(1): 362–72.

Rudd, A. 2021. Interview. Brexit Witness Archive. London: UK in a Changing Europe.

Runnymede Trust 1997. *Islamophobia: A Challenge for Us All*. London: Runnymede Trust.

Runnymede Trust 2006. *Connecting British Hindus: An Enquiry into the Identity and Public Engagement of Hindus in Britain*. London: Runnymede Trust.

Rutter, J. & A. Menon 2020. "The mysterious story of how a split-down-the-middle nation killed off the chance to be half-in and half-out of Europe". *Prospect*, November.

Rzepnikowska, A. 2018. "Racism and xenophobia experienced by Polish migrants in the UK before and after Brexit vote". *Journal of Ethnic and Migration Studies* 45(1): 61–77.

Saddique, H. 2020. "'Divisive tactics': WhatsApp messages urge Hindus to vote against Labour". *The Guardian*, 9 November.

Saini, A. 2019. *Superior: The Return of Race Science*. London: Fourth Estate.

Sanni, S. 2019. Tweet, 6 January. And cited by Martin Shaw, Twitter, 8 January 2019. https://twitter.com/martinshawx/status/1082643952644313088.

Saul, J. 2019. "Immigration in the Brexit campaign: protean dogwhistles and political manipulation". In C. Fox & J. Saunders (eds), *Media Ethics, Free Speech, and the Requirements of Democracy*, 21–37. Abingdon: Routledge.

Schwartz, C. *et al.* 2020. "A populist paradox? How Brexit softened anti-immigrant attitudes". *British Journal of Political Science* 51(3): 1160–80.

Schwarz, B. 2019. "Forgetfulness: England's discontinuous histories". In S. Ward & A. Rasch (eds), *Embers of Empire in Brexit Britain*. London: Bloomsbury.

Seldon, A. 2019. *May at 10*. London: Biteback.

Shah, B. & J. Ogden 2021. "Immigration, race, and nation in the UK: the politics of belonging on Twitter". *Sociological Research Online*. https://doi.org/10.1177/136078042110 29968.

Shaw, M. 1991. *Post-military Society: Militarism, Demilitarization and War at the End of the Twentieth Century*. Cambridge: Polity.

Shaw, M. 1996. *Civil Society and Media in Global Crises: Representing Distant Violence*. London: Pinter.

Shaw, M. 2011. "Britain and genocide: historical and contemporary parameters of national responsibility". *Review of International Studies* 37(5): 2417–38.

Shaw, M. 2015. "Conceptualising and theorising antisemitism and racism: the structural context of Israel–Palestine". *Journal of Holy Land and Palestine Studies* 14(2): 149–64.

Shaw, M. 2019. "Going native: populist academics normalise the anti-immigrant right". https://www.politics.co.uk/comment-analysis/2018/10/31/going-native-populist-academics-normalise-the-anti-immigrant-right.

Shaw, M. 2020. "Racial self-interest, Max Weber and the production of racism". *Patterns of Prejudice* 54(4): 347–65.

Shilliam, R. 2018. *Race and the Underserving Poor.* Newcastle upon Tyne: Agenda.

Shilliam, R. 2021. "Enoch Powell: Britain's first neoliberal politician". *New Political Economy* 26(2): 239–49.

Shipman, T. 2016. *All out War: The Full Story of How Brexit Sank Britain's Political Class.* London: William Collins.

Shipman, T. 2018. *Fall out: A Year of Political Mayhem.* London: William Collins.

Shipman, T. & C. Wheeler 2019. "General election 2019: if Tory lead falls below 10 points, prepare for 'squeaky bum time'". *Sunday Times*, 3 November.

Sian, K. 2013. *Unsettling Sikh and Muslim Conflict: Mistaken Identities, Forced Conversions, and Postcolonial Formations.* Lanham, MD: Lexington.

Siapera, E. 2019. "Organised and ambient digital racism: multidirectional flows in the Irish digital sphere". *Open Library of Humanities* 5(1): 1–34.

Siddique, H. 2017. "96% drop in EU nurses registering to work in Britain since Brexit vote". *The Guardian*, 12 June.

Sime, D. *et al.* 2017. *Young People in Brexit Britain: Racism, Anxiety and a Precarious Future.* Racism, Research and Policy Briefing No.1. Glasgow: Strathclyde University. http://www.migrantyouth.org/files/2016/08/Briefing1-Here-to-Stay-Racism_web.pdf.

Singh, M. 2016. "The 2.8 million non-voters who delivered Brexit". Bloomberg. https://www.bloomberg.com/opinion/articles/2016-07-04/the-2-8-million-non-voters-who-delivered-brexit.

Singh Investigation 2021. Independent Investigation into Alleged Discrimination Citing Protected Characteristics within the Conservative and Unionist Party in England, Wales and Northern Ireland. London: Singh Investigation.

Sivanandan, A. 2001. "The emergence of xeno-racism". http://www.irr.org.uk/news/the-emergence-of-xeno-racism.

Skandachanmugarasan, M., L. Devine & J. Hopkins 2019. *EU Settlement Scheme: Why Are Children and the Elderly Being Left Behind?* https://eachother.org.uk/eu-settlement-scheme-why-are-children-and-the-elderly-being-left-behind.

Skopeliti, C. 2019. "How Leave.EU dominates the Brexit conversation on Facebook". https://firstdraftnews.org/latest/how-leave-eu-dominates-the-brexit-conversation-on-facebook/.

Smith, M. 2020. "Most Conservative members would see party destroyed to achieve Brexit". YouGov. https://yougov.co.uk/topics/politics/articles-reports/2019/06/18/most-conservative-members-would-see-party-destroyed.

Smith, M. & C. Colliver 2016. *The Impact of Brexit on Far-right Groups in the UK.* Research Briefing. London: Institute for Strategic Dialogue.

Sobolewska, M. & R. Ford 2018. "Brexit and identity politics". In A. Menon (ed.), *Brexit and Public Opinion*, 21–3. London: UK in a Changing Europe.

Sobolewska, M. & R. Ford 2019. "British culture wars? The politics of immigration and ethnic diversity after Brexit". *Political Quarterly* 90(S2): 142–54.

Sobolewska, M. & R. Ford 2020. *Brexitland: Identity, Diversity and the Reshaping of British Politics*. Cambridge: Cambridge University Press.

Sodha, S. 2020. "Priti Patel may have experienced one form of racism: that doesn't mean she gets to dismiss others". *The Guardian*, 12 June.

Spours, K. 2020. *Shapeshifter: The Evolving Politics of Modern Conservatism*. London: Compass.

Stacey, M. 1960. *Tradition and Change: A Study of Banbury*. Oxford: Oxford University Press.

Stone, J. 2020. "Tories running targeted anti-immigration ad campaign against Labour MPs in marginal seats". *The Independent*, 21 July.

Surridge, P. 2020. "EU referendum identity and the 2019 election". https://medium.com/@psurridge/eu-referendum-identity-and-the-2019-election-a4c513574b13.

Swami, V. *et al.* 2018. "To Brexit or not to Brexit: the roles of Islamophobia, conspiracist beliefs, and integrated threat in voting intentions for the United Kingdom European Union membership referendum". *British Journal of Psychology* 109(1): 156–79.

Sweney, M. 2021. "Grant Shapps will do 'whatever it takes' to fix lorry driver shortage". *The Guardian*, 24 September.

Taggart, P. & A. Szczerbiak 2004. "Contemporary Euroscepticism in the party systems of the European Union candidate states of central and eastern Europe". *European Journal of Political Research* 43(1): 1–27.

Tell MAMA 2017. Annual Report 2016: A Constructed Threat: Identity, Intolerance and the Impact of Anti-Muslim Hatred. London: Tell MAMA.

Tell MAMA 2018. Annual Report 2018: Normalizing Hatred. London: Tell MAMA.

Thompson, H. 2017. "Inevitability and contingency: the political economy of Brexit". *British Journal of Politics and International Relations* 19(3): 434–49.

Threadgold, T. 2009. *The Media and Migration in the United Kingdom, 1999 to 2009*. Washington, DC: Migration Policy Institute.

Tice, R. 2021. Interview. Brexit Witness Archive. London: UK in a Changing Europe.

Tidman, Z. 2020. "White supremacist posters appear around UK town". *The Independent*, 4 February.

Titley, G. 2020. *Is Free Speech Racist?* Cambridge: Polity.

Travellers Times 2020. "Home Secretary Priti Patel under fire for telling Jewish leaders that 'traveller family' murdered police officer". https://www.travellerstimes.org.uk/news/2020/09/home-secretary-priti-patel-under-fire-telling-jewish-leaders-traveller-family-murdered.

UNESCO 1968. "UNESCO Statement on Race and Racial Prejudice". *Race and Class* 9(3): 365–8.

Vathi, Z. & R. Trandafoiu 2020. "EU nationals in the UK after BREXIT: political engagement through discursive awareness, reflexivity and (in)action". https://research.edgehill.ac.uk/ws/portalfiles/portal/22759272/Migrants_Political_Engagement_Revized.pdf.

Versi, M. 2019. "Denial, obfuscation, apathy: why it's so hard to get Islamophobia on the political agenda". *The Guardian*, 6 December.

Virdee, S. 2014. *Racism, Class and the Racialised Outsider.* London: Palgrave Macmillan.

Virdee, S. & B. McGeever 2017. "Racism, crisis, Brexit". *Ethnic and Racial Studies* 41(10): 1802–19.

Vote Leave 2016a. Video. https://www.youtube.com/watch?v=yIYq5xMW98I.

Vote Leave 2016b. "5 positive reasons to vote leave and take back control: Europe yes, EU no". Leaflet. LSE Digital Library: "The Brexit Collection: The 2016 Referendum". https://digital.library.lse.ac.uk/collections/brexit/2016.

Vucetic, S. 2011. *The Anglosphere: A Genealogy of a Racialized Identity in International Relations.* Stanford, CA: Stanford University Press.

Walker, P. 2019. "Amber Rudd says prime minister's Brexit rhetoric 'legitimises violence'". *The Guardian*, 27 September.

Walt, S. 2021. "Breaking up is bad for the United States". *Foreign Policy*, 18 November

Weber, M. 1964. *The Theory of Social and Economic Organisation.* Ed. Talcott Parsons. New York: The Free Press.

Weber, M. 1978. *Economy and Society.* Berkeley, CA: University of California Press.

Webster, E. 2021. "UK's East Timorese population faces loss of rights after Brexit". *The Guardian*, 27 June.

Wellings, B. 2012. English Nationalism and Euroscepticism: Losing the Peace. Oxford: Peter Lang.

Wellings, B. 2015. "English nationalism and Euroscepticism: a response". *British Politics* 10(3): 373–7.

Wheeler, B. 2016. "Ad breakdown: Vote Leave EU referendum broadcast". *BBC News*, 24 May. https://www.bbc.co.uk/news/uk-politics-eu-referendum-36367247.

Williams, M. *et al*. 2020. "Hate in the machine: anti-Black and anti-Muslim social media posts as predictors of offline racially and religiously aggravated crime". *British Journal of Criminology* 60(1): 93–117.

Wright, O. 2016. "EU referendum: 'it's project hate, not project fear' – Sadiq Khan attacks Boris Johnson over immigration". *The Independent*, 21 June.

Yeo, C. 2020. *Welcome to Britain: Fixing Our Broken Immigration System.* London: Biteback.

Yeo, C., N. Sigona & M. Godin 2019. "Parallels and differences between ending Commonwealth and EU citizen free movement rights". Eurochildren Research Brief Series, No. 4.

YouGov 2020. "When in the UK, are you bothered when you hear those from a non-English speaking country talking to each other in their own language, or not?" 3 February. https://yougov.co.uk/topics/politics/survey-results/daily/2020/02/03/66818/3?.

Younge, G. 2019. "Given Britain's history it's no surprise that racism still infects our politics". *The Guardian*. 29 November.

Yuval-Davis, N., G. Wemyss & K. Cassidy 2019. *Bordering.* Cambridge: Polity.

Zavos, J. 2010. "Situating Hindu nationalism in the UK: Vishwa Hindu Parishad and the development of British Hindu identity". *Commonwealth and Comparative Politics* 48(1): 2–22.

INDEX